THE AMERICAN TAKE-OVER OF BRITAIN

THE AMERICAN
TAKE-OVER OF BRITAIN

James McMillan
and Bernard Harris

LESLIE FREWIN : LONDON

Also by James McMillan
The Glass Lie

First published 1968 by Leslie Frewin Publishers Limited,
15 Hay's Mews, Berkeley Square, London W1

This book is set in Baskerville,
printed by Anchor Press and
bound by William Brendon,
both of Tiptree, Essex

Contents

'It is perhaps no longer an exaggeration to use the trite phrase—which is sweet to American capitalists, but the dirge of culture to British and European critics—the Americanisation of the world. . . .

There may have been some excuse for Britain on her poor island to go imperialist. There is none for us on a near-continent on which to thrive. But we are not without cunning. We shall not make Britain's mistake. Too wise to try to govern the world, we shall merely own it.'

The American writer, Ludwell Denny

'It is essential that public opinion be enlightened.'

George Washington

I

Mrs John Bull's Diary

7 am My Westclox alarm rings. Rouse John; lay out his shaving things : Gillette razor, Personna blade, Colgate shaving stick, Old Spice after-shave lotion.

7.15 John clear of bathroom. Bring in my toilet things. Phillips Magnesia toothpaste, Camay soap, Odorono deodorant.

7.30 Dress. Maidenform bra, Playtex girdle, Max Factor lipstick, Avon preparations. Give John Alka-Seltzer to help him get over effect of too much Long John whisky. Take Anadin for my own headache.

7.45 Breakfast. Maxwell House Coffee for us, Tetley Tea for the children. Kellogg's cornflakes for Susie and Michael, Weetabix for John and myself. See that Quaker Oats has interesting competition—First prize Vauxhall Car.

8.30 They're away! Get down to dishes with Fairy Liquid. Use Brillo pads to clean Prestige pans. Use Ajax on the sink.

8.45 Put Pepsi-Cola into my Kelvinator refrigerator.

8.50 Start Hoovering. Acrilan carpet only needs Ewbank sweep, Susie's room needs Johnson's Wax on furniture. Kitchen could do with Flash cleaner.

9.30 Hoover washing machine going strong. Daz washes whiter !

9.45 Fill Ideal Boiler.

10.00 Shopping time. Take the Ford Anglia to garage. Fill her up with Esso. Get two new Champion sparking plugs. Air for Goodyear tyres. Check pressure with Schrader gauge. Havoline Oil for engine. Order Turtle polishing wax.

10.40 To the Safeway Supermarket for some Mars, Maltesers, Wrigley Spearmint and Spangles. Then to pick up from repairers

John's Ronson lighter and Michael's Timex watch. Collect latest gadget for our Black and Decker tool kit.

Buy Andrex tissues, Andrews Liver Salts, Johnson Baby Powder, Vaseline, Jansen swim suit, hand in Kodak colour film for processing, pay at the National Cash Register desk.

Packet of Ritz biscuits, three tins Campbells soups, two packets Nabisco breakfast foods. For the pets—two tins of Kit-e-Kat and one of Pal.

12.30 Home—prepare lunch. Heinz beans with potatoes cooked in Brown and Polson's Mazola Corn Oil, followed by Bird's Custard and Carnation Milk. Frears biscuits with Kraft Cheese. Get Betty Crocker mix ready to make cake.

2.00 Write to mother. Can't find Venus pencil, borrow John's Parker pen.

2.45 Type out recipe on John's Remington Rand typewriter.

3.30 Work with Simplicity Pattern dress on Singer sewing machine.

3.45 Michael brings in Revell model kit.

4.00 Prepare present for mum—Scripto pen; seal envelope with Scotch Tape, get her a Hallmark birthday card.

5.00 Relax with Corgi paper back.

5.40 Questions from Susie. Check answers in Encyclopaedia Britannica.

6.30 Lay out bills for John to pay; premium to Lincoln Dominion Insurance. Subscription to *Reader's Digest*. Account for Diners' Club.

7.15 John home—opens door with Yale key. He had to lend his Hillman Imp to customer so returned in Hertz hire car. Very smug. Has been presented with MacGregor golf clubs for success in IBM computer course.

9.00 Watch Columbia film on television. Break for commercials include Mobil economy run; Clairol hair shampoo; Firestone tyres, Coca-Cola and Limmits slimming biscuits.

10.40   Switch on Monogram electric blanket.

11.00   And so to bed. John swears he will dream of his firm, J Walter Thompson, which advertises many of the products I have mentioned.

And what is remarkable about Mrs Bull's diary? Simply this. Every single brand mentioned is American.

And that is only the domestic tip of the iceberg.

2

All the way with LBJ?

THE PACE OF America's take-over of British industry has increased enormously in the years since the war. America's stake in the UK is now fifteen times greater than in 1939. Indeed, the annual increase of US investment in England is twice as large as the total sum invested before the war.

Over 1,600 US firms are established in Britain. More than half-a-million workers are employed in US concerns which produce about one-tenth of British manufactured goods. Hundreds of millions of pounds flow yearly across the Atlantic in the form of dividends from British subsidiaries.

But simple quantity does not adequately convey the full scope of the American take-over.

The US penetration of British business is concentrated on those science-based, service and consumer industries which are growing fastest. Thus the proportion of American-owned concerns may well reach twenty per cent or more of British manufacturing by the end of the seventies.

Already a number of key British industries are dominated by US companies. Motor manufacturing; tyres; oil and petrol; car accessories; computers; office equipment; accounting machines; photography; chemicals; chemical engineering; film industry; paper-back publishing; drugs and medicines; roadmaking machinery; agricultural tractors and harvesters; razor blades; electric shavers; toilet accessories; cosmetics; soap; detergents; consumer durables—vacuum cleaners, sweepers, refrigerators, washing machines, heating appliances, telephones; electric tools; pens and pencils; typewriters; canned, tinned and packaged foods of all kinds; advertising; film production; news magazines; mining equipment; manmade fibres; radio equipment; electric

4

switchgear; shoemaking machinery; machine tools; cigarette lighters; clocks and watches; women's foundation garments; car hire; cine-projectors; dental goods; sewing machines; locks; beverages and chewing-gum.

The chances are that of the advertisements on British television at least half—often more—will be of American goods advertised by American agencies.

In some cases American firms virtually monopolise the market. Practically every door in the country is opened by a Yale key.

Seventy-seven per cent of colour film is produced by Kodak, yielding (according to the Monopolies Commission Report) a return of fifty-five per cent on capital employed.

Singer is the name for sewing machines. Ronson for petrol lighters and so on.

In a society which is becoming increasingly consumer orientated that, in itself, is important. But of far greater significance is the growing supremacy of American industry in Britain's technology.

The old staple industries—coal, cotton, shipbuilding, iron, railways—are declining. There is no American stake in any of them. America's money is in the future: aviation; fuels; computers; cars; consumer goods; the 'leisure' industries.

Sixty per cent of the firms exploring the North Sea for natural gas are American. The most modern and expensive oil refinery plant in the United Kingdom, Esso's at Fawley, is American. Britain's chemical plants are built by US engineers. Britons' American-owned cars run on American-owned petrol. The British, clothed in American-owned fibres, walk on shoes made by American machinery. Their business accounts are prepared by American-owned computers and when they pay cash they pay it to American-owned cash registers. They may soon draw their cheques from American-owned banks, for in the last few years twelve US banks have opened branches in London. And as Sir George Bolton, Chairman of the Bank of London and South America, has remarked: 'With the growth of large-scale American industry, particularly noticeable in Western Europe, there seems little doubt that more and more American banks will endeavour to establish themselves abroad.'

Hardly a week goes by but the British financial Press records another take-over bid for a British engineering firm—often a very small one. But adding all the time to the size of the US stake in Britain which by the end of 1967 amounted to close on £2,500 million (more than $7,000 million).

The benefits of American investment are loudly trumpeted and US public relations are superbly good. But in an age of competitive coexistence, when technology is power, do the British want to surrender completely to the United States?

From the moment an English baby is weaned on American-owned baby food, until he is carted away in an American-owned funeral car he is, to that extent, American-orientated from the cradle to the grave. Must it now be universal? Is it to be 'all the way with LBJ'?

3

'Transformation of a Debtor'

IT ALL BEGAN more than a hundred years ago. In 1856 five American partners in the US firm of J Ford & Company set up a vulcanised rubber factory in Edinburgh. The factory was entirely American designed; key workers were brought from across the Atlantic and all the capital was subscribed by the US investors.

The reason for the factory being established in Scotland was because at that time English patents were not protected north of the border and so could be exploited without payment of royalties.

Later in the same year the partnership was incorporated into a limited company, the North British Rubber Company, which is still in thriving existence today.

The choice of Scotland is also symbolic. For in the years to come more American firms were to be established there than in any other part of the United Kingdom, or Europe for that matter.

The reason why the five Americans decided to go into business in the Old World rather than concentrate on expansion in the New is simply that they reckoned the chances of getting a good return on capital were better in Britain than in the United States.

Certainly in setting up their factory in the UK they were going to the home of capitalism.

In 1856 there was only one major industrial nation in the world and that was Britain. Fed by a stream of inventions, supported by a sophisticated capital market (in Edinburgh there were more lending houses than pubs) British traders and entrepreneurs dominated the markets. Well over half the ships on the seas in the latter half of the nineteenth century were British built and most of them were British owned. Strangely enough, the Americans had led the British in the building of wooden ships in the years after Waterloo but fell away badly with the introduction of steam and left Britannia in command.

England's coal fuelled England's ships as it did the grim factories which poured out iron machinery of all kinds. Abundant water supplies in the moist, rainy climate of Lancashire combined to promote a flourishing textile industry. King Coal and King Cotton ruled in dual hegemony.

In 1851 England presented in the Great Exhibition a demonstration of industrial supremacy so overwhelming that the rest of the world could only stand in awe.

Sponsored by the precise, learned, scientific-minded Prince Consort—who, in modern-mindedness if not in the saltiness of his language, bore more than a passing resemblance to a later consort, the Great Exhibition bore witness to a century of British thrift, enterprise and inventive genius.

This was the age of absolute assurance. The key to unlimited prosperity had been discovered. All that was needed was capital in the right hands and goods would pour out in abundance. Given enough capital orchids could bloom in Soho. Nothing was impossible as long as the employer was free to practise enterprise and the employee to advance by means of self help.

Political power was passing, had indeed largely passed, from the broad acres to the factories. The capitalists, large and small, were taking over from the landowners.

On the throne sat Victoria, the embodiment of middle-class virtues and prejudices. By her side Albert, the cool, dedicated managing director, who made up in ability for what he lacked in grace and popularity. Then there was Palmerston, the super sales manager for all things British, scorning Whig detachment and rumbustiously advancing his country's interests.

Palmerston was quite ready to give instructions for a note to be sent to a defaulting country stating 'that the patience and forbearance of HM's Government have reached their limits, and if the sums due to the British claimants are not paid within the stipulated time and in money, HM's Admiral commanding on the West India Station will receive orders to take such measures as may be necessary to obtain justice in this matter.'

Secure in a legal system which protected their investment at home, British capitalists sought outlets abroad.

British capital financed the railways of the New World, the tramways of Buenos Aires, the copper mines of Chile, the forests of South America, the cattle herds of Texas. British money found its way into the pockets of Turkish pashas (who promptly spent it on developing their harems instead of their country); it financed irrigation in the Nile, floated barges on the Irrawaddy, generated electricity in Bangkok. The pound-sterling was the medium of exchange for the whole world.

The Times newspaper asked: 'Of what use is India to England?' and answered: 'In calicoes and bitter beer. We fought and conquered for our export trade in cotton stuffs and pale ale. The Hindus find our calicoes so cheap and so comfortable that they buy them by the ship load; the Englishmen who guard and govern them find bitter beer a necessity of tropical service.'

But it was not just beer and calicoes. Sir Alexander Cairncross in his book, *Investment at Home and Abroad,* estimates that by the late nineteenth century Britain had invested overseas about as much as her entire industrial and commercial capital excluding land. One-tenth of her national income came to her as interest on foreign investments.

The ownership of such wealth was spreading, too. During the nineteenth century the number of people holding Government stock increased tenfold from 17,000 to 170,000. The list of shareholders in Selfridges, the big London store, included a dressmaker, a valet, a housekeeper, a caretaker and a grocer. For the thrifty individual with an eye for the future, slender means were not necessarily a bar to investment. And for those with more than slender means capitalist Britain was an Aladdin's cave.

As Lord Keynes, the economist, wrote of this period: 'The inhabitant of London could order, sipping his morning tea in bed, various products of the whole earth, in as much quantity as he

9

might see fit and reasonably expect their early delivery upon his doorstep; he could at the same moment and by the same means venture his wealth in the natural resources and new enterprises in any quarter of the world and share in their prospective fruits and advantages. He could secure forthwith, if he wished it, cheap and comfortable means of transport to any country or climate without passport or other formality, could dispatch his servant to the neighbouring office of a bank for such supply of the precious metals as might seem convenient and could then proceed abroad to foreign quarters without knowledge of their religion, language or customs, bearing coin wealth upon his person, and would consider himself greatly aggrieved and much surprised at the least interference. But, most important of all, he regarded the state of affairs as normal, certain and permanent, except in the direction of further improvement. And any deviation from it as abhorrent, scandalous and avoidable.'[1]

How different from the passport, exchange control and travel allowances of today. And how incredibly affluent it must have appeared to the American workers in the North British Rubber Factory in Edinburgh. They must have felt very humble in this citadel of capitalism whose industries were germinating the globe with money equivalent in present-day terms to £20,000 million (nearly $50,000 million).

The North British Rubber Company was on its own for quite a time. Between 1856 and the end of the century American economic expansion was concentrated almost entirely in the United States.

The Civil War did for the US what the Seven Years War, the Napoleonic wars and the conquest of Empire all rolled into one did for England. It called forth an immense industrial expansion to arm and equip the victorious armies of the North. It speeded up industrial processes which might have taken generations to develop in peacetime. The course of war—or rather its aftermath—

1. *Economic Consequences of the Peace,* Lord Keynes, Macmillan, 1919

opened up the wonderful lands of the West to displaced soldiers and desperate Southerners seeking a new life.

The Americans, deriving the same drive and self-reliance from their English (and, more especially, Scottish) puritan forebears, turned an untamed continent into the richest community on earth. They sometimes accomplished this by cruel and ruthless measures —killing their natives in contrast to the British who converted them. The destruction of the Red Indian is a grizzly episode in the unfolding of 'Manifest Destiny'. It cannot be excused but it does help to explain the colossal achievement of America in material terms. For it means that great tracts of land were transformed from subsistence economy to intensive cultivation and later urbanisation. Between 1869 and 1909 the annual value of United States output rose sevenfold from 3,400 million dollars to 20,000 million dollars.

Unrestricted free enterprise was the driving engine of this fantastic growth. Millions upon millions of poor immigrants poured into America during these years—sixty million in all. They came from the economically depressed areas of Europe, such as Ireland and Southern Italy, and from politically oppressed regions like Russia, Austria, Germany and Poland. They filled the empty spaces. They provided the hard-hearted and hard-headed leaders of American capitalism—Rockefellers, Morgans, Carnegies—with eager levies for the new railways, steel mills and factories; levies made all the more eager to toil after, strive for and save because they knew that by doing so they could become leaders themselves.

America was 'God's own country'; 'the land of opportunity'; 'the melting pot'.

The Statue of Liberty proclaimed America's message to the world:

> *Give me your tired, your poor—*
> *your huddled masses yearning to breathe free.*
> *The wretched refuse of your teeming shore—*
> *send these, the homeless, tempest-tossed to me.*

And the 'huddled masses' came. But rather than 'refuse' they were the most active and enterprising—the risk-takers, ready to take a chance with the perils of the New World rather than accept their status in the Old.

The most venturesome of the Irish, for example, were willing to brave the tempest-tossed Atlantic waves to reach America. The not-quite-so-enterprising chanced the shorter passage to Glasgow and Liverpool. On that deal the Americans got the best of the bargain.

It is fashionable to picture the US as a society of equals where, miraculously, races coalesced, where merit and toil claimed the reward which only birth and breeding—and not always breeding —could command in Europe.

That is not quite the whole truth. The American miracle was not created by God but by Britons. America's greatest asset was that she was settled by the English and Scots.

She was a colony of the Crown for at least a hundred and fifty years before independence.

Her laws, her religion, her lines of thought, her speech were English. The foundation of the land was English puritan with a strong mixture of Scottish Presbyterian. That may be an uncomfortable mixture to live with, but it is an uncommonly good basis on which to build a nation.

The races which came after, the immigrants, did not arrive in a vacuum; they poured into a mould and the mould was white Anglo-Saxon Protestant.

Each race brought its own distinct contribution to America, but they all conformed—they had to conform if there was to be a nation at all—to certain clear standards. These standards were laid down by the men who drew up the Declaration of Independence and the Constitution. They were, almost without exception, English and Scottish colonial gentlemen. Free from old prejudices perhaps, but clinging strenuously to old virtues, too. Chief of which—ironically for rebels—was loyalty.

The Flag, the Constitution, the Laws, provided the essential framework within which liberty could flourish and happiness be pursued. 'We, the people', had to make sure conformism came first. That was the unspoken clause in the Declaration of American Independence.

And if the leading men in the thirteen colonies were determined to keep the mob in place by a most elaborate system of checks and balances, how much more necessary was it to implant loyalty and conformism in the huddled masses of immigrants.

It is not too fanciful to trace from the flag-pledging ceremony in America's schools the corporate loyalty which young and ambitious American executives display for their firms—loyalty which brings tears of envy to the eyes of employers in other countries, and which helps to explain the tremendous zest and drive of America's young businessmen. 'The Company' represents to them what the eagle-topped standards did to the soldiers of Napoleon, it inspires an élan wholly lacking in other business communities. It gives the Americans an advantage to which the British have no right answer.

When to these advantages are added the manifold blessings of nearly three million square miles of the richest soil on earth open to exploration by the most vigorous of the world's inhabitants, it is hardly surprising that America should produce wealth in super-abundance.

Given vast expanses to be cultivated, given the resources, minerals, cotton, tobacco, oil in bewildering quantities and given a relative scarcity of labour, high wages and lush living were the natural consequence.

Somewhere in the 1890s America's average standard of living passed England's. For example, there were at this time 135,000 telephone subscribers in the US against 12,800 in the UK and from then on the disparity increased as the accumulated technical wisdom of Europe was added to the colossal natural wealth of the New World.

Up to 1900 the US bought 45,000 patents from this side of the Atlantic. In the following three decades they purchased another 123,000. Along with the know-how they bought machinery; as much as £100 million worth a year by the outbreak of the 1914 war.

Guarded by the British Navy (whose strength alone provided the reality of the Monroe Doctrine by which America 'forbade' any foreign interference in the Western Hemisphere); enriched by the skills of European peoples and the invention of European engineers and scientists, blessed by peace and bounteous nature, America thrived mightily.

The aid the US has given Europe in the past twenty years has been very generous indeed. But it is no more than a part repayment of a very large debt.

The US was in fact heavily in debt to Britain until 1914, while at that time her stock in the UK was comparatively small.

Then there were only seventy US manufacturing subsidiaries or jointly owned Anglo-American concerns in the UK—compared with 1,600 today. Many of these old-time businesses were patent medicine enterprises driven out of their homeland because of tighter laws governing contents and seeking pastures new.

Big US shipping interests were also active in England and for a time White Star, Dominion and Atlantic Lines were under their control.

Even so, the labour force of US-owned firms in Britain amounted only to about 12,000 and the combined capital to only about £25 million ($100 million). Britain's investment in the USA on the other hand amounted to no less than £700 million.

At one stroke, Britain put everything to the hazard. In going to the defence of Belgium (for remember England was neither directly attacked nor threatened by any of the participants in World War One) Britain risked all and very nearly lost all.

The causes of the 1914 war have no part in this book. But the results are central to its theme. For had there been no war in 1914 there would have been no World War Two; no draining away of British strength and no mounting danger of American take-over of England.

In four years of bloody struggle England squandered the patrimony built up by ten generations. Put in simple, stark terrifying terms:

—She lost 750,000 of her finest young men, killed in action. Another 500,000 were permanently disabled.

—She lost 2,479 merchant ships aggregating 7,759,000 tons.

—She borrowed from the US £842 million to pay for food, munitions and vital war supplies of all kinds.

—She lent to her allies (particularly France and Russia) almost £1,740 million, hardly any of which was repaid.

Keynes commented: 'Almost the whole of England's indebtedness to the United States was incurred not on her own account but to enable her to assist the rest of her allies who were for various reasons not in a position to draw their assistance from the US direct.'

England disposed of £1,000 million ($4,000 million) of her foreign securities and in addition incurred foreign debts of £1,200 million ($4,800 million).

How different was America's war! True her ardent youth proved magnificent on the battlefield. But they did not arrive there in any number until the last six months.

US war dead in the years 1917–18 totalled just over 100,000 or about the same as were killed on America's roads in the years 1965–66.

The US, far from selling foreign investments, bought back £1,000 million of these—largely from the UK.

Keynes summed it up like this: 'Including loans to allies, the war expenditure of England was three times that of the US. And, in proportion to industrial capacity and population, Britain's contribution to the war was some eight times greater than America's.'

Britain may have defeated Germany in the war of 1918. It was America who emerged as the real victor.

4

Balance Sheet
of World War Two

'WE MUST MAKE the world safe for democracy.' With these sonorous words, President Woodrow Wilson ushered in a new era —the era of the common man, fashioned in the likeness of Madison Avenue.

For now began the age of zany jazz, Hollywood, cocktails and crooners, slang, sex and no-stuffiness. The captains and the kings —or most of them—departed smartly amid the tumult of revolution. The pomp of yesteryear was no more.

The United States in 1919 was indubitably the strongest and most powerful as well as the wealthiest nation on the globe. Moreover a special halo of morality encircled her. For she was untouched by the pitch of war guilt, or the shoddiness, intrigues and pettiness of Europe. Here was a young giant, fresh, clear-eyed, unspoilt, who could cleanse and invigorate a tired and weary continent.

Of course it did not work out like that at all. No nation could possibly have lived up to that reputation. Woodrow Wilson tried. But the loftier his speeches, the more down to earth were the re-actions of the American people. They wanted to enjoy life and to hell with leading others to the Promised Land—especially as the others were making no noticeable efforts to get there under their own steam.

'America's business is business,' intoned the Republican Party. Theirs was the winning slogan. The Democrats and Mr Wilson (who, to judge from his diary, seemed to have wished he was an Englishman, anyway) disappeared from the seats of power.

To the Americans 'finance' was not to be confined to their own land. Returning soldiers, who had tasted foreign travel, were eager to try their luck in foreign investment: 'How do you keep them down on the farm, now that they've seen Paree'? And there were a lot of good bargains to pick up in depressed, war-torn Europe.

The dollar, which before 1914 had been simply one currency among many, and a long way behind sterling, now took on a magic hue as the outward, visible, sign of America's inward grace and material prosperity. For the first time the term 'almighty' began to be applied to it, not in derision, but in awe.

The settlement of war debts proved beyond the wit of man. President Coolidge's curt remark about the financial plight of his erstwhile allies—'they hired the money, didn't they?'—was considered by some to be in doubtful taste. The truth of his comment was, however, undeniable.

Britain attempted to repay despite the fact that those countries in debt to her were either near bankruptcy or, in the case of Communist Russia, had no intention of paying anything to capitalism.

Stanley Baldwin went off to the States to see what he could do. In defiance of instructions from his Prime Minister, Bonar Law, he agreed to repay England's debts not, admittedly, at the five per cent demanded in Washington, but at three and a half per cent per annum. According to Bonar Law's biographer, Robert Blake, the British Prime Minister contemplated resigning in disgust at these terms and Maynard Keynes denounced them in scathing terms.

International finance was in a bad way. The delicate system of exchanges, built on gold and confidence, had been destroyed. A nation at war did not permit the elegant theories of economists to interfere with the pressing task of spending billions to blow another to kingdom-come. At the end of the '14–18 war there was precious little gold or confidence—and what there was of either was in America.

Striving to regain prewar normality in wholly changed circumstances the British committed blunder after blunder. They tried to return to free trade where America relied on protection, Germany on borrowed capital, Russia on self-sufficiency and Japan on undercutting her competitors. The experiment was not a success.

Hard money and a balanced budget was another nostrum. Mr Winston Churchill, then in 1925 Chancellor of the Exchequer, put the pound back to its parity with the dollar—worth $4.80. Alas, Britain's economic resources could not match his brave gesture. Her exports, overpriced at such a parity, found fewer and fewer customers. The English share of international trade steadily declined.

To put matters to right, stern unwavering economies were imposed on home consumption. Subsidies to sheltered industries, notably coal, were ruthlessly pruned. Wages and public expenditure were cut back. As effective demand slumped, unemployment rose (it never fell below a million in the twenty years from 1919 to 1939). Labour stoppages culminating in the General Strike of 1926 climaxed the misery. Britain was sick.

To the brisk, efficient, courteous but slightly contemptuous American visitors—and there were plenty of them—England must have seemed played out and effete.

P G Wodehouse, sketching his chinless wonders in constant search of American heiresses to bolster crumbling family fortunes, struck a note in the twenties which was funny and sadly accurate.

America was setting the pace. *There* was the action. US business enterprise positively crackled with a fierce energy.

Electricity was changing the face of the earth. 'Communism', Lenin had declared, 'is Socialism plus electricity.' An American somewhere ought to have answered him by saying 'Capitalism is electricity plus dollars'.

The dollars flowed into British electricity; into generating companies, into distributing companies, into electrical engineering companies.

By 1930 US interests owned or effectively controlled no fewer than seven electricity concerns including the thoroughly English-sounding Worcestershire, Shropshire and Staffordshire Electric

Power Company, which was bought up by the Utility Power and Light Corporation of Chicago. Three massive firms, which today dominate British electrical engineering—Associated Electrical Industries, General Electric Company and Electric and Musical Industries were in American hands.

How much further the penetration might have gone is anyone's guess. Presumably as the marginal profitability of capital diminished in the US, with more and more investors chasing fewer and fewer worthwhile opportunities, US money expertise would have been directed in an ever-increasing flow to England. Other growth industries would doubtless have been snapped up; motor manufacturers for a certainty.

Lord Nuffield revealed at a luncheon in 1935 that, some years previously, an American bid of £10 million was made for his firm: 'A cheque was shaken in front of my face. At the same time I should have been selling the Old Country to another country and I could not do that.'

It is a sobering thought that, had Lord Nuffield given way, virtually the whole of the British car industry would be today in American hands.

In this period—the mid to late nineteen-twenties—Boots Cash Chemists had been sold to US interests.

So, conceivably the biggest chemist chain, most of the car industry, practically the entire electricity industry and much of Britain's shipping industry (for remember the Americans had taken a big stock of shipping companies in the early 1900s) could have been owned by the US, to add to their many acquisitions since.

It is often claimed that the Americans are infinitely better at exploiting an idea and selling the merchandise than are the British. That may be. But it is difficult to imagine a more successful sales operation than the launching of The Beatles pop group.

Much of this was due to the initiative and intensive sales technique of Electric and Musical Industries on whose label The Beatles made their records.

British-owned EMI reaped the rewards of enterprise. If EMI had remained under American control The Beatles might well have gone to the top—but they would have been shipped Stateside first. The profits, and the showbiz glory, would have gone to America.

If EMI had stayed American . . . but it did not.

Just as the US business invasion of England waxed in prosperity, so it waned in adversity. On 29th October 1929 Wall Street suffered its blackest day. The Stock Market collapsed. Banks called in their overdrafts and America slid into the deepest depression in her history.

'Cut, cut, cut' was the order from boards of directors to executives. Sack, sack, sack was the response. US production plummeted by fifty per cent. Unemployment soared to fifteen million, proportionately very much greater than Britain's at its worst. When Americans do things they do them big—including slumps.

The taste for foreign investment (for any investment for that matter) went sour. Those who had been so keen to get into Europe (and each year in the 'twenties US overseas holdings grew by over £200 million) were the first to sound the retreat.

Within four years of the crash most of the big American-owned firms in the UK had been sold back to British shareholders. Boots, held by the Pure Drug Co, was the first to go, bought by a group of businessmen headed by Mr Reginald McKenna, a former Liberal Chancellor of the Exchequer, whose duties on imports in 1915 ended a century of Liberal free trade.

The same body re-purchased Associated Electrical Industries in 1934, Mr McKenna having been told by a casual American acquaintance: 'You Britts have bought back Boots the Chemists, you ought to have a go at the electrical group.' The American retreat was in full spate.

Repatriation of EMI holdings was secured from Radio Corporation of America. GEC was recovered. Pressed Steel (a vital component of British Motor today) was won back from Budd International of Philadelphia. Tobacco Securities Trust was surrendered by the Americans—also to the McKenna group.

England owes much to Mr McKenna's foresight and commercial acumen. Fortunately for the UK the money was available. So was the will to use it for national needs.

Given a comparable situation to 1930 could Britain mobilise a similar reverse take-over to rescue subsidiaries stranded by their US parents? Or would the Government have to step in to provide the purchase capital? In which case US private enterprise would have paved the way to the biggest exercise in involuntary nationalisation in history!

Of course we are told that 1930 could never happen again; that the techniques of pump-priming, of state intervention to sustain demand, of sophisticated methods of taxation rebate, guarantee the free enterprise system against a repeat performance of the Great Slump. That is probably true.

But the American economy is still far more volatile than the British, or that of any other European country. The mystical, though by no means mythical, imponderable of business confidence wields far more influence on the other side of the Atlantic than in Europe.

Waning confidence in European prospects, or a chilly climate for US investment engendered by Common Market policies, or a big switch to Asian development—any one of these may provide a cut-back in American investment, leaving the host countries with the dilemma of what to do with America's industrial orphans.

It may never happen. But it has happened before. As the frightened 'thirties showed, capital scares easily. What goes up can come down—even America's prosperity.

Between 1935 and the outbreak of the Second World War in 1939 US investment in England was static. The big withdrawals had to some extent been compensated by the establishment of American firms on the outskirts of London; the North Circular

Road, the Slough Trading Estate, and the Hillington Estate near Glasgow. The US plants were set up not, as in the 1920s, as catchment areas for the overflow of American prosperity nor to take advantage of the greater profitability in the UK, but because of the erection of the Imperial Preference system. This made their location in England a necessity for corporations wishing to do business within the British Empire.

As a consequence of the 1930 slump the last remnants of free trade had been discarded and at Ottawa in 1932 the Empire countries had fashioned a new deal. Briefly the homeland, the dominions of Canada, Australia, New Zealand and South Africa plus India and the colonies granted each other preferential tariffs on manufactured goods and virtually tax-free entry for foods and raw materials.

In the depressed and desperate conditions of the 'thirties there was little the Americans could do about this. They resented the whole idea of a preferential area which gave England access to raw materials on privileged terms and secured markets for British manufacturers, but the Americans could hardly complain on the grounds of equity considering that they themselves had erected the highest tariff walls in the world to keep out other people's goods. The Smoot-Hawley tariff made Imperial Preference look like chicken feed.

If the campaigners of the Empire Free Trade Campaign had had their way the British Empire would have become a completely closed economic block with internal free trade protected from external competition by tariff barriers of Smoot-Hawley proportions. That would have been still less to the Americans' liking.

Things did not happen that way because the confused coalition which comprised the British National Government from 1931 onwards contained a fairly high proportion of free traders. The Empire Free Traders did not get what they wanted. But the possibility that they might at some future date was a factor in American economic calculations.

With the outbreak of war in 1939 (once more a case of Britain going voluntarily to the aid of an invaded ally !) England became economically vulnerable.

If the Americans wanted to punch holes in the Imperial Preference system, now was the moment. England, after the fall of France in 1940, was in dire straits. To re-equip her armies she was heavily dependent on America for munitions of war, strategic materials and foodstuffs.

There is no evidence that President Roosevelt exploited this extremely powerful bargaining position for political purposes.

Personally he did all he could to bring Britain aid and comfort, not because he was particularly pro-British—he was not—but because he well knew that America's fate hinged on England's survival. His generosity was a perfectly natural, legitimate, exercise in self-interest. Britain would have followed the same policy for the same motives had the roles been reversed.

However, not all of America felt as Roosevelt did that Britain was worth helping and saving for America's sake. Some elements believed that England's war was none of America's concern and that if England fell she would not necessarily be the loser.

Colonel Lindbergh took this view. President Kennedy's father, Joe Kennedy, Ambassador to the Court of St James's, held not dissimilar notions.

These two apart, the invididuals holding such views were not terribly numerous, nor were they particularly influential but they were noisy and in their propaganda they played on the understandable fears of Americans becoming involved in Europe's war. They sounded the note of high patriotism and combined it with self-righteous pacifism. The Roosevelt Administration was obliged to pay heed to such powerful sentiments.

So Britain could not be let off too mildly in economic transactions. The American taxpayer had to be shown he was getting his money's worth and that America was not being dragged at England's coat tails. The fact that a stern policy also corresponded with US commercial objectives did nothing to lessen its attaction.

Consequently when the British went to Washington to negotiate for supplies they came up against fair but tough and uncompromising bargaining. Cash down, or gilt edged promises were the requirements. In the official *British War Economy*,[1] authors Hancock and Gowing commented: 'The United States administration was fertile of suggestions (in 1940) to the British of stripping themselves bare. They might sell . . . their direct investments in America, their South American securities, Malayan tin and rubber.

'Some of these things the British did. They sold British ownership of the Viscose Corporation at a self-sacrificing price. The Americans decided not to buy Malayan shares because that involved responsibility for the territory. But as for gold, the US cruiser *Louisville* put in at Simonstown and took on gold to the value of 149 million dollars . . . by 1941 British exports were fifty per cent down on prewar so that labour could be released to maximise her armed forces. But such as were maintained went largely to pay for direct American contracts.'

As Winston Churchill was later to say to President Roosevelt, quoted in the book *As He Saw It*, by the President's son, Elliott: 'Mr President, I believe you are trying to do away with the British Empire. Every idea you entertain about the structure of the postwar world demonstrates it. But, in spite of that, we know that you constitute our only hope. And you know that we know it. You know that we know that without America the Empire won't stand.'

In March 1941 the British, having fought alone against Germany and Italy for nine months and having mortgaged most of their possessions in the Western Hemisphere in the process, the US administration introduced Lend-Lease.

Roosevelt had won the presidential elections. He was no longer afraid of being punished at the polls for pursuing an unequivocally pro-Allied policy. He knew America would soon be in the war. He was practically provoking Japan to start a conflict by

1. *British War Economy*, W K Hancock and M M Gowing, HMSO

24

denying her vital raw materials, including oil. Now was the time, in Roosevelt's judgement, to fling America's cap into the ring and provide all-out support for the British war effort.

Churchill has called Lend-Lease 'The most unsordid act in history'. Set against the cold-eyed bargaining of the previous period, the tribute is deserved. Lend-Lease was a mammoth operation which ultimately yielded England £5,000 million-worth of war supplies.

But it was not all one way. Under its terms the first consignment from the US was a small fleet of fifty World War I destroyers which had been in mothballs for twenty years. In return the US was granted a ninety-nine-year lease in various parts of the British West Indies to build naval bases.

In truth the US destroyers were a decisive contribution to the battle against the U-boats. But the deal was not universally popular in England. It was felt that Britain was exchanging real estate of permanent value for ageing warships with a strictly limited future. So limited indeed—so the story goes—that Churchill bleakly growled on seeing them, 'Cheap and nasty!', swiftly assuring an American officer who had overheard, 'I mean, of course, cheap for us; nasty for the enemy'. The cheap-and-nasty tag remained however to sour Anglo-US relations.

As the war progressed, especially after Pearl Harbour, the balance of power between Britain and America tilted more and more in America's favour. This was inevitable. The US was by far the stronger partner. She had three times the population and thirty times the area of England. She was immune from bombing. Her vast industrial might was being fully employed and she had great unused resources. Britain was the most fully mobilised nation of all the combatants—including Nazi Germany—and had no resources to spare. The US had ten million unemployed to pump into the production system.

So, in the division of labour between allies, the big bomber programme went to the States as did the building of transport planes and Liberty ships and the atom bomb—along with the

British nuclear research team which had been working on the project for two years.

It is impossible to quarrel with this distribution. The demands of total war required that production be allocated to the areas which could deliver 'fastest with the mostest'. In most cases America fulfilled these requirements. The fact that wartime production of large aircraft, welded ships and nuclear power had profitable civil application in peacetime was incidental. 'Just the way the cookie crumbles', as the Americans might put it.

Nevertheless this understandable division of effort gave the Americans an overwhelming advantage in post-war competition and reinforced their economic superiority. Where America was building factories—some with money provided by the liquidation of British assets—British factories were being bombed out of existence by the Luftwaffe.

In the years 1940–45 Britain's real wealth declined by £7,000 million ($28,000 million), or about thirty per cent. In the same period America's real wealth increased by about the same proportion.

Three in every ten of Britain's houses were destroyed or damaged. The standard of living fell by sixteen per cent (for the middle classes the fall was much more severe).

The total stock of homes in America increased during the war. The standard of living of American families went up by sixteen per cent, much more for those who had previously been unemployed.

England suffered sixty thousand civilian dead and four times that number wounded. America lost six civilians, killed when they picked up a Japanese balloon bomb which had floated across the Pacific to the west coast of Oregon.

Britain's gold reserve was almost exhausted : a mere £3 million ($12,000,000) being left in the national kitty.

America had acquired gold to the tune of 29,000 million dollars —seventy-seven per cent of the world's known reserves.

Britain had liquidated hundreds of millions worth of private securities in the US. America had gained correspondingly.

By the conflict's end the British weekly meat ration could be put in a match-box. America's only notable consumer shortage was an occasional difficulty in getting one's favourite brand of cigarette.

Such was the balance sheet of World War II.

It is not surprising that the German rocket scientists drew the obvious conclusions, and whenever they could escape from the Russians, flocked to the US. If any came to the UK they remained singularly anonymous.

To those who have, shall be given,
From those who have not, the little they have shall be taken away.

5

On the Dollar Trail

ON A GREY December day in 1945 the noble peers of England met to discuss the terms of the American loan to England. They gathered not in their traditional meeting place but in the Robing Room; their own chamber having been given to the MPs until the Commons' bomb-blasted chamber could be rebuilt.

The House of Lords is not normally an emotional assembly. The atmosphere is best summed up by the story of the peer who dreamed he was addressing the House—and woke up to find that he was!

Yet in the two-day debate on the American loan their lordships expressed their emotion fiercely and often bitterly. Self-pity is a bad counsellor and the exhibition of war wounds is a pretty weak argument.

At any rate it could be said that had England not acted like a zombie in the 1930s there need never have been a war; that she got what was coming to her and neither the world in general, nor America in particular, owed her any debt. Equally it could be said that for nearly two years the US let England fight America's battles while raking in the blood money—and offering 'all aid, short of help'.

Such arguments are pointless and offensive and to their credit the Lords did not indulge in them, preferring honest anger to the 'we was robbed' whine.

The peers had indeed little quarrel with the actual terms of the American loan. They were not onerous. Britain was given £937 million which was to be repaid over fifty years starting in 1950. Repayment could be waived in certain defined and limited circumstances and interest—at the far from severe rate of 1·6 per cent—was to be charged only when British exports rose above a certain level.

It was the principle of a loan between two old friends and allies which raised wrath.

The most remarkable speech of the debate came from Lord Woolton. This large, jovial, shrewd, businessman was perhaps the greatest popular success, Churchill apart, of the wartime coalition. Unlike the redoubtable Lord Beaverbrook (who also spoke), Woolton was no 'wild colonial boy' charged with furious energy and an impish desire for battle.

Woolton was a political moderate, a superb salesman, chairman of the Lewis's Store group; a man who had achieved the incredible feat of keeping Britons on iron rations—and winning their affection in doing so. He was so well liked that a pie was named after him. He was 'the housewife's friend', 'Uncle Fred'. Later he went on to create a supremely efficient Conservative Party machine by the same bland combination of good humour and sound sense which had won him fame as Minister of Food.

Woolton was not a crusader, nor a prophet, nor a flag-waving jingoist. He was, in the best sense of the word, an organisation man, the kind of man for whom the Americans had immense respect; almost one of their own.

Which makes his contribution to the debate all the more astonishing—and significant.

Thus he spoke:

'We reduced ourselves to the miserable, poverty-stricken position of having a gold reserve of only £3 million in this country. We fought, we "paid on the barrel" for the means to fight . . .

'America came into the war not to save Britain but so that we might together defeat the nations that assailed us. The war has left us poor. It has left us the largest debtor nation in history. America, on the other hand, has been left by the war rich beyond her dreams. I ask the American people whether, in justice and in honour, they ought not to return to us, without conditions, those securities we were compelled to deposit with them in 1940. I do not ask for a loan. I do not ask for a gift. I ask for rightful restitution of the dollars we paid in advance of what became a common cause.

'For fifty years we are faced with the prospect of labouring to pay toll to America for financial transactions in munitions. For fifty years we are going to face the prospect of possible default because our creditors (by virtue of their tariff barriers) may not allow us to pay our debts with our labours.

'American traders need us as much as we need them. There is neither need nor justification for this cringing appeasement of their immediate power.'

Such eloquence is almost Churchillian. Was there perhaps a touch of the master in Woolton's words?

Officially Churchill could never make such on attack on the US. As Leader of the Opposition he had actually approved the loan, though without any demonstration of enthusiasm. But did Churchill inspire Woolton—who had but recently announced his allegiance to the Tory Party after years of being an independent —to utter views which he, as the Party Leader, could not publicly express?

For Churchill, the patriot who had strong ties with and a great love for America, that might have been one way of getting important points across.

Other peers, notably the Canadians, Beaverbrook and Bennett, opposed the loan. Another, Lord Sempill, pointed out that the Americans had pushed down the price of the Viscose Corporation (Courtauld's US subsidiary) so low that the British Government had had to fork out £30 million to compensate shareholders for 'daylight robbery'.

Lord Balfour of Inchrye who feared that the Americans were using the loan to pursue their policy of undermining imperial preference—a policy objective of which the Americans made no secret—declared : 'If we do not make a stand now we shall retreat from position to position until there is nothing left.' As a prophecy it was, for whatever reasons, pretty accurate.

Sensing the bitterness, Lord Keynes, the outstanding economist of his day and chief British negotiator on the loan, tried to present the case as Washington saw it.

He stressed the 'practical realism' of the Americans, contrasting it by implication with the sentimentalist approach of the critics of the agreement. He emphasised the reasonableness of repayment terms which required the UK to pay a sum in interest and principle representing a mere fraction of her prospective dollar earnings.

But he failed to answer Lord Woolton's principal charges : that the Americans could have restored the dollar securities to England and that US protective devices would make it hard for Britain to earn the dollars with which to meet the debt obligations.

Keynes was a sick man. Within four months of the Lords debate he was dead. The mental strain of long months of negotiating the Bretton Woods agreement on international monetary arrangements had sapped his strength.

Moreover, he had a poor hand to play in Washington. Virtually all the trumps were held by the Americans. In the end he had no alternative but to accept what was offered.

It would be a gross exaggeration to say that the American loan put Britain in pawn to the US. The total outstanding debt today represents under three per cent of the UK's annual national output. The yearly payment is a fragment of that figure.

But in the late 1940s the debt bulked large in British eyes. It symbolised the overwhelming power of the dollar. Earning dollars became the obsession with the then Labour Government and undoubtedly made them welcome with open arms US investment in the UK—even though such capitalist penetration conflicted with their declared socialist ideology.

In accepting the American loan the British accepted the condition that the balance of payments must have overriding priority in economic policy. The ironic feature is that had the British but waited for a couple of years they would have received all the dollars they wanted in Marshall Aid—gratis !

The Americans have been praised to the skies for their generosity in furnishing Europe with financial succour. If Lend-Lease was 'the most unsordid act in history', heaven knows what words could be found to describe Marshall Aid. No less than 30,000 million dollars was poured into the shattered Continent by means of the Marshall Aid Administration. It was magnificent. But it was not entirely altruistic.

As Chester Bowles, chief of the Economic Stabilisation Bureau, put it :

'The US is heading towards some sort of recession which can be eased by the quick approval (in Congress) of the Marshall Plan.' And again : 'The real argument for the Marshall Plan is a bolstering of the American system for future years.'

As has been said, America's wealth had doubled during the war. Much of this extra productive capacity could be devoted to serving the American public. But there were—or at any rate there was thought to be—limits to what the Americans themselves could consume. The spectre of over-production still haunted a US Administration scared by the Great Slump.

On the production side the US, with six and a half per cent of the world's population, harvested one-third of the world's grain; half its cotton; melted 55 per cent of its steel and other basic metals; pumped 70 per cent of the world's oil; used 50 per cent of its rubber; generated 45 per cent of its mechanical energy; produced 60 per cent of its manufactured goods and enjoyed 45 per cent of the entire annual income of humanity.

On the consumption side—the US owned 50 per cent of the world's telephones; 50 per cent of its radios; 75 per cent of its baths; 71 per cent of motor cars; 83 per cent of civil aircraft and 85 per cent of refrigerators and washing machines.

With such production and so much satisfied demand at home was not there imminent danger of a recession from lack of customers? Economists and politicians thought so. Therefore it was no more than enlightened self-interest to put the European economy back on its feet and so provide a huge new market for

America's burgeoning output. Additionally, the compassion and generosity of the American people, stirred by the sufferings in Europe, provided a powerful stimulant to action.

There was a further and more urgent reason for rushing to help Europe. Americans had, at long last, awakened to the Soviet threat.

But for President Roosevelt's naïve obduracy, a great portion of Eastern Europe would have been saved from Communism at the end of the war. Churchill wanted to move Anglo-American armies into South-East Europe before Stalin's troops got there. Roosevelt however would have none of it. He was determined to concentrate all allied strength in the West, leaving the Russians to take Eastern Europe including Berlin. Furthermore he trusted uncle Joe Stalin. He boasted to his cabinet how well he got on with the master of the Kremlin and gleefully contrasted this happy relationship with the less cordial atmosphere existing between the increasingly suspicious Churchill and the increasingly demanding Stalin.

Some Americans saw the Russians as being more their natural allies than the British. Wendell Willkie (Roosevelt's Republican opponent in the 1940 presidential elections) never tired of urging the British to give up their wicked empire—along with imperial preference! Yet somehow Mr Willkie could find little to criticise when he visited Stalin's Russia, next to Hitler's, the most brutal dictatorship of all time.

Willkie's deep faith in Stalin's good intentions and concern for democracy—a faith shared by many intelligent Americans at this period—is beautifully illustrated by an episode from Willkie's book *One World*,[1] an account of his travels in 1942.

'On the personal side Stalin is a simple man, with no affectations or poses. He does not seek to impress by any artificial mannerisms. His sense of humour is a robust one, and he laughs readily at unsubtle jokes or repartee. Once I was telling him of the Soviet

1. *One World,* Wendell Willkie, University of Illinois Press, 1966

schools and libraries I had seen, how good they seemed to me. And I added, "but if you continue to educate the Russian people, Mr Stalin, the first thing you know you will educate yourself out of a job".

'He threw his head back and laughed and laughed. Nothing I said to him, or heard anyone else say to him, seemed to amuse him as much.'

Which is hardly surprising considering that Mr Stalin had polished off everyone who had ever tried to work him out of his job—and a few million more besides.

Contrast these Kremlin capers with Mr Willkie's stern, unforgiving, upbraiding of British colonialism: 'Millions of people in Eastern Asia are no longer willing to be eastern slaves for western profits. They are resolved, as we Americans must be, that there is no place for imperialism . . .

'Freedom means an orderly but scheduled abolition of the colonial system . . . China will help towards this end.'

China certainly has done just that. But it is not on record that Mr Willkie's Republican Party is cheering its head off at this particular triumph of anti-colonialism.

The miasma of American goodwill to Soviet Russia was swiftly cleared when it became obvious that Stalin was intent on extending the rule of Communism throughout Europe by subversion and military threat.

Churchill's famous 'Iron Curtain' speech in March 1946 at Fulton, Missouri, finally alerted America to the menace which her stubborn blindness to previous warnings had done so much to create.

The Marshall Plan was the economic buttress just as NATO was the military one to counter Soviet aggression. By 1949 America was back in force in Europe and as the dollars flowed to former defeated foes like Germany and Italy, thereby helping to build them into formidable competitors, so Britain began to search still more anxiously for means of strengthening her economy, for fresh injections of dollars to meet her heavy national and international obligations.

The Scots, always the pioneers, were the first to set out on the dollar trail and the first to put down the welcome mat for America's dollar invasion.

6

Hail, Caledonia!

A BURLY FIGURE of determined gait, sandy hair and set expression made his way to the rostrum of the United Nations General Assembly in New York. American delegates sat back in gleeful anticipation. 'Hector' was about to have a go at the Commies.

Hector was indeed. In the pugnacious accents of Clydeside the 38-year-old Hector McNeil, Minister of State to the Foreign Office in HM Government, demolished the latest Soviet propaganda gambit and proceeded to construct in telling, commonsense fashion, the arguments of the free world. His performance evoked warm appreciation from the Americans who were now, in 1948, locked in a grim struggle with the Russians for the hearts and minds of mankind.

McNeil, like his chief, Ernest Bevin, was their kind of man. He was respected for his hard work, abilities and devotion to the Anglo-American alliance. Even more entrancing was the fact that as a Labour politician of working-class origin he was a far more effective champion of anti-Communism than the English old-school diplomats with their old-school tie and their strangulated public-school accents. To the Americans at the UN Hector was a local hero. He confirmed them in their affection for the Scots. His tough realism did much to reinforce the belief that the 'Caledonians' had plenty in common with the 'Yankees'.

This bond of affection, of which McNeil was both a reminder and a symbol, was to prove a considerable asset when, two years later, as Secretary of State for Scotland, he was trying to attract American firms to his native heath.

In one sense McNeil was lucky to get the job which put him right in the foreground of international politics. He was not hand-picked for the post. When Ernest Bevin was appointed Foreign Secretary after Labour's landslide victory in 1945, he looked around for an Under-Secretary. Although he had been in the Coalition Government for five years, Bevin knew few MPs. An indifferent parliamentarian himself, he was ill-acquainted with the talents on Labour's side in the Commons. Moreover many of his party's MPs were newly elected. He had no natural choice.

So a list of possible candidates was provided. He eliminated known left-wingers and, largely by a process of saying who he did not want, Hector McNeil emerged as the one he would accept. McNeil turned out to be an excellent selection. Not only for Bevin, but for Scotland's aim of attracting American business.

The US move to Scotland had, of course, begun before McNeil became Secretary of State. He simply gave it impetus as well as creating a shining bright image of Scotland in American newspapers and radio.

National Cash Register was in the van of the post-war invasion. Indeed NCR arrived before the war was ended. Anticipating a dollar shortage and a demand in Europe and the Commonwealth for accounting machines, NCR's Nelson T Larne surveyed seven possible areas in the UK. He chose Dundee, a somewhat bleak town on beautiful Tayside; the city of jute, jam and journalism— principally jute, a commodity notoriously fickle in supply and liable to booms and slumps.

The work force in Dundee was largely unskilled in engineering and pretty radical in its political attitudes. This was the town which had exhibited 'an unexampled ferocity' at Winston Churchill's meetings in 1922, at which election they dismissed him as their MP, provoking him to the mournful reflection that he had lost his post in the Cabinet, his seat in Parliament and his appendix at one and the same time.

Considering that virulent anti-Socialism and an almost paranoic fear of Communism gripped America in the late 1940s it is a remarkable tribute to Scottish persistence and character that

37

they overcame the gory reputation of 'Red Clydeside' and 'dour Dundee'.

This reputation for militant Marxism was of course greatly exaggerated (Jimmy Maxton, 'the Scottish Lenin', was the kindest soul and a past president of Glasgow University Conservative Association!); even so the Americans were not to know that the reputation was false. At the very least they might have expected severe labour troubles. In Scotland they have been remarkably free from these difficulties.

Certainly Nelson Larne was entranced with what he saw at Dundee. It was, he discovered, a port with excellent rail communications. It had plenty of adaptable labour, keenly aware of the need to diversify and lessen dependence on jute. The local authority was only too anxious to be of assistance whilst the Government made special arrangements to ease the import of parts and materials and to provide planning permission to build a factory.

In addition, Dundee has one precious asset which does not appear in balance sheets. It is only forty miles from St Andrews, home of golf.

It is impossible to over-estimate the influence golf has with US businessmen. In deciding where to locate their factories no red-blooded self-made tycoon is going to admit that he was influenced by any factors other than strictly commercial ones. The fact remains however that many Americans look to the Royal and Ancient in much the same way as devout Moslems look to Mecca.

Scotland has more good golf courses than very nearly all the rest of the world put together. And Scotland, in relation to its population, has attracted more American firms than any other part of the world.

After National Cash Register—which by the mid 1960s had about one million square feet of factory space with five thousand employees—the flood of US firms to Scotland began. Beckman Incorporated, Burroughs Adding Machines, Caterpillar Tractor, Cessna Aircraft, Cleveland Twist and Drill, Cummins Engine,

Dayton Rubber, John Deere, Euclid, Honeywell, International Business Machines (secured by Hector McNeil for his home town of Greenock), Anglo Enterprises, Parke-Davis, Remington Rand, International Latex, Joy Sullivan, Simplicity Patterns, Schenley, Sunbeam, US Time, Westclox, Wilsons Sports Goods. And the latest big acquisition, Rootes of Linwood, a Chrysler subsidiary. In all, sixty corporations have established plants in Scotland since 1945 to add to North British Rubber and Singer Sewing Machines (established on Clydeside in 1867). They employ close on sixty thousand workers, a figure which represents, in family terms, a city the size of Aberdeen.

Such is the scale of American invasion of Scotland.

The man who did so much to promote it, Hector McNeil, became a director of the American concern Encyclopaedia Britannica. Tragically he died at the age of forty-five on his way to New York.

No one can question the success of the American firms in terms of output, efficiency, competitive keenness and labour relations, although some firms are not members of the Employers' Federation in union negotiations. They have sent a fresh wind blowing through areas which had decayed through neglect and where, too often, nineteenth-century ideas and pay rates matched nineteenth-century equipment.

Sympathy can be spared those Scottish employers who bemoan the loss of cheap labour to better-paying American factories which offer cleaner work in congenial surroundings.

But there is another side of the picture.

The American invaders have been given highly favourable treatment. Unlike domestic producers they have been able to choose the location of their new factories to suit their convenience, free from responsibility to any other plant. They have been able to go to those parts where labour has been most plentiful, rents the cheapest, local authorities most accommodating.

The Scottish Council for Development and Industry (a non-profit-making organisation devoted to the modernisation of Scottish industries) advertises factories to Americans in the new industrial estates. 'These,' it says, 'are fully serviced, modern, steel-framed buildings to a standard design or to customers' requirements. Rentals for such factories range from 0.32 dollars per square foot per year to 0.52 dollars per square foot per year.' By contrast, factory space in London is £5 per square foot ($12.00), or approximately forty times the cost in subsidised Scotland.

Unlike those aged American Lend-Lease destroyers, that is 'cheap and good'!

Scottish employers trying to make do with obsolescent equipment in cramped conditions in the industrial part of the Central Lowlands may have themselves to blame for many of their shortcomings. But they *do* have a grievance when their results are compared—discreditably to them—with the achievements of the Americans. There is no comparison, for it is not comparing like with like. Where English firms have set up on these new industrial estates their success compares favourably with US business in the same areas. Thus, output per head in English-owned concerns established in Scotland is about £43,000 ($103,000) per annum while output per head in US-owned concerns is £34,000 per annum.

Yet according to a survey conducted by the Scottish Council, English companies tempted North represent in total only about half the American stake.

Why have successive governments since the war failed to pursue imaginative policies giving exclusive advantages to British concerns?

The reason is not hard to seek. Owing to the dollar shortage caused by the war, Britain was desperate to attract US capital. The Americans, having unwittingly gained so much by the conflict, were offered still more in the form of large tracts of Scottish real estate and subsidised, custom-built plant to enable Britain to pay her way.

Ironically, belated attempts to rejuvenate the old depressed areas of Scotland—now known as development regions—will

mean that US firms will benefit disproportionately from investment grants and increased Selective Employment Tax rebates,
at the expense of the British taxpayer.

If successive governments after 1945 had been less concerned
with doling out welfare benefits and more with strengthening
the nation's industrial base—if necessary, by using Exchequer
funds to develop new industries—British firms, rather than American ones, would today be the beneficiaries of state encouragement.

Scots who congratulate themselves on their acquisition of so
many internationally-famous corporations, with their brisk management techniques and pace-setting innovations, should remember that these glittering plants are but small branch factories to
the parent concern.

So long as they fit into the world-wide dispositions of the parent
in Chicago, or Dayton, Ohio; or Fullerton, California; they will
survive and thrive. However, if circumstances change; if, for
example, the parent firm itself were to be taken over by another
corporation in the States (and this may well happen on an increasing scale) then the future of the Scottish factories might be
in serious doubt.

For suppose American Corporation A has a subsidiary in Den-
mark making the same products as American Corporation B which
has a branch in Scotland and Corporation A takes over Corporation B, will the new boss continue to operate two identical subsidiaries in one corner of Europe? Hardly.

It can be argued that the same set of circumstances could apply
with Scottish subsidiaries of English organisations. Very true.
But UK firms, however large, must always take into consideration
the views of the British Government. Abrupt closures, drastic
changes in policy likely to harm factories in the development areas,
are far less likely with UK corporations than in the case of companies domiciled outside the British Isles.

There is another important factor which puts the huge US
stake in Scotland in a darker hue. The opportunity for Scottish
subsidiaries to contribute much to new processes is remote. Re-

41

search and development are almost wholly confined to the parent corporation in the US. It is cheaper to centralise 'R and D' and it also wins the approval of the US Government which, naturally enough, wants to secure for its nationals—and its tax revenue— the first fruits of innovations.

C H Offord, director of Honeywell operating at Newhouse, Lanarkshire, admits : 'While local initiative is important, and is being encouraged, it is also essential to avoid duplication of effort. There has to be integration of ideas, knowledge and planning to ensure making the best of available resources both here and in the USA.' Quite so. In other words, what Big Daddy says, goes.

Beckman Instruments Inc of Glenrothes, Fife, 'still leans to a very large extent on American electronics know-how which is, of course, among the most advanced in the world.' With the best will in the world it is unlikely that Beckman Instruments Inc of Glenrothes will develop a personality of its own. It is likely to be leaning pretty heavily on Beckman Inc of California until king-dom-come.

'The impact of this invasion,' says the Scottish Council, 'has been very great indeed.'

It has. Production of goods worth £175 million ($420 million) a year; diversification of large industrial areas too heavily dependent on shipbuilding, coal and steel; the introduction of advanced techniques—all these have been rightly stressed.

But the drawbacks; repatriation of profits to the US; vulnerability to changes in US commercial policies and the almost complete lack of original research and development undertaken in Scotland have been completely ignored.

The Council exults in 'the first welcome invasion in Scotland's history.' It is nice that they are happy, but is it altogether healthy that Americans own :

—95 per cent of the office machinery industry in Scotland?

—92 per cent of the household appliances trade?

—66 per cent of computer output?

42

Plus dominant shares in earthmoving equipment, agricultural machinery, electrical goods and instruments?

The Scots, regarded around the globe as a self-reliant people, ought really to ask—could not we have done much of this ourselves?

7

Drugs—American Style

To Enoch Powell the problem posed a particularly sharp dilemma. The Minister of Health, with the flat Midlands accent, grammar school background, brilliant academic record (Professor of Greek at twenty-six), and dazzling wartime career (from private to brigadier), was the rising hope of that diminishing band of Tories who really believed in private enterprise.

Enoch was their prophet; the stern unbending exponent of the gospel according to Adam Smith—that which is in the private interest must always be in the public interest, given a free market.

But Powell, in 1961, was also the Minister charged with safeguarding the people's health and ensuring that they received value for money.

His plight was this : A British pharmaceutical company, DDSA, was selling tetracycline, an extremely effective antibiotic, at £6 10s (nearly $16.00) per thousand tablets. The patent holder, Pfizer, an American drug company established in the UK, was selling the same drug at £60 per thousand.

On the sound principle of buying in the cheapest market, DDSA ought to get the contract for supplying Health Service hospitals. The cause of public economy pointed in the same direction and Mr Powell was constantly being reminded by the Cabinet of the need for thrift. It was 1961 and Britain was, once again, caught in the toils of inflation.

There was however one big snag about buying from DDSA. It had purchased supplies from Italian and Iron Curtain sources which had pirated tetracycline. That is to say they had ignored Pfizer patent rights.

If Powell gave the order to DDSA he would save the taxpayer £53 10s ($130.00) on every thousand tablets. But he would

44

rouse the fury of Pfizer, a private concern which had spent time and money researching the drug. He would be using the power of the State to deny the company the fruits of its labours.

The choice was cruel for a man who matched honesty in politics with a near fanatical adherence to the free enterprise system.

In the end Powell chose DDSA and gave them an order for £240,000 (nearly $600,000) worth of tetracycline for NHS hospitals.

Pfizer fought him in the courts right up to the House of Lords where, in November 1964, the Health Ministry won with a three-to-two decision on a technical point.

Powell's decision to buy from DDSA was based on Clause 46 of the Patent Act, 1949, authorising a Minister to override patent claims in the service of the Crown.

Pfizer averred, understandably perhaps, that the 'Crown' must surely mean the armed services, not the hospital services. The wording of the Act however was not explicit and the verdict was given for the Ministry.

But the point at issue, the point which roused public interest and concern, was not the court's findings, but the huge difference in price between Pfizer's tetracycline and DDSA's. Pfizer's price —which had come down from £90 per thousand in the early 'fifties to £60 in the early 'sixties—was still almost ten times that of the British company.

True DDSA's supplies came from manufacturers who had borne none of the research costs. But these manufacturers would not sell to DDSA without making a profit and DDSA would not sell to the Health Service without also making a profit. If DDSA could show a surplus at £6 10s per thousand, what kind of profit must Pfizer be making at £60 a thousand? Thus reasoned the public. And though the calculations were unsophisticated and the conclusions doubtless unfair to Pfizer the fact is that from that date on the drug industry, despite its glittering achievements, never quite recovered the trust of the customers.

45

Pfizer could legitimately claim that in charging £60 a thousand it was recovering development expenditure not only on tetracycline but on the many, many other drug experiments which had proved abortive. The company argued that if firms were to be penalised for their triumphs when they were never compensated for their failures, they would go out of business, or, at the very least, diminish their efforts to discover new life-saving medicines.

The public, however, was not greatly impressed with this line of talk. After all Pfizer had held the patent for tetracycline since 1955. It had had plenty of time to recover the research outlay and bring the price to within measurable distance of DDSA's. It had not done so. The public felt aggrieved. The Labour opposition demanded an enquiry into drug prices and on achieving office set up a committee to investigate the industry. And Britain woke up to the fact that the drug trade was very largely a non-British concern; not much more than a branch office of big US corporations.

Brian Inglis, in his book, *Drugs, Doctors and Disease*,[1] asserts: 'The pharmaceutical industry in the UK is British only in name . . . within the past twenty years American companies have been taking over British firms and introducing their policies; with a remarkable rapidity, they have acquired a dominant position. British firms now hold less than one third of the market. The individual companies tend to present the same image as they have in the US.

'It is disturbing,' he goes on, 'that the market for a group of drugs in England can be controlled by a US ring. . . . The British market has happened to be singularly vulnerable because of its own past incompetence which made take-overs easy for US firms . . . and private enterprise has largely collapsed in the US industry owing to the companies' realisation of the greater profitability of avoiding competition.'

Thus, because in the US free competition cannot freely operate in the drug business it does not operate fully in Britain, either.

1. *Drugs, Doctors and Disease,* Brian Inglis, Andre Deutsch, 1965

It may have been awareness of this sad fact which led Mr Powell to break the Pfizer patent.

No one should suggest that a British company would not have acted in precisely the same way as Pfizer to protect what it regarded as its legitimate patent interest. The rub is that whether the British like it or not, they must abide by policy decisions on drug prices and promotion taken in foreign lands.

Every second bottle of medicine or packet of tablets or capsule of pills handed over the chemist's counter is American. Fifty per cent of the Health Service prescriptions are American-owned drugs. Six of the top ten companies supplying the NHS are American (two of the remainder are Swiss).

The Health Service has been a great attraction to US drug companies who have clustered around it as bees round a honey pot.

Until the Health Service was established in 1948 only one major US corporation, Merck, Sharp and Dohme, operated in the UK.

Since 1948 American companies have flocked in: Eli Lilly, Pfizer, Cyanamid, Abbott Laboratories, Smith, Kline and French, Parke Davis, Bayer, Squibb, Wyeth, Lederle, Upjohn. In addition, the Americans after the war took over some German drug concerns represented in England.

The lure of the Health Service to US firms was not so much the primary profits that could be made in the UK, but the opportunity to penetrate a large, stable market which could be exploited after initial research and development costs had been recovered in the US. The American pharmaceutical industry is seven times larger than the British and spends thirteen times as much on experimenting with and promoting the sale of drugs.

Selling in Britain is in reality 'found money' for the Americans. Having discovered a popular and successful method of winning custom in the US they simply repeat the formula in the UK. Whether such methods are always entirely suitable for the British market is immaterial. The Americans have such a hold that the British must simply like it or lump it. The US firms are the pace

47

setters and even British competitors, notably Glaxo and Beecham's, are obliged to adopt transatlantic attitudes.

As with practically all industries in America the pharmaceutical one is 'consumer orientated'. The customer, whether he be general practitioner or layman, must be convinced that only the latest medicine, the very newest brand, can meet his needs or cure his complaint.

With engaging frankness John T Connor, President of Merck Corporation, admitted : 'The simple, most effective way to earn profits is by making products obsolete—including our own.'

The Kefauver Committee which conducted a Congressional investigation into the US drug industry reported that : 'It would take eight hundred postmen to deliver the daily load of drug circulars and parcels to American doctors if mailed in a single city.'

Competition is by product differentiation and packaging rather than by price. This is, perhaps, inevitable with the present system. But it does mean that salesmanship is carried to extreme lengths and that a disproportionate amount of money is spent 'pushing' the drugs.

What happens in America happens, albeit on a smaller scale, in England.

Thus free golf balls, socks, even pillows, emblazoned with the company's name are offered to doctors as an inducement to order the firm's drugs. One enterprising US concern in Britain distributed a gramophone record consisting on one side of a tone poem on a bladder operation and, on the other, or flip-side, a description of the company's products.

The ever active Pfizer Corporation offered doctors in Glasgow two guineas for each card they filled in detailing the response of patients to treatment by one of the company's drugs.

The hard sell of direct mail and free gift offers is buttressed by personal calls on doctors carried out by detail men, frequently ex-medical students who have failed in their exams after a year or two at university.

According to one such detail man, 'the name indicates the

essential purpose of the work; to persuade the general practitioner to prescribe the company's drugs by serving him with suitable tempting details.'

Advertising on this scale is costly. It is reckoned for every pound spent in research almost as much is spent on promotion. But it pays off. The average profit on capital employed by eight American drug subsidiaries operating in the UK was 72.8 per cent. In a single case it was as high as 184 per cent.

Admittedly much of the research costs had been borne by the subsidiaries' parents in America. But, even allowing for this, the American companies make about three times as much on capital employed as the average industrial firms in Great Britain.

Brian Inglis points out that, 'Of the £7 million ($17 million) paid in a year by the National Health Service to US drug houses, £5 million ($12 million) was over and above what can be regarded as normal profit.'

The Health Service has what amounts to an open-ended commitment. There is no limitation on what the public can demand in the way of medicaments from their doctors; no pricing system to impose a schedule of priorities (the last frail barrier to unrestricted demand, the prescription charge, having been swept away by the Labour Government). As a result, the NHS is both vulnerable to public pressure for the supply of certain popular drugs and subject to the requirements of economy in meeting those demands.

In a sense, therefore, the more successful the American drug houses are in promoting sales in England, the more authoritarian will the Health Minister become in dealing with the pharmaceutical industry—as the case of Enoch Powell and Pfizer demonstrated. And as has been shown too by the bleak attitude adopted by the Sainsbury Committee on drug prices.

Here clearly is a field where considerable caution and restraint ought to be exercised.

The voluntary price regulation scheme has undoubtedly played a big part in keeping UK drug prices down. Even so the drug bill doubles every eight years and with the total cost of health reaching towards the £2,000 million ($5,600 million) a year mark, British governments of whatever political hue must look for economies.

The drug companies provide the largest and most plausible target for savings because, in most cases, there are standard (*i.e.* proprietary) alternatives for the doctors to prescribe.

The pharmaceutical industry is quite naturally bitterly opposed to the Government's policies of encouraging doctors and chemists to provide natural chemicals as against branded products. The battle for public opinion has been going for a long time and has become still more intense since the tetracycline case and the publication of the Sainsbury Report on Drugs and Prices.

In this struggle the American firms play a leading part, which is only right, considering they form the biggest single group in the British pharmaceutical industry. But can the Americans adopt the right tactics to suit British requirements? Is it fair to expect them to exercise a moderation which they would not dream of exercising in the US?

In short, will the case for the private enterprise drug industry in Britain be weakened simply because the Americans, with a wholly different ethos, are conducting it?

The argument put forward by the US pharmaceutical companies—instanced by their defence in the Kefauver hearings—is that the public unquestionably benefits by the sales methods they adopt.

'OK, it's vulgar, noisy, brash,' they say, 'but it works. Just because companies are constantly trying to get the better of each other, they come up with answers which no state monopoly would ever reach.

'So there is the odd weakness where a "new" drug that is really just a different colour from the "old" one is sold at fancy prices for a time! Proper government supervision—with which the companies will happily co-operate—will see that no one gets away with trick-stuff for long.'

There then follows an impressive list of successful drugs which might never have been developed as swiftly as they have been without the spur of rivalry and the tempting prize of lush profits.

'Why,' say the drug house advocates, 'should drugs be any different from soap flakes? Both are commodities. Both yield to the same sales treatment. If it is said that life-saving medicines should not be treated commercially remember that if they had not been treated so they might never have made their appearance. Better a whopping profit for some firm which produces a life-saver amid the hustle and bustle of the market than no profit, no bustle—and no life-saver.'

That, in essence, is the US drug companies' case. It is an extremely powerful one. It echoes the general argument for free enterprise. But it does so with a megaphone and this difference in degree is colossal.

The British public (no doubt an altogether different view is taken by the American people) cannot help wondering if some of the hypochondria today is not in direct proportion to all this high-pressure salesmanship. Drugs are taken almost like sweets. The very variety of medicaments on offer encourages consumption. Product differentiation and ceaseless propaganda have certainly produced drugs in abundance. But have they not also perhaps done something to create the very tensions they are designed to smooth away?

There is no way of comparing Western health with Russian health as there is, say, of comparing Western wealth with Russian wealth. It may be that the Russian people are suffering from the lack of a driving, aggressive, consumer-orientated drug industry; but the suffering is not particularly noticeable to the outside world.

And although the British are, for the most part, favourable to free enterprise they are not devoted to it. They have to be convinced that its benefits outweigh its debits. They remember the case of Sir Alexander Fleming and penicillin and this tends to make them take—probably unjustly—a surly view of the money-making propensities of US drug firms and a suspicious attitude towards the pharmaceutical industry as a whole.

Fleming's discovery of penicillin was one of the great landmarks in modern medicine. Just as the failure of British companies to follow it up was one of the minor mishaps. As it happened, the onset of war in 1939 led to the development of penicillin—along with the development of so many other things—being concentrated in the US.

Penicillin had not been patented in the UK but it was patented in the US, for the Department of Agriculture held the rights. After the war the department permitted a free-for-all and prices fell quickly, from an original cost of two hundred dollars for a million units to sixty cents a million a year later. From penicillin was developed a broad spectrum of antibiotics, chief among them being Pfizer's terramycin and later tetracycline which, selling at £60 a thousand, caused Enoch Powell so much heartache.

On a visit to America, Sir Alexander Fleming, the Scotsman who started it all, was asked by the head of the firm which had made most out of penicillin why he had not insisted on the full rights and rewards of his discovery.

Replied Sir Alexander, 'I never thought of it.'

That little story is still widely recalled in the UK. It sticks in the gullet. And it has not done the public relations of the US pharmaceutical industry any good.

Just as Britain is the first stepping stone for US firms after their own home market, so the UK is itself a stepping stone for the penetration of Europe.

The advantages of England as a base are obvious. First, the existence of the comprehensive Health Service provides a solid foreseeable demand for drugs (Aneurin Bevan, who launched the NHS, was later to lament that the British people had taken to 'pouring a Niagara of medicine down their throats'). Second, a common language. Third the existence of a pool of technological talent. Lastly the ease with which British companies, many of long standing, succumb to US take-overs.

Operating from English plants the US corporations have boosted sales quite dramatically to the Continent. Winthrop Products, for example, recorded a sixteenfold increase in six years.

This certainly helped to increase UK drugs exports—they reached £75 million in 1966. The American contribution should not be exaggerated, for a sum equivalent to the entire export earnings of the US companies is remitted annually by the subsidiaries to their parents in the USA. The most that can be said is that the American companies save imports by manufacturing in the UK.

Financially then, Britain does not lose from the American invasion. Does she gain?

A spirited defence of the American stake in the pharmaceutical industry, written by Harry Morgan, points out that if the US companies had not started to manufacture in the UK Britain would either have had to import the drugs or produce them under licence and pay a stiff royalty.

The US firms, he says, have saved the UK these costs and brought employment, research knowledge and dynamic management to England's shores. F H Happold, author of *Medicine at Risk,* goes so far as to claim that, 'by selling in Britain from their UK factories at much lower prices than in their home market the American companies are, in fact, causing American consumers to subsidise the National Health Service.'

Which is a very large claim indeed and can hardly be seriously entertained considering the very large profits made by the US corporations. The idea that they were in any way subsidising the NHS would, quite properly, cause apoplexy among their shareholders in the States.

Yet this curious exaggeration of the benefits showered by American companies on the UK is all too typical of the justification of US involvement in the British drug industry. It is too shrill by half.

The Association of the British Pharmaceutical Industry, the trade's pressure group, is an especially strong champion of the US firms.

To quote again from Mr Morgan, writing on the association's

behalf: 'It has been argued with good reason that American industries setting up in our midst introduce advanced management ideas and practices and help to decrease the time lag between their introduction in the USA and their adoption over here. The Esso experiment in labour management is a case in point which is still on the way to becoming a classic.'

It is hard to see what the Esso oil company has to do with prescription medicines. It is stranger still to see the British Pharmaceutical Association acting very like a mouthpiece for American interests.

Quite fairly Mr Morgan emphasises the international quality of pharmacy. 'The activities of the American-owned companies emphasise the interdependence of nations in medical technologies and the co-operative basis of a vigorous national pharmaceutical industry. To be fully effective the industry should pick other brains and lend its own not merely to an interchange of ideas but an intermixing of effort in every phase of activity—research, development production and organisation. This cross-fertilisation may be unequal between partners of unequal size . . .'

And there's the rub! While some British concerns, notably Beecham, Burroughs Wellcome and Glaxo, manufacture in the US they are but a fraction of the total American industry. The Americans in the UK are dominant. That is what gives the peculiar flavour to the British drug industry and one which is not completely to the liking of the British people.

The US firms in England, despite the fact that many of their top managements are British subjects, are simply branch offices.

Policies are decided in New York or Chicago or San Francisco. The British plants follow instructions, based primarily on American experience and American requirements. The sales philosophy is wholly American; the rumbustiousness of the marketing is American; the bewildering clamour which resounds around the ears of consumers to 'try the latest—it's new! New! New!' is American. Sometimes the 'newness' is in the colour of the pill.

This method may be the right one. It may be the best way of

curing illness. But it is not the British way. That is why suspicion of motives and methods of drug companies flourishes among the people. They reckon they are being conned, although there is no evidence whatsoever of any deception.

The Americans are rightly determined to defend their own way of life. The British are no less entitled to do likewise.

But so long as the US drug companies in England are merely extensions of corporations in the States the behaviour of the pharmaceutical industry will be a cause of friction between the two countries, made especially abrasive by the fact that the National Health Service is a tax-financed organisation with strong political overtones. The drug industry in Britain should realise that it is in politics as well as in business.

It is not easy to suggest a solution. But some form of share exchange by which British shareholders could take a major stake in the principal US subsidiaries would help to answer the charge that the British pharmaceutical industry is only an appendage of the American.

Every sensible person wants to maintain and extend worldwide collaboration in medicine. National boundaries should not be a hindrance to development. But equally it is entirely fallacious to pretend that US corporations are 'international' simply because they happen to manufacture in a number of countries.

What is wanted is a genuine association—such as was practised for many years before the war between the US and British drug houses—rather than domination, however friendly disposed the States may be to the natives.

The British public has an instinct for compromise and it certainly does not want to drive the Americans away. But it does seek a more honourable arrangement than that which exists at present. The Association of the British Pharmaceutical Industry should strive to bring this about. And the American drug companies would do well to agree to a compromise and give practical expression to the concept of partnership about which they speak so eloquently.

8

Three Out of Five

NOTHING SYMBOLISES THE age of materialism so truly as the motor car. And as the age owes almost everything to the techniques of American mass production, it is fitting that America should be the land where the automobile has become a way of life.

All sorts of reasons have been dreamed up to explain why Americans took so lovingly, so lavishly, so effectively to the motor car: The call of the wide open spaces; the restless urge for movement; even the desire of the American male to find a sex substitute more manageable than the one provided by nature. The more prosaic reason is probably the correct one—America had first-class engineers and clear-eyed businessmen who honed down the costs of a machine until it could be sold to the masses at a price the masses could pay.

Henry Ford's admonition: 'They can have any colour they want as long as it is black', has become a classic joke. Yet it represented, at the time, exactly the right approach.

While in Europe the motor car before World War One was regarded, significantly, as a 'horseless carriage' hand-made for the wealthy few, in America the Model T was already on the road in its hundreds of thousands.

If ever the class structure inhibited the growth of industry it was cars in Europe. More than a generation was lost before Europe caught up with the US in techniques by which time America had won a handsome share of European car production.

And nowhere has that share been greater than in the UK.

The attractions of Britain for the Detroit manufacturers in the early 1920s were compelling. Tariff barriers were going up and American-made models—which had proved remarkably popular among Englishmen who were becoming motoring enthusiasts—

were likely to be excluded from the British market. Moreover from the UK American manufacturers could penetrate the Empire markets on the same advantageous terms as those enjoyed by British-owned firms. And in every case where America has involved herself in the English economy the common language provided a bonus incentive.

Yet even more important than such economic criteria was the pathetic amateurism of much British car production. A market so lamentably served cried out to be exploited.

By the 'twenties motoring had ceased to be wholly the preserve of the leisured classes and had moved into the orbit of the upper middle-classes. Kipling wrote amusing poems about the perils of motoring; *Punch* filled pages with jokes on motoring. Basically it was treated as a pleasant, slightly 'nor'-nor'-west' fringe activity confined to Bright Young Things, students and aged dowagers who could afford chauffeurs.

The superb talents of British engineers were devoted to providing supercharged models for a tiny minority of racing enthusiasts or large elegant models built for wealthy customers with the care and craftsmanship worthy of the Pyramids—and liable to last as long.

For ordinary folk, for those able to put £20 down and another £100 or so in instalments, there were only two manufacturers, William Morris, later Lord Nuffield, and Herbert Austin. In the 'twenties Austin was producing 12,000 cars out of a total British output numbering less than 160,000 vehicles of all kinds, split among a host of manufacturers.

Morris, as Lord Nuffield recalled (page 19), was tempted with a big cheque. Austin, too, very nearly fell to America. Had it done so the British car industry would today be American controlled.

The story of the one that got away and the one that was landed is told by Alfred P Sloan, Jr, former joint chairman of the mighty General Motors, of which another chairman remarked: 'What is good for General Motors, is good for America.' As GM extends its international operations, a future chairman may well alter the phrase to read: 'What is good for General Motors is good for the world.'

Back in the 'twenties, however, the welfare of GM was not yet equated with the welfare of humanity. It was just a big company on the make.

Alfred P Sloan viewed the prospects of exporting cars with no high degree of optimism. 'Superficially our export trade to the continent appeared to be thriving' (he wrote in his book, *My Years With General Motors*[1]), 'but it became increasingly clear that in the long run our European export and distribution systems were threatened by economic nationalism. We continued to press our export business there as best we could, and we backed up this position by building assembly plants in several European countries.'

This, however, was not enough. A manufacturing beach-head was needed. The first choice was France (Ford having already been established in the UK since 1917) where negotiations were opened for the acquisition of a half interest in Citroën. The French Government opposed the take-over and General Motors withdrew.

Continues Sloan: 'Our next effort to secure a manufacturing position abroad was made in England. The so-called McKenna duties raised a formidable tariff barrier to all foreign vehicles. In addition motor car licences were assessed per unit of horse power. The formula for determining horse power greatly favoured a small bore, long-stroke, high-speed engine and penalised the American engine, the bore of which was nearly equal to the stroke. And since insurance costs were generally related to the licence fees the owner of an American car was doubly penalised. Altogether the fees, insurance and garage charges on a Chevrolet touring car in England in 1925 came to £1 (then the equivalent of $4.80) a week—all this before normal operating costs.

'By contrast, the owner of an English-made Austin had fixed

1. *My Years With General Motors*, Alfred P Sloan, Jr, Sidgwick & Jackson, 1965

58

charges of 11s a week—and his first cost was lower, too.

'While the export of American cars to England was inhibited by these circumstances, British manufacturers faced difficulties of their own. A large number of British producers had come into the auto industry but their combined output of cars and trucks, 160,000, was split up into a large number of design and price levels. The British producers therefore lacked many of the economies associated with American mass production techniques. Mr Mooney, then vice-president of overseas operations, discussed the prospects of acquiring Austin with me and with others in the Corporation several times during 1924 and 1925. We saw that Austin had managed to build up its volume and profits even when the protection of the McKenna duties was temporarily suspended (from August 1st 1924 to July 1st 1925). Mr Mooney inspected the Austin properties in the spring of 1925 and wrote a report recommending that we buy them. In July the committee went to England to look into the question further. In August the Committee sent home the following cable :

Committee agrees unanimously English company will be of advantage to General Motors stop Think we can buy all certificates of common stock Austin million pounds sterling leaving outstanding £1,600,000 cumulative preferred stock requiring £130,000 dividend stop Think we can earn at least 20 per cent on our investment stop Conservative estimate net assets £2,000,000 plus £600,000 goodwill ($12,610,000) stop Are we authorised to close in the event of the unanimous agreement among ourselves?

'On the same day I cabled this answer :

Finance Committee stated June 18th would approve any recommendation Executive Committee stop Assuming your Committee unanimously agree without reservation desirability purchase and fairness price we satisfied go ahead and authorise you to do so stop Impossible we here pass any judgement propriety of purchase or the amount proposed pay stop Conditions here continue very satisfactory stop All well stop regards.'

This swift, meticulously planned descent on the British car industry is a model of American thoroughness. No easy-going amateurism here. The market situation sized up; advantages of going ahead with manufacture in the UK weighed against the disadvantages of staying out; the plant inspected; the prospective yield on capital calculated; the deal drawn up—all within the space of a few months. And when the price was not right, why the deal was dropped straight away.

Mr Sloan explains: 'The principal disagreement concerned the manner in which Austin valued its assets.

'On September 11th Mr Mooney cabled me that our offer had been withdrawn.

'As I recall the incident I was actually relieved to hear the news. For it seemed to me that Austin had largely the same disadvantages that had bothered me about Citroën: Its physical plant then was in poor condition and its management was weak. And I still had some doubts whether our own management was strong enough to make up for Austin's deficiencies.'

The impression is left that Austin asked more than GM was prepared to pay—given the Americans' aim of making twenty per cent.

At any rate there were no lingering regrets, no protracted discussions, no half measures. Austin was forgotten and another target was selected—Vauxhall.

Founded by a Scottish engineer, Alexander Wilson, in 1857, Vauxhall originally produced marine engines for river craft. The first car was rolled out of the factory in 1903—a 5-hp tiller-steered job. In 1905 the firm moved to Luton and went over entirely to car manufacture.

In 1913 the famous 30/98 model was introduced. By 1925 the company employed 1,820 people and sold just about the same number of cars per year from a plant covering ten-and-a-half acres.

This much smaller concern was more to Sloan's liking. 'Vauxhall,' he says, 'manufactured a relatively high-priced car roughly comparable in size to our Buick. It was in no sense a substitute for Austin; indeed I looked on it only as a kind of experiment in overseas manufacturing. The experiment seemed appealing however and the investment required of us was only $2,575,291.

'Vauxhall lost money in the first few years after we took it over and it gradually became clear to us that we would have to develop a smaller car if we were to capture a much larger share of the British market. We also saw Vauxhall as a precedent for expansion of our production operations in other countries.'

Sloan reveals that Vauxhall was very nearly a write-off as a bad investment. In 1928 the question was asked: 'Was it really necessary to manufacture in Europe or could a modified Chevrolet, exported from the US, compete with European cars in the European market?'

'Mr Mooney pointed out that the Chevrolet cost the user approximately 75 per cent more in world markets than it did in the US (presumably due to higher taxes and petrol price) and the user in the world market had approximately only 60 per cent of the money of the US user to pay for it. Therefore the Chevrolet when put down in world markets was not in the largest volume area and was in a relatively high price class.'

Mr Mooney pressed his case. He emphasised that the best way to safeguard GM's investment was to make a success of it and he hammered home the big selling point that the British Empire represented 38 per cent of world markets outside America.

So Vauxhall was reprieved. A brand new popular model was prepared; commercial vehicle production was planned and the decision taken to expand General Motors empire in Europe.

In 1929 GM bought the firm of Adam Opel, the largest car manufacturer in Germany producing 44 per cent of all German cars. GM paid $33,367,000 for this investment—twelve times what they paid for Vauxhall.

By 1933, after four years of slump, Vauxhall and Opel sales were greater than exports of General Motors American-made cars. The case for subsidiaries was triumphantly vindicated and GM was launched on overseas expansion which was to earn it the title of The Biggest Firm of Them All.

From England came a querulous footnote. In *The Vintage Motor Car*, authors Cecil Clutton and John Stamford commented, 'The Vauxhall story is rounded off in a rather dismal fashion. General Motors assumed control of the concern in 1925 and although production continued normally for a few years the old line was discontinued in 1927 and an entirely new one-model policy adopted. This was the K type 20/60 . . . although a sound enough car in its way it was an unworthy successor to the immortal 30/98.'

Words like these explain why the British automobile industry is 50 per cent American-owned and why the UK had by 1967 fallen to fifth in the league of car producers, trailing behind America, Germany, France and Japan.

The 'immortal' 30/98 may have been a collector's piece. But cars are for drivers, not collectors, and it is because of this unrealistic attitude to cars, treating them like petrol-drinking pets, that the UK has never been able to match the astonishing success of one-model lines such as Ford's T and the German Volkswagen.

Nostalgia for old names and old ways, a not unattractive trait in the English character, has proved a distressing liability in car production. Models were continued long after they had ceased to be commercially viable and a leisurely, not to say slap-happy approach characterised motor manufacturing.

Perhaps the worst thing to happen to the British industry was World War Two. The aftermath of this provided full employment and captive markets based on insatiable demand. The inevitable consequence was to convince both workers and employers that Utopia had arrived. Delivery dates to foreign customers slipped; dealers were slack, after-sales service poor or non-existent; workmanship on them frequently shocking. Freed from French, German and Italian competition, British manufacturers enjoyed a field day—and practically wrecked Britain's proud reputation for quality.

Nemesis befell when the Europeans re-entered world markets and the fragmented army of British cars, the Singers and the Wolseleys, the Humbers and the Hillmans, and the Triumphs fell before the disciplined assault of the Volkswagen. The fat days gave way to lean.

Under the compulsion of events the British industry coalesced into three principal groups and three specialised quality manufacturers. The big ones were British Motor Corporation, merger of Austin and Morris, Rootes which cast its mantle over Singer, Hillman and Humber, and Standard which accounted for cars of that name and for the Triumph brands. In addition Rover continued as an independent concern, serving the market for £1,000 cars and over, as did the incomparable Jaguar and the unapproachable Lord of the Highways, the Rolls-Royce. The British, as usual, had a corner in top-quality cars for top people. However, down the price scale they suffered savagely from foreign competitors both at home and abroad.

Rationalisation had gone far, but it had not gone far enough. Standard/Triumph, the smallest of the big five manufacturers (for to British Motor and Rootes must be added the American-owned Vauxhall and Ford), was the first to knuckle under. By great good fortune it was taken over by the bustling, superbly run Leyland bus-to-trucks group which extended its operations to passenger cars and has since taken over Rover.

That left Rootes in the unhappy position of bottom of the league. A family firm, with a strong paternalistic streak, Rootes fought a losing battle. It tried, at enormous cost, to re-establish industrial discipline by facing down a three-month strike and then it launched with insufficient resources into the small-car market dominated by BMC's Minis.

This venture was doubly handicapped. It involved occupying a brand new government factory in the development area of Clydeside and it meant using untried labour which was especially sensitive about Rootes's 'rough' policy and ready at the drop of a hat to go on strike. As a result, production was plagued by stoppages and the 'Imp'—a good enough car—was years behind schedule and failed utterly to win anything like a sufficient share of the market to justify the costs.

Rootes was in trouble. By the early 'sixties profits were being transformed into huge losses and with the fatal illness of Lord Rootes, the firm's number one salesman, the fight went out of the company.

At this moment the Chrysler Corporation of America appeared on the scene. Chrysler, which itself had gone through a testing period only a few years previously, was the third largest American car manufacturer and the only one of the top three without a British subsidiary.

It owned Simca in France and was eager to develop its European potential and compete more vigorously and on more even terms with General Motors and Ford.

Rootes was the ideal base for such operations. The British firm enjoyed preferential treatment by being in an area of high unemployment. There were no traditional practices to overcome because Rootes had not been long enough in Clydeside to establish any traditions. The poor state of Rootes's finances and the low morale of its management and the fact that Rootes's models did not fit into the production schedule of either BMC or Leyland promised an early and easy conquest.

There was just one possible snag. An American take-over of Rootes would mean that more than fifty per cent of British passenger car output would be US-controlled. Would the British public stand for this? More to the point, would the British Government which could ban the sale of assets?

Chrysler need not have worried. British politicians were hardly of the calibre to stop the onward march of the dollar, even supposing they had the wish to do so.

As Chancellor of the Exchequer, Harold Macmillan had presided over the sale of Trinidad Oil to the Texas Oil Company. As Prime Minister he had happily concurred in the sale—for £129 million ($350 million)—of the British minority holding in Ford to the parent company in America. He was known to talk of England being Greece to America's Rome; trying perhaps to smooth the rough corners, aspiring maybe to be principal toga-bearer, but in no way frustrating the designs of the new Caesars. Resistance to an American take-over from such a quarter was not to be expected. And none was forthcoming.

Reginald Maudling, the amiable, ineffectual Chancellor in the last years of the Conservative regime, gave the green light to potential American buyers of British industries when he declared in February 1963: 'If, as appears, there may be some growing opposition to American investment on the Continent of Europe, let us make it quite clear that American investment and American know-how are welcome in the United Kingdom.'

The Treasury's welcome was echoed by the Board of Trade which announced that 'existing arrangements will be carried out exactly as with any other firm which is helped by the Government with inducements to go into developing districts.' In other words, the arrangements made to help the British firm of Rootes would be transferred to Chrysler should the American firm choose to move in. The welcome was rapidly taking on the character of a submission.

Even so, Chrysler moved cautiously. To start with it purchased 30 per cent of the voting equity at twice the market value (and 50 per cent of the non-voting 'A' shares at three times the market value) leaving control theoretically in the hands of the Rootes family. Chrysler promised that should it wish to protect its investment by taking control it would first ask permission of the UK Government.

Mr Maudling professed himself satisfied with this commitment, as well he might considering that he was apparently delighted at the prospect of an American take-over without qualification. The Labour opposition noisily objected to the 'sell-out' to American capitalists. Harold Wilson thundered: 'The Conservatives' interest is not in production. They are too busy drooling at the mouth over increased share values which benefit speculators and bear no relation to national needs.' There were murmurings about 'nationalisation' but the general consensus was that it was far better to save Rootes with American capital than lose it altogether.

Rootes's salvation was finally consummated when, in the spring of 1967, Chrysler bought outright control of the company. Anthony Wedgwood Benn, the Socialist Minister of Technology, explained that efforts to find an alternative solution, involving British capital, having failed the Administration had no choice but to confirm the sale to Chrysler.

It was quite true that Rootes's range of cars was competitive with rather than complementary to those of British Motor and Leyland/Triumph. Chrysler, on the other hand, could pour money into Rootes, bear years of losses if need be, vastly strengthen the local management and provide world-wide sales machinery from which Rootes cars would benefit.

Short-term the argument for Chrysler appears conclusive. But what of the longer term?

The three major American car companies now each have two major plants in Europe. Chrysler has Simca in France, Rootes in the UK. General Motors has Opel in Germany, Vauxhall in England. Ford has one plant in Dagenham and another in Cologne.

Britain is the only country where all three US manufacturers are engaged. Part of the historic reason for this, at least as far as Ford and Vauxhall are concerned, was that Britain was the centre of an imperial preference area. Production in Britain meant entry into the empire at special tariff rates. But with Britain in the Common Market imperial preferences will cease to exist. What then will be the point of American manufacturers maintaining a plant in the UK and another on the Continent? The case for streamlining, for one-firm-one-factory will be overwhelming.

British politicians may find that their obsession with the next election, with short-term objectives, has cost the domestic car industry dear. It would have been painful if Rootes had gone to the wall in 1964; painful but bearable. What if Rootes's best men and much of its production are transferred to Chrysler's French subsidiary in 1974 or 1984? Will not the blow be far more severe —especially as in the intervening period Rootes may well have captured custom previously held by British Motor and Leyland/ Standard Triumph?

What is good for Chrysler is not necessarily good for Britain. Just as what is good for General Motors or Ford may quite possibly be bad for Great Britain.

Detroit will divide its world-wide dispositions in the best interests of the people who own the American car corporations— the American shareholders. In advancing these interests the US car bosses can be ruthless and relentless, as they showed in the case of Ralph Nader.

Mr Nader, a young technical writer, had the temerity to criticise the safety factors of US cars in a book called *Unsafe at Any Speed*.

Unwilling, or unable, to believe that anyone would criticise US automobiles unless he were a Communist or a madman, US car chiefs hired private detectives to delve into Nader's private life. Was he perhaps a Jew with a chip on his shoulder and a grievance against life? A homosexual? A disgruntled discharged employee? Nader reacted against this campaign by suing General Motors and winning substantial damages.

The significant point is not the scurvy treatment meted out to Nader, but the absolute conviction of the US manufacturers in the virtuousness of their policies and the perfectness of their products.

Blessed by riches beyond compare (General Motors' income is larger than the national product of most states of the United Nations), anointed by decades of achievement, the men in charge of America's auto production are the high priests of the Cult of Success. They know the secret. They have the key. Let other markets follow the rules, obey the instructions and abundance will pour forth. But let them kick against the starter . . . !

To Detroit, Britain is a branch factory, of some strategic significance—though lessening as the Commonwealth diminishes—and a rather backward approach to the philosophy of business: Somewhere between the bloody-minded French and the good, hardworking, efficient Germans.

As long as the UK does its job all will be well. Local obligations will be scrupulously adhered to and pay and conditions will rank with the best. But it is a branch. It can be closed or expanded; transferred or transformed at the whim of men sitting three thousand miles away. To remove possible local obstruction Ford bought out the British minority shareholdings in 1960. Americans have replaced Britons in the boardrooms. Once the managing directors of Ford and Vauxhall were British; later they became American.

It is perfectly natural that the US car chiefs should want their instructions to be acted on by men trained in American ways and wholly devoted to American interests. And if the British should squawk there is the ultimate deterrent to local rebelliousness: 'You wanna we quit England and go set up elsewhere?' Whenever labour is particularly troublesome or backbench MPs set up complaints about American domination this is the inevitable rejoinder. Then the smiles of American executives come to resemble the glint of moonlight on a tombstone and the ruthlessness exhibited in the Nader case shows through.

Politicians, in the end, tremble before this threat and recalcitrant union leaders come to heel.

Any reorganisation which the car chiefs in Detroit determine to carry through in their branches must be accepted by the locals lest worse befall.

Thus, if General Motors for example were to decide to eliminate the passenger car production in its UK plant at Luton (182,000 cars built in 1966) and concentrate passenger car production at its Opel plant in Germany (output in 1966—649,000 cars) Britain would have to like it or lump it and accept as 'compensation' the concentration of GM's European truck production in the UK.

Such is the measure of England's dependence on America. In the greatest mass industry of the twentieth century, she must be grateful for small mercies conferred by others, she must abide loyally by the decisions of the gentlemen of Detroit. And there is no sign on the horizon of a Declaration of Independence.

9

Star-Spangled Computers

'WHAT WERE YOU doing on the second Friday in April 1946? Well, no matter how old you were at the time there were many things you weren't doing. You weren't lifting the phone to make a reservation on a transcontinental jet airliner. You weren't wondering when the next live television programme would be broadcast from Europe, or when the next astronauts would be launched into orbit, or what the next Mars probe would reveal. Or, on a more mundane level, you weren't trying to decide which of several credit-card organisations to join. And a thousand other things we take for granted weren't even contemplated in 1946.

'But on that April day in 1946, two men at the University of Pennsylvania's More School of Engineering were at work on a project that would lead to jet propulsion in instant reservation systems, space probes and countless products and services that didn't exist at that time. Dr J. P. Eckett Jr, Dr John W. Maunchly and some colleagues were building the first electronic digital computer in history. Life hasn't been the same since.'

So begins an account of the computer revolution published by the American Federation of Information Processing Societies. And it ends with these words : 'The computer is an information processor whose liberation potential for mankind is greater than that of any other invention in history.'

Twenty years after that Friday in April, nearly seventy per cent of the western world's production of computers is in the hands of a single American company—International Business Machines. Rarely, if ever, has a single commercial organisation captured such a colossal share of the market for a machine so fundamental to industrial progress.

A computer is a fast calculating machine with a built-in filing

70

system, or memory, which can choose between several courses of action as it goes through a problem by reference to predetermined rules; just as a train is directed into the correct line by a series of preset points. It is a machine for marshalling facts and printing out required answers to abstruse scientific or engineering problems.

The human brain takes in news, information, instructions through the eyes and ears. Some of it is stored in the memory. The brain thinks about it, works out the implications and, if necessary, instructs the hand to write or the body to do something. Memory and brain, store and calculator, are distinct.

The computer works in a similar way. It takes in information via punched cards or punched paper tape, stores it in a memory, works out its implications according to a set of instructions which it has been given, calculates the answers according to those instructions and prints them. This ability to follow slavishly prearranged instructions is the nearest a computer gets to the human brain.

There is no value judgement in a computer—but there is a phenomenal speed in its calculation. Thus, if a man lives to ninety and performs one calculation every second for twenty-four hours a day for the whole of his life—doing without sleep—he will do in ninety years what the computer can do in three seconds. A computer can print the Bible in an hour. It can store on a single magnetic tape half a mile long the contents of one hundred books.

It can 'talk' to students, providing them with the wisdom of the ages as long as they ask the right questions.

The engineer designing a machine will be able to draw a beam and then have a discussion with the computer which will tell him if that beam is strong enough for the purpose he has in mind.

Here then is a tool of fantastic possibilities in business, science, engineering, education. A tool which may well alter the behaviour patterns of the users as well as the business patterns of their enterprises.

How then did it happen that a single company came to command such a domination over computers as did IBM?

Chance. The chance that brought a brilliant commercially-minded man, Thomas J Watson (once a £2-a-week bookkeeper), into touch with the talents of an electronic genius, Herman Hollerith of Buffalo, New York. Hollerith—a census clerk—developed a tabulating machine which was used in the 1890 census, cutting the data processing time from $7\frac{1}{2}$ years to $2\frac{1}{2}$ years.

As patents poured from US and foreign inventors in the first thirty years of the twentieth century—more than 1,300,000—so the demand for electronic computing machines grew. Hollerith's company merged with others and became the Computing Tabulating and Recording Company. In 1911 it came under the control of the Watson family. Thomas J, Sr, became chairman. He stuck one-word notices round the company's offices. The word: 'THINK'. His employees 'thought' to such purpose that when Thomas J died in 1956 the company, now International Business Machines, had a market capitalisation five times as big as Britain's largest company, Imperial Chemical Industries, and an annual turnover well in excess of £1,000 million. Such was the colossus which invaded Europe in the 'fifties.

Initially some of the shares in IBM United Kingdom were issued privately to British investors through the merchant bankers, Helbert Wagg. Among the lucky chaps who obtained shares in the English IBM were the Duke of Marlborough, Lord Howard de Walden, the Earl of Listowel, Lord de L'Isle and other members of the nobility.

In 1959 IBM decided to buy out the private shareholders. They offered 165s (approximately $23.50) for shares which had cost 29s ($4.10) only eight years previously, an appreciation of very nearly 60 per cent a year. Lord Howard de Walden cashed in to the tune of £260,000 ($750,000) for shares which had cost him £45,000 ($125,000) in 1951. Emmanuel College, Cambridge, got £130,000 ($360,000) for an investment of £23,000 ($60,000).

The personal fortunes of those fortunate enough to have a tiny temporary stake in the company measures the enormously swift growth of IBM in the UK. With factories in Scotland and England it expanded at a tremendous rate.

But Britain is only one branch of a gigantic world-wide network centred, of course, in the United States. The scale of IBM's global operations can be gauged by the methods used to launch System/360.

To quote the US business magazine, *Fortune* : 'When Tom Watson Jr made what he called "the most important product announcement in the company's history" he created quite a stir. The elaborate logistics that IBM worked out in order to get maximum Press coverage—besides a huge assembly at Poughkeepsie (company headquarters) IBM staged Press conferences on the same day in twenty-six states in the US and in fourteen foreign countries—underscored his view of the importance of the event. But then no company had ever introduced in one swoop six computer models of totally new design in a technology never tested in the market place and with programming abilities of the greatest complexity. Once the announcement was made, it was no wonder that in the scattered locations where IBM plans, builds and sells its products there was, on the evening of 7th April 1964, a certain amount of dancing in the streets.'

Fortune goes on : 'Two and a half years later it would seem that there was good reason for the celebrations in which IBM staked its fortune of five billion dollars, its reputation and its position of leadership in the computer field on the decision to go ahead with System/360. It is forecasted that by the end of 1968 ten billion dollars worth of IBM's new computing equipment will be in the field.'

The cost of preparing the programming was staggering. In a single day estimates were changed from fifty billion dollars to sixty billion dollars. But money was not the only thing employed on a gigantic scale. There was talent. British talent. German talent.

The company's Hursley laboratory in England was set to work. So were engineers in Germany. To link them with supreme headquarters in America, IBM leased a special transatlantic line between the US and Europe. The international engineering group was woven together into an effective whole—at the service of IBM and its American shareholders.

Indeed, so impressed were the IBM chiefs with this world-wide hook-up that they decided they ought to bypass the common carriers and get direct access to COMSAT space satellite.

Why not machines talking to other machines across the Atlantic —defining, analysing, correlating? Instead of nation speaking to nation, IBM should speak to IBM. *Fortune* declared that it was 'conjectural' what such visions would mean in dollars.

'The company,' went on *Fortune*, 'sees itself playing a critical role in a brand new kind of international data communication based on computers that work and talk with each other.'

In this Wellsian vista it seems the space communication satellites will be American and they will carry American computer messages to American receivers, to be analysed and codified by American machines. The British—and others—may however be allowed to make the tea.

Certainly the control exercised from the centre at Poughkeepsie during System/360 appears to justify the conclusion that the outlying branches did not have much independent existence.

Let *Fortune* tell the story: 'Long after the 360 concept had been endorsed by IBM's top management there were enormous development efforts going on outside the company that offered continuing alternatives to the concept—and they were taken seriously enough, in some cases, so that there were fights over the jurisdiction over them. Early in 1963 for example, there was a row over development work at IBM's San José laboratory, which belonged to the General Products division. It turned out that San José—which had been explicitly told to stop the work—was still developing a low-power machine similar to one being worked on in World Trade's German laboratory (World Trade being a subsidiary of IBM). When he heard about the continuing effort, A K Watson—Head of World Trade and brother of IBM's Tom —went to the laboratory and seems angrily to have restated his

demands that San José cut it out. Some people were then transferred to Germany to work on the German machine.'

Well, at least they were not sent to Siberia! But the somewhat
brusque treatment meted out to the branches by the supreme
headquarters had its consequences in England.

In May 1967 three of IBM's top marketing men in the UK
quit the company for jobs with British firms. Their reason? They
were irked that all the real decisions were made in America.

Flushed with success, filled with an almost mystical belief in its
omnipotence, IBM enraged its rivals and provoked them into a
massive counter-attack at home and abroad.

The dominance of IBM was certainly wondrous to behold. With
something approaching three quarters of the American market,
IBM's control in Europe was also impressive. In 1964 the share-
out of the European computer market was:

IBM	62 per cent
ICT (British)	9 per cent
GE Bull (French domiciled, owned by GEC of America)	7 per cent
English Electric (British)	3 per cent
Elliott-Automation (British)	3 per cent
Univac (American)	2 per cent
Olivetti (Italian, but US controlled)	2 per cent

These figures however mask rather than reveal certain facts.
Only in Britain was there a real challenge to American leadership. There the computer market was split almost fifty-fifty between domestic and US companies. In Europe as a whole the US
was supreme, with IBM so far ahead that it was practically in a
league by itself.

Then on the scene came Honeywell, another American concern,
which had eaten into part of IBM's market in the States, and
now decided to challenge the master in Europe. Honeywell, established at Newhouse only a few miles from IBM's plant at Green-

ock, jauntily announced that it was going to crash into Europe and aimed to take IBM apart.

So there were the US giants squaring up to each other for a knockout, drag-down fight for which Europe provided merely a ring, and a secondary ring at that, considering that the main bout took place in America.

It is hardly surprising that President de Gaulle was distressed. The vast bulk of his country's computer industry—like that of Germany's—had passed out of domestic control into US hands. Even the French nuclear defence programme had been delayed —and hindered—by the French industry's dependence on US computers. In his shame and irritation de Gaulle looked round for a possible ally to fend off American hegemony. He looked to the one country capable of offering a technological challenge to the US—England.

The British had some claim to be first in promoting computers. A moody, eccentric young Englishman, James Babbage, devised the first digital computer in 1823 at the age of thirty-one. He persuaded the British Government to finance this invention which he called 'The Difference Engine', later evolving into an analytical engine design to perform complex calculations and to possess a memory device.

But the technology of the day was not sufficiently advanced to construct the parts needed and when Babbage died, in 1871, he had only a small working model to his credit.

Before he died, however, he had met the daughter of Lord Byron, the young Lady Lovelace, another mathematical genius, who devised a form of binary arithmetic still used in computers today. She worked out some very complicated programmes, but again the lack of a sophisticated technology prevented them from being transformed into practical machines.

It was left to Hollerith, the American, to take up the challenge twenty years later, by which time engineering advances did permit actual building. Such are the fortunes of history.

Yet there was one crumb of comfort for England, and a substantial one. An off-shoot of the original Hollerith firm was established in the UK. It merged with British Tabulating Machines Co and Powers-Samas and together they brought into being International Computers and Tabulators. Later it was joined by the computer divisions of GEC, EMI and Ferranti.

According to Brian Murphy in his book, *The Computer in Society*, ICT is the biggest rival to IBM.

Certainly it is one of the most aggressively-minded. It achieved a brilliant success with its 1900 Series, selling close on a thousand of these machines to practically every part of the world—except the US.

Buoyantly British in outlook, ICT set itself on a pro-European course as the only means of meeting and beating the US technical supremacy. Its optimism was needed for the odds were massive. ICT's annual turnover in the mid 'sixties was £70 million a year. IBM's was close on £1,500 million—a twenty to one lead. And if to IBM were added the fierce number two challenger, Honeywell, and Univac and General Electric of America and Radio Corporation of America and National Cash Register and Sperry Rand and Burroughs, the array of technical might facing ICT and its prospective allies—Elliott and English Electric plus the rump of the nationally-controlled French industry—was formidable indeed.

ICT, strong, modern-minded, restless, had to face the fact that its 23,000 employees were outnumbered five-to-one by IBM's 118,000 and the economics of scale were on IBM's side. For in this highly-sophisticated kind of production, total cost per unit can fall by one third if the production run is increased threefold.

Prospective demand for computers in the UK is likely to be six hundred installations a year until the early 1970s. Demand in the US will be many times this. More significant, companies with enormous resources can rout their small competitors by imposing fundamental changes in design.

Thus a report by the National Institute of Economic and Social Research states: 'IBM introduced transistorised computers, so

77

made the first generation of valve computers obsolete and so forced their competitors to develop transistorised models if they wished to remain on the scene.'

The conclusion reached by this report: 'If the threshold set by leading American firms for particular products is beyond the resources of European firms then—barring mergers with American firms—they can only survive by the rationalisation of the industry on a national, or European basis.'

These are precisely ICT's views. It is putting twelve thousand students through its technical training courses each year because it believes it must prepare for the future, *ie* education for Europe. The technological alliance with Europe is central to the task of building a computer industry capable of holding its own with America. To accomplish this ICT is prepared to endure the storm and stress of an economic war against the American companies, always with the proviso that British and other European governments favour the home side.

US firms in Europe naturally take umbrage at this idea. Honeywell asserts that it is a British company using British labour in a British factory, exporting British goods. True, it does not go as far as Bechtel, the US chemical engineering firm, which displays the Union Jack in its newspaper advertisements, but Honeywell would like to be known as British in Britain, just as it would doubtless like to be known as German in Germany or Dutch in Holland. Anything to get even with IBM!

The value of US concerns established in the UK is however diminished by the lack of genuine, independently-orientated research efforts. The story of IBM's 360 model illustrates the fact that overseas satellites of US corporations are integrated into plans prepared, designed and launched by the company in the USA for the USA.

One of the beauties of IBM's 360 was that it met the needs of a world market. In the words of *Fortune* it 'integrated the domestic and foreign operations' but, while the foreign operations were peripheral to the central strategy, the US operations were basic.

The foreign ends of IBM could if necessary be sacrificed. The needs of American customers never could be.

'Where the boss is—there is power,' said Basil de Ferranti, joint managing director of ICT. And where the Boss is there is fundamental research, too.

A Political and Economic Planning report on competition in Europe concluded: 'There is good evidence that where the US enterprise has a subsidiary in the UK the research intensity is much lower than in the US and in some cases there is no British-based research at all.'

It is in the nature of things that it should be so. No matter how generous-minded the men in charge of European operations may be, they must abide by company policy and company finance. The policy is made in America and the finance is provided by America. And he who pays the piper calls the tune.

It may be that the Americans do not want their European subsidiaries to be, technologically speaking, mere hewers of wood and drawers of water but business logic requires that it be so.

The situation can only be altered by structural changes in the ownership of companies and by unashamed government discrimination in favour of British and European concerns.

If Britain and Europe do not have a computer industry they will have no advanced technology in the future. And they will not have a computer industry unless they fight for it—against America.

For as Thomas Edison once wrote: 'Our chief want in life is someone who will make us do what we can.'

The American challenge ought to make Europe do what it can. Which is to build a computer industry of its own.

10

The Second Battle of Britain

'LET US GUARD against the unwarranted influence, whether
sought or unsought, by [America's] military-industrial complex'
—Dwight D Eisenhower

The aim of the American aircraft industry has been to destroy
the British aircraft industry. There is nothing nefarious or even
shocking about this objective. It is the natural consequence of
rigorous competition that the strong survive and the weaker perish.
The British aim has been to devise means of staying alive; to reduce wherever possible opportunities for the Americans to inflict
damage and to strike back, at least occasionally, at markets the
Americans believe to be their inviolable property.

It is unlikely that the US corporations actually expect to take
over British aircraft firms—of which by the mid 'sixties there were
only three sizeable ones, British Aircraft Corporation, Hawker
Siddeley and the much smaller, but aggressively active, Handley
Page. Not even the most supine British Government—and that
is saying something!—would willingly agree to the outright purchase by American interests of the British aviation industry. Although such suggestions have been made, notably by the aviation
consultant to the Labour Party, Richard Worcester.

But there are other ways of eliminating an opponent than by
capturing him. If sufficient British military and civil contracts
could be given to the US the British aviation industry would die
of anaemia. Its designers and engineers would either emigrate to
the US, or be employed in the UK doing sub-contract work for
Boeing, Lockheed, Douglas or General Dynamics. This, indeed,
has already begun to happen.

Britain is the prime target for the US aerospace corporations because she alone in the West operates—or tries to—a world-wide aviation industry offering short, medium and long range aircraft in direct competition with US manufacturers. France, it is true, has a substantial aviation capacity, but its products are confined to short-range civil airlines like the Caravelle, and helicopters. At any rate the French Government is (in American eyes) so besotted with nationalism that it would 'buy French' even if the aircraft were made of wood and string and stuck together with glue.

Not so the British. Their nationalism being of an apparently watery variety, the Americans reckoned they could be persuaded that it was in the wider interests of the free world and of cost effectiveness to submit to an international division of labour. This is known as 'inter-dependence'.

In theory, it is supposed to provide a splendid model of brotherly co-operation. In practice, it has turned out to be something less than ideal so far as the British are concerned. For the huge American corporations with their protected home market, many, many, times the size of the English, can reserve all the important work to themselves. Carried to its logical conclusion, division of labour in the aviation industry would end up with the British designing the ash trays! Effectively, international dependence would mean that America was international and Britain was dependent.

All is fair in love and war—and the same goes for the aviation business. It is not a matter of innocent, cut-throat competition in which the best man wins on account of his lower price, faster delivery date and superior quality. Politics are involved to a degree far in excess of anything experienced in other branches of international commerce.

The British, contrary to their own simulated modesty, are no sluggards at winning orders by bland ruthlessness from which chicanery and polite blackmail are not entirely excluded. But in the aviation game their cards are pitifully weak in comparison with the Americans'.

A host of fortuitous circumstances have combined to reinforce

81

America's natural advantage in size.

The war gave the US a head start. While the British, trying to make up for the years of prewar neglect, were producing military aircraft in quantity which were not always of the best and were sometimes obsolescent, simply in order to be able to fight at all, America, 'The Arsenal of Democracy', was able to plan and produce on a longer-term, more rational basis. She could afford to scrap her mistakes. The British had to fly theirs!

The scale of the American effort was daunting and truly magnificent. When, in 1941, Lord Beaverbrook, then UK Minister of Supply, asked the US for a supreme endeavour, the Americans responded by doubling their target for airplane output to 45,000 planes a year.

During this period they expanded the production line of the fabulous Douglas Dakota, which later became the work-horse of the world's airlines and gave foreign operators a taste for US products.

After the war, Britain and the US were the only two nations in the West with aviation industries. For a while the British, using their political control of Middle Eastern nations, did quite well. Arms sales, including a high proportion of aircraft, almost entirely offset UK defence expenditure overseas. But with the establishment of the North Atlantic Treaty Organisation, the US moved in in a big way.

The price of America's wholehearted military commitment to the defence of Western Europe was that the countries of Western Europe should purchase American weapons. Increasingly the allied air forces of the Continent were equipped with American planes, made either in the US or under licence in Europe. Initially, funds from Washington were provided to finance these purchases; later, when the economies of the Western European countries had recovered, they paid for what they got.

Germany was a particularly rewarding market for the US. The Germans are very impressed by power and success: 'Either at your throat or at your feet.' In the case of America, the Germans were in the prostrate position. They had at any rate little choice. With the Russians on the Oder they had no alternative but to placate the Americans at every turn. The Germans would have 'bought' the Brooklyn Bridge if they had been ordered to do so.

They bought American aircraft right along the line. A great slab of Central Europe was closed to British manufacturers. And, of course, the sale of military aircraft led to European airlines expressing a preference for US civil aircraft, because many of the technical chiefs and pilots had gained their postwar flying experience in US-made planes.

The British had a one-shot triumph, the Viscount, a short-range turbo-prop airliner of which more than four hundred were sold overseas. They also established a remarkable technological lead with the Comet, the first pure jet to go into commercial service. The tragic accidents to this plane, due to metal fatigue, dealt a crippling blow to the British aviation industry from which it never really recovered.

But even if the Comet had been a roaring sales success, like the Viscount, the Americans would still have remorselessly tightened their grip on the world's aviation markets.

They had the resources. They had the military stranglehold on Western Europe. For without American power, NATO was nothing. So who can blame them if, on occasion, they exerted a certain gentle pressure to make sure that national airlines, as well as national air forces, 'chose American'. Would not the British have done the same in America's position?

Of course the American planes chosen were good. But had they been less than first class they would still have been gratefully accepted. A poor tenant does not argue when a kind landlord offers to sell him furniture, even when some of the furniture demonstrably fails to give satisfaction, if the alternative is notice to quit.

Over a three-year period the Germans lost seventy US designed Starfighter aircraft in accidents—ten per cent of their total fighter forces. Yet they bore the loss stoically, concluding, no doubt correctly, that it was a small price to pay for maintaining US good-will.

As the British saw their markets dwindle they gathered their scattered strength, spread over as many as half a dozen independent companies, into two major corporations and launched six big projects, three civil and three military. Each of these projects was matched, or matched twice over, across the Atlantic.

Here, in the late 1950s, was the confrontation to decide whether or not Britain could sustain a viable aircraft industry, or whether it was doomed to be reduced to the status of a sub-contractor owing its soul to the 'company store' in the States.

The contest was really no match. It was like setting a bantam against a heavyweight. For Britain, one slip would be vital; a knockout. Costs rising too far above estimates; snags in performance; failure to land that early and substantial overseas order—any one of these would almost certainly ruin a project.

There were other complications. By 1960–61 the Conservative Government was under severe financial and political pressure to cut State spending. Chief target of the Labour Opposition's wrath was the aircraft programme, requiring many millions from the Exchequer. To Labour, this programme appeared a wasteful misuse of resources, which ought to be applied to better uses than a prestige stunt to indulge the Tories' delusions of grandeur.

The Labour Party was in a specially vindictive mood as it had lost three General Elections in a row. A principal object of its derision, amounting in some cases to hatred, was the TSR2, the technical strike reconnaissance aircraft, built by the British Aircraft Corporation. It was by far the most important of the military contracts by which the aircraft industry hoped to recover lost ground.

The TSR2 was a supersonic bomber capable of acting in a nuclear or conventional role, flying very high out of range of anti-aircraft fire or hedge-hopping under an enemy's radar screen. In public relations parlance it was to be the 'all singing, all dancing star' of the RAF's repertoire.

84

Its nuclear capacity however roused the especial ire of the Opposition which was at that time trying to appease the pacifist Left Wing by denouncing Britain's atomic weapons and their delivery system.

Moreover the TSR2 was the pet project of Julian Amery, a tough-minded right-wing Tory who did not court popularity and did not receive any gratuitously. He was a man whom many people loved to bait.

The critics of the TSR2 were not confined to Labour politicians. The aviation consultant, Richard Worcester, directed an unwavering fire at the plane. He had for two years been employed on an aviation journal in the United States and had returned to edit his own paper in the United Kingdom. He commanded considerable respect and following among Labour leaders who were looking round for technical reasons to cancel the plane once they got office. Mr Worcester was later to boast that he had in fact been a prime mover in grounding the TSR2.

Backing Mr Worcester's effort was the highly vocal air correspondent of the weekly journal, *The Economist*, Miss Mary Goldring. *The Economist* has always shown a touching fidelity to American interests and admiration for American achievements. In turn, US businessmen demonstrate faith in *The Economist*'s pulling power by regularly taking as much as forty per cent of the journal's display advertising.

Another outspoken foe of the TSR2 was *The Observer*, the Sunday newspaper owned and edited by one of the Astor family which has strong American affiliations.

Such a formidable front not surprisingly attracted a number of Conservatives who were more than half-convinced anyway that the country's financial difficulties were caused by extravagant defence spending.

As opposition to the TSR2 swelled, so the plane's advocates compensated for their declining numerical strength by redoubling their claims for its performance, thus making themselves more vulnerable to counter-attacks. The more boasts, the more hostages to fortune.

As the debate in the UK over the TSR2 grew in bitterness, so the contrast with American aviation grew even plainer, to America's undoubted advantage.

In the US the major complaint about the Administration's aviation policy was that it was not bold enough, not big enough.

Stung by Russia's triumph in being the first nation to launch a satellite into space (in November 1957), the American people and politicians were resolved to advance in overwhelming techno-logical array, to remind the world that the USA was still the scientific-engineering super power without equals and without rivals.

Military projects involving sophisticated hardware were urged forward at maximum speed. General Dwight Eisenhower's warn-ings in his final address as President to 'guard against the unwarranted influence, whether sought or unsought, by military-industrial complex' was swept aside. America's pride was at stake. Her superiority had been challenged. So the crowds cried 'shoot the moon' and the whizz kids, led by the redoubtable Defence Secretary Robert McNamara, the man born to be a computer, applied their cost effectiveness technique to expedite projects among which was a controversial aircraft known as the TFX.

In range and performance the TFX was slightly inferior to the TSR2 but it was good enough. Here was the substitute sought by the British critics. 'Let's save the £750 million developing our own plane,' they said, 'and buy American instead.'

This argument was clinched when the US sold twenty-four TFX's (later renamed F111) to the Australians. The Australians might have preferred the British plane but they could not resist the American price. With a secure home demand of 1,600 planes for the US Army and Navy, unit costs on subsequent orders were so much lower than for the British TSR2 which had a secure home contract for 160 planes, at the most. The Americans had a ten to one advantage which they duly pressed home.

As usual, God was on the side of the big battalions. So was Harold Wilson. Within a few months of winning the General Election of 1964 he cancelled the TSR2 which shortly before had performed faultlessly in test flights. The prototypes of the plane were destroyed. So were the jigs and tools. In its place the American F111 was ordered for the RAF. Two other British military aircraft, a supersonic vertical take-off fighter and a transport aircraft, were also abandoned. The American Phantom fighter and Hercules transport were ordered in their stead. Thus three of Britain's six air hopes were demolished for ever.

The echoes of the affair still resound. Stephen Hastings, a Conservative MP, wrote a book called *The Murder of the TSR2*,[1] in which he alleged that: 'The Americans, under arms salesman Henry J Kuss, were so keen to break into the British aircraft industry that they offered C130 transport aircraft (the Hercules) to the British Government at a figure between £700,000 and £800,000, while the unfortunate Australians had to pay £1,300,000 for the same aircraft. So the Australians were persuaded to buy the American F111 at cut rate and the British were persuaded to buy the Hercules at cut rate.'

Hastings makes a further and more serious accusation. 'There can be only one reasonable deduction [from the decision to cancel the British projects], the Prime Minister had to have backing for sterling. The Americans would provide the backing necessary, but at a price—the British would be well advised to abandon expensive projects which could be duplicated in the USA.'

The clear implication is that the Americans twisted Mr Wilson's arm by promising him financial support in return for giving up the military planes. They seem also almost to have succeeded in persuading him to give up a major civil project—the Anglo-French supersonic Concorde.

According to Hastings, the Labour Government, on the day it took office, despatched Sir Eric Roll (then a distinguished civil

1. *The Murder of the TSR2,* Stephen Hastings, Macdonald, 1966

servant, now a director of numerous companies including American ones) to Washington with a draft statement which declared : 'The UK Government have already indicated to the French Government their wish to re-examine urgently the Concorde project.'

Hastings infers that this paragraph—none of the statement having at that time been published in the UK—was added after Roll's discussions with the Americans. In other words the British Government announced its intention to consider cancelling Concorde as a result of pressure from the Americans.

The French, under de Gaulle, being much less amenable to American wishes, refused to drop the Concorde threatened to take the issue to the International Court and obliged the British to go on with the airliner.

The effect of the cancellation of the military aircraft did, however, reverberate through British aviation.

Production on the civil side was denied that technical 'spin off' from weaponry development which the Americans had found so useful in promoting civil aviation. Morale among those employed in the British industry plunged, and dived lower still when a committee under Lord Plowden—another civil servant turned businessman—declared that 'really advanced aviation systems should always be purchased from the USA'.

The credibility of British aviation with a labour force of 200,000 men and annual exports worth £220 million was ravaged. The deadly question went round the foreign airlines : 'Why buy British, when all the indications are that these people are going out of business?' Ludicrous notions of American duplicity were circulated. Among the more extreme of them was the belief that 'the Yankees' would sabotage the VC-10 airliner on its maiden flight to New York.

Such hysteria was a symptom of widespread defeatism caused by muddle in the aircraft industry, and vacillation at Whitehall, but also by the Americans' colossal strength and ability to exploit their rival's blunders.

Stephen Hastings makes the point that 'The American campaign to dominate the aerospace industry of the West has been long drawn out, insidious and effective. Two of the principal targets have, I believe, been the British Joint Services Mission in Washington (originally established during the war) and the technical staffs of the main British air carriers.

'The attitude of mind the campaign has induced among senior officials and officers has ranged . . . to an outright and avowed preference for American equipment, sometimes assiduously pressed upon colleagues.

'The American technique with the airlines is to select, after careful study, some of the younger, more ambitious and able engineers, and to subject them to a long campaign of conditioning in the hope of a dividend in due course. It has not been entirely unsuccessful.'

The dividend has indeed been a considerable one. Whatever the reason—whether as a result of long-term persuasion or from sterling's weakness or from the sheer incapacity and political stupidity of the British—the rewards for America have been most gratifying.

Apart from the direct orders for US planes already described, large sections of the British industry have been turned over to making parts for American aircraft which the British Government has contracted to buy. This is a psychologically important achievement in that it ties British management to winning the goodwill of American main contractors and conditions British technicians to working to American instructions.

With that readiness to spot talent and employ it to maximum advantage, American aviation interests have recruited hundreds of British engineers for their US plants. They have also given jobs to displaced British aero-engineers at a specially designed centre in Southern England. They are to concentrate on tasks set them by US companies. The Americans amiably argue that they are doing Britain a good turn as they have not actually drained brains away to the States. Anyone, even British firms, can use the centre for a fee, although in fact most of the talent will be employed on US projects. The design centre is like the Ritz : open to everyone, but more open to those with money—and that happens to be the Americans.

The rout of British aviation was completed by the signing of an agreement by which the Americans promised to offset some of the $1,000 million it was costing the UK Government to buy American equipment.

Under this extraordinary arrangement the Americans did not actually promise to buy anything specific, they merely agreed to allow the British to tender on equal terms with American concerns for certain non-sophisticated weapons. The Americans waived the requirements of the Buy America Act (which lays down that, to be acceptable, foreign bids must be at least fifty per cent lower than the lowest US bid) on a strictly limited list of items. They also allowed the British to sell equipment to Saudi Arabia, long regarded as a US client state. This sale was to count as a sale to America in computing the offset total.

Here was agreement of a kind . . . the kind between a shrewd young boss and an aged retainer of unsound mind. It was remarked by some embittered individuals in the British aviation industry that the 'special relationship' between Britain and the United States had become one of servant and master.

Of course the British had no one to blame but themselves for the sorry state of their once proud aeronautical industry. No one forced them to commit their follies. However much propaganda the Americans disposed of, it could never have triumphed without the sheer ineptitude of British firms, the civil service and the political parties. Well might the Americans echo Cromwell's words when his foes charged to disaster at Dunbar : 'Now thank thee Lord they have delivered themselves into our hands.'

Credit in no small measure should be given to the quality of the American aviation industry in all its branches.

The salesmanship is slick and professional, combining the technical training of the Service Departments with the excellent presentation methods perfected by the United States. In clinching the F111 deal with Australia, General Dynamics left nothing to chance. Each question was anticipated. The answer to every problem was on hand, so that the man on the spot handling enquiries did not have to refer back to base.

If, in the days of Empire, the British soldier serving abroad was an ambassador for his country, so today the US serving officer is a salesman for his country's products.

Utter conviction in the superiority of American equipment, buttressed by a command of technical details, together form an impressive front, and foreign buyers cannot help but be struck by the sheer efficiency of a sales operation conducted by such able individuals.

When it comes to selling arms, the fact that American military personnel are imbued with as much business sense as martial training gives US negotiators a big advantage over their rivals.

They used this advantage to the full in the F111 transactions, where the Australians must have compared the smooth, well-integrated manœuvres, conducted jointly by the USAF and General Dynamics, with the halting, barely co-ordinated efforts of the RAF and the British Aircraft Corporation.

British professional soldiers were taught, at least until recently, to hold trade in some contempt. American professional soldiers are brought up to respect business and, in a material world where arms salesmen are at least as important as vacuum salesmen, the American tradition is more in keeping with the times.

Slowly and sadly, consciousness of England's inadequacies and shortcomings sank into the minds of political leaders and public alike.

The Conservatives had been rudely reminded of their dependence on the US when, in 1962, Mr McNamara cancelled the Skybolt airborne missile, intended for use by the RAF, thus leaving the British nuclear bombers without the means of reaching their targets.

Not long after being returned to office, the Labour Party, too, acknowledged that unless Britain was to decline to the status of an industrial satellite, a new policy must be hammered out. So the British aviation industry was duly proclaimed dead, and in its place there arose the concept of an Anglo-European partnership, not confined to one aircraft, the Concorde, but spread across the whole spectrum of aerospace.

By her very success in eliminating British aviation as a sovereign force, America had called into existence a European counterforce big enough on its own to compete with the US.

Could the Americans have prevented the creation of a European-wide aviation industry—which must necessarily cut deeply into their overseas sales—by being 'kind' to the UK? By holding back the killer punch so that the UK industry, albeit sick and groggy, could have survived? The answer must be no. There was a deadly inevitability about the process.

First, US involvement in the defence of Europe led to the Americans supplying the weapons to the alliance. Then as the West European markets recovered economically, and as the bill for the American taxpayers mounted, so the Americans determined to sell their arms and aircraft to offset the cost of sustaining the American defence of Europe. After that economy and skill took over.

Because America was big and her mass production techniques were highly advanced she could meet her own requirements—and fill the wants of her allies from the over-spill. Short of reserving a portion of the aviation industry exclusively to the UK there was no way in which British aircraft production could live beside that of America.

Why was not a portion reserved for the UK? Because neither the military authorities nor the aircraft firms were prepared to accept a situation in which America relied on another country for the supply of any type of aircraft. The United States could supply all her needs from her own resources, therefore she would do so. American boys must never be denied American-made planes; American plant must never be rendered idle in order to cosset fumbling foreigners unable to compete on their own merits.

The sheer size of America, the deep, abiding competitive instinct of her people and their will to win made it impossible for the US to adopt an aviation policy other than the one she followed. To restrain business enthusiasm in the interests of diplomacy (even though it were to the ultimate advantage of the United States), to pass up a business opportunity for the sake of an alliance, are calculations alien to the American nature. Give things away? Yes. Refrain from making them so that others can make them? No.

The Americans acted with the grain of their character, and Britain and Europe reacted to circumstances in the only way they could.

I I

The One That Got Away

FREDERICK EDWARDS WAS disconsolate. His job as lecturer in science at Northampton Polytechnic was in jeopardy, probably doomed. The college was cutting down its budget and preparing to get rid of staff. In the slump-ridden England of 1920 there was no room for 'frills'—as science education was so regarded.

Frederick decided not to wait to be sacked. He quit. In partnership with his father he established a small business buying and selling laboratory equipment. Edwards senior's skill as a carpenter helped in the display and saleability of the company's products. The business prospered and it was not long before Edwards junior became aware of another potential outlet: the growing demand for high vacuum pumps vital to the production of electric lamps and radio valves.

Borrowing £25 from his wife, Frederick established a firm to import pumps from Germany. He realised that a whole new technology was opening up with the opportunity of carrying out many industrial processes in the perfectly inert environment of a vacuum.

The experimenter began to stir in the businessman. Why not manufacture these pumps himself? Why not develop new types? In 1937 Edwards produced his first vacuum pump. With the war, output grew. With peace—and boom conditions—demand outpaced both his factory facilities and his capital resources. He applied to the Government-backed Industrial and Commercial Finance Corporation for support. It was provided to the tune of a £130,000 loan. Edwards High Vacuum was on its way to the big time.

By 1954 the company was installed in a new factory in Crawley and was employing close on 1,500 workpeople, most of them highly skilled. That same year Edwards 'went public'. The shares, given a high-growth rating, swiftly found favour among investors and soared so high on the market that the dividend yield was barely two per cent.

Success followed success. New factories were opened at Eastbourne and Shoreham; subsidiaries were established in Canada, Italy, United States and Germany. Fifty per cent of the company's output was exported and a very high percentage of the staff, including virtually the whole of the management, were recruited from universities.

Edwards High Vacuum was a model of what British industry was supposed to achieve : talent plus science plus investment resulting in exports being substituted for imports.

Indeed Edwards' was so good that it attracted the attention of the New York Society of Security Analysts. This body of investment advisers had sent a study group to England to discover promising prospects for American money; the team picked Edwards High Vacuum as one having outstanding possibilities for the long term.

New York analysts did not exaggerate. The prospects for Edwards were truly dazzling. By the early 'sixties Edwards had developed into the world's largest independent vacuum equipment manufacturer : the only one of the six major companies spanning vacuum technology not allied to any other group.

The company could simulate on earth the almost complete vacuum conditions that exist outside the earth's atmosphere and the whole of space technology depends on vacuum technology.

There was much more besides. High vacuum technologies are required for the manufacture of telescopes; for scanning systems used in colour television; for enabling small electrical components to be made smaller still (micro miniaturisation). Vacuum technology is indispensable in the nuclear power establishments throughout the world.

The firm also contributes to medical science on a large scale. By freeze-drying, its vacuum equipment transforms life-saving vaccines into a dry porous sponge which can be reconstituted with distilled water. The freeze-drying product is much easier to transport than vaccine in liquid form; it has almost unlimited shelf-life and so is vital to underdeveloped countries where communications are poor.

Road travel is being made safer by the elimination of misting or icing of windscreens. Removal of this hazard has been made possible by using film-heated windscreens—and their manufacture depends on vacuum technology.

Space, communications, nuclear power, medical science, the motor industry, Edwards' is intimately concerned in every one of these growth industries. To the Americans such a mouth-watering prospect was worth more than mere portfolio investment. It was worth a take-over bid.

So in the autumn of 1966, just five months after the death of Frederick Edwards, the firm's pioneer founder, the bid came—from Varian Associates of California.

Varian were in trouble. They had a turnover of $180 million a year, but much of that was dependent on US Government orders —which showed every sign of falling off. Diversification was indicated. Varian already had a small interest in the vacuum industry. It was here that expansion looked most promising. And expansion could most readily be achieved by taking over the outstanding performer in high vacuum technology—Edwards' of Britain.

The letter to Edwards made a tentative offer of 11s (approximately $1.60) a share for shares which were then standing at 7s 4½d.

Eleven shillings a share represented a total purchase price of £5,200,000 ($15 million). From a purely financial angle it looked very attractive. The Edwards' family trusts held twenty-two per cent of the equity and the board was prepared to recommend acceptance.

But before the directors could send out a letter to shareholders giving details of Varian's proposals there was a leak which sent

Edwards' shares soaring on the Stock Exchange.

W A Smith, Edwards' managing director, decided that in view of the rumours that were circulating he ought to tell his senior executives precisely what was happening.

And now occurred one of the most startling developments in the history of the American take-over of Great Britain. The executives of Edwards High Vacuum said 'No'. They made it plain that if control of the company passed into American hands they—and their highly skilled staffs—would leave. It would be wrong, they said, to allow the benefit of years of highly technical research to be lost to Britain.

Here, at last, was Bunker Hill in reverse!

Varian was not mainly interested in Edwards' plant or equipment. What was sought above all was its brains, represented by the top men at Crawley. So when Varian heard of the executives' attitude, it swiftly withdrew its tentative bid.

Not everyone was pleased at the failure of the take-over. Some shareholders were deeply upset at not getting 11s for their shares. Some economic commentators took time off from foretelling the future to point out that the American company would not have sought to buy Edwards' unless it had seen a big growth potential and that American ownership and American money would have expanded the output and exports from Crawley. How foolish, they said, to resist the Americans who brought only gifts!

US businessmen must be eternally grateful for such blinding shortsightedness. Never mind if first-class scientists are turned into servants of foreign countries; never mind if some of them are shipped across to the United States; never mind if the real research and development is switched from Crawley to California; never mind if America's lead in advanced technology is reinforced; never mind if America's gain is England's loss; never mind all that —if the shareholders get their price all is for the best in the best of all possible worlds!

Economic commentators who take this line may be divided into two classes. Those who worship bigness for its own sake and

97

would enthuse just as shrilly over China were it to transplant the US as the number one commercial power. The other, more honourable class, clings to the belief, neither ignoble nor fatuous, that profit is the only true determinant of materialist satisfaction in a materialist world.

If the profit is maximised by the Americans rather than the British, why worry? In a world of free trade it matters not who owns what, for in the end everyone will benefit through the free interchange of goods and ideas.

Carried to its logical conclusion, every single industry in Europe would sooner or later become American property and everyone would become in fact, if not in name, an American citizen. Such a prospect may not be altogether displeasing to a good number of people. Only they forget one thing. Every citizen would not be equal; in George Orwell's immortal phrase, 'some would be more equal than others'. The 'some' would be the genuine American citizens of the USA.

Just as the rules of theoretical competition have had to be altered over the years to take account of the imperfection of competition in practice, so the rules of free trade laid down by Adam Smith in the eighteenth century have become unrecognisable and unworkable in the twentieth century. The trouble is that many British economists—taught by free trade professors—are still thrilled by the old dogmas; splendid old dogmas maybe, but no longer conforming to reality.

Goods and labour and capital do not flow freely across the frontiers. Governments exercise powers over business undreamed of in Adam Smith's days. Politics are enmeshed in commerce. To maintain that, in these conditions, the rights of shareholders are absolute and that they should be free to sell their companies to the highest bidder is wholly absurd.

A sensible resolve to defend British (perhaps, one day, European) interests, would seem to be the proper antidote to the unworldly theories of the free traders.

Unfortunately the argument in England about the shareholders' right, the place of profit, and the national interest, have been clouded by the arid controversy between Socialism and private enterprise.

Faced by the demand for 'the nationalisation of the means of production, distribution and exchange', enshrined in Clause IV of the Labour Party's constitution, the defenders of free enterprise felt obliged to be as dogmatic as their opponents in upholding the claims of international capital against the challenge of international labour.

If, as appears likely, Socialism in the Labour Party is giving way to the acceptance of a mixed economy and of pragmatic politics the chances are that the militants of free enterprise will modify their views. Then a national, rather than ideological, approach will be applied to industrial problems and a climate of opinion may be created far less favourable than at present to American infiltration.

The significance of the Edwards High Vacuum case lies in the attitude of the scientists and the effect of that attitude on the board of directors.

Thirty years ago a transatlantic bid might have been welcomed by scientific staff as a way of improving their pay and conditions; or rejected because it was a capitalist device abhorrent to Socialist conscience. Instead it was the Americanisation of Edwards' to which objection was taken. The national view was adopted and the national view prevailed over short-term economic advantages to men who undoubtedly would have benefited from higher American salaries.

Similarly, the board's reaction to the scientists' ultimatum displayed a conscious identity of interest with the employees. At one time a board of directors would simply have dismissed the opinions of its staff, even of senior personnel, as of no significance. But the Edwards' board took the national requirements into account and so the Americans were turned back by a consensus of opinion in which patriotism played its part.

Is this a special case? Perhaps. In so far as it was the skills of

99

Edwards' scientists that was the main attraction for Varian then the employees obviously carried more weight than they would in other firms. But no company today can afford to ignore the views of its leading employees. Talent is the most valuable commodity in commerce. It is in short supply and is an asset which must be increasingly cherished.

The Edwards' case may have special features but it does establish a precedent which will surely inspire others.

Whatever the future holds for Edwards' (and it is probable that it will eventually link up with a broader-based British group), the firm has shown how to fight back against the American invasion—and win.

12

The One That Should Have Got Away

IN ONE OF Sherlock Holmes' cases the master remarks on the curious incident of the dog that didn't bark. The silence, Holmes decided, was the most significant factor in the case.

The silence of the Hoover Company is equally significant. A six-page review of the company's performance referred in glowing terms to the achievements of Hoover since the British subsidiary of Hoover of North Canton, Ohio, was established in 1919. 'Sales rapidly increased and in 1932 the first British Hoover factory was built at Perivale, Middlesex. Hoover Ltd was established as a public company in 1931. Today British shareholders own some forty-five per cent of the equity, the remaining fifty-five per cent being owned by the parent American company.'

And who was responsible for that 'rapid increase in sales'? Who decided to build a British factory? Who built the British Hoover concern to several times the size of its parent back in North Canton, Ohio?

The review is silent on these points. And behind that strange silence lies the story of a disagreement between the head of an American parent company and its 'child' which has no parallel in the history of US infiltration into British industry.

The man who made English Hoover and showed the Americans how to conduct business was Englishman Charles Colston, son of a village schoolmaster in Gerrards Cross, Buckinghamshire. Colston joined the newly formed Hoover concern in 1919 at the age of twenty-eight. The business was backed with only $60,000 of capital and was simply a distributing and marketing agency for the American-made vacuum cleaners.

Colston's engineering experience had been gained in the tough school of the Royal Engineers in which he served from 1914–18, holding every rank up to Company Sergeant-Major. The ex-CSM had just the right combination of drive, flair and guts to make a triumphant success of the tiny company. He it was who turned it from a £20,000 midget into a giant worth £15 million.

Nine years after joining, Colston was made managing director. The company was still merely an importing and sales agency but in 1932 came the break into the 'big time'.

The devaluation of the pound and the system of tariffs imposed after the great slump made Hoover machines imported from America too expensive. The British branch had to expand or expire. Colston decided the cleaners must be made in the UK.

So he organised the plans and superintended the building of the factory at Western Avenue, Perivale. Year after year the factory was extended to cope with the demand for a product that could ease the housewife's burden and take the drudgery out of floor cleaning.

Came the war and Hoover engineering talent was enlisted by the Ministry of Aircraft Production. Colston's genius was used to speed the flow of engineering goods. And his conviction in personal initiative went into the slogan, which his brother coined, 'It all depends on ME'.

Peace brought boom with returning soldiers setting up home and the virtual disappearance of domestics (there had been some three million before the war). The demand for labour-saving devices soared. 'At the same time,' the company's review records, 'Hoover began to expand its range of products.'

Again no name is mentioned. The review carefully omits the information that in 1945 Charles Colston bought the world rights, outside Canada and the US, for a Czech-invented washing machine. Colston was sure this machine could be mass-produced on a scale which would bring it within the range of nearly every household in the country—this, at a time when hardly one British household in fifty had a washing machine. Colston wanted to make luxuries into necessities. He also wanted to make lots more money for Hoover. He did both. If any man is responsible for the kitchen revolution which freed British housewives from dreary chores it is Charles Colston.

At Merthyr Tydfil, in depressed South Wales, a fine new factory began producing washing machines in 1948. And one of Colston's brainwaves also began producing results. This brainwave was a major reason for the chill silence with which Hoover was later to envelop his activities.

Colston believed passionately in incentives. Give the right men the right rewards and any target could be reached. Such was his basic philosophy. As he thought, so he acted.

Following discussions with financial experts in the City, he introduced the controversial Hoover 'A' share scheme. These were 1s shares entitled to a fixed dividend of a mere four per cent but given the right to participate to the extent of one-eighth of profits, provided profits rose above a defined minimum—£650,000.

The shares were confined to 110 executives with a minimum allotment of two thousand shares (*ie* a £100 investment).

Colston naturally sought the views of the directors of the American parent company before going ahead.

Frank Hoover, younger brother of the boss H W Hoover, Sr., said : 'If Charles Colston is enough of a fool to believe that with this scheme he and his colleagues will do without pay increases while sharply pushing up the English profits, then let him go ahead'—so the board agreed.

Colston recalls : 'The 110 people who were allotted the shares would have backed me through hell and high water. I had frequent meetings with them—sometimes "black tie" affairs at Claridge's. The scheme kept their enthusiasm at fever heat. Our profit estimates, which the folk in Canton, Ohio, had been inclined to scoff at, were realised over and over again.'

As the profits soared, so did the value of the 'A' shares. The man holding the minimum two thousand saw his holding doubled by a one-for-one bonus and then looked on as it increased substantially again. When H W Hoover, Jr, joined the English board in 1954 he offered 1.45 Hoover ordinary shares for each of the 'A' shares. Since Hoover's were then standing at over £2 each that meant the original £100 holding was now worth almost £13,000!

Partly as a result of this incredible advance English Hoover became five times larger than its American parent.

After 1947 the Continental branches of Hoover flourished mightily, too. (In 1962 control of these branches was transferred to Hoover US which reckoned it ought to have the fruits of this enterprise, which were calculated to grow still more lush following England's expected entry into the Common Market.)

An exuberant Colston crowed: 'I don't mind how you measure size, you can do it by sales, by profits, by employment, by exports —by any test you like, the answer's the same. We could have paid the shipping charge on British-made Hoovers plus the import duty and still undersold the American company on its own doorstep.

'The market valuation of American Hoover was actually less than the sterling value of its investment in British Hoover. So if someone could have bought up the American Hoover they would have got all their money back from the English shares and obtained all the other Hoover assets for nothing. Of course, it wasn't possible to do a deal like that with the Hoover family in control.'

But suppose Hoover of England were divorced from Hoover of America? Suppose the British began to get uppity—as well they might having so completely overshadowed the US principal?

Was this fear, coloured, too, perhaps by jealousy of Colston's extraordinary achievement, the reason why he was squeezed out?

Into England to learn how it was done came Herbert W Hoover, Jr, grandson of the founder. The thirty-two-year-old American seemed amiable enough on his arrival in 1951. He and Colston appeared to get on well together. The surface appearance was deceptive, however. Colston found the newcomer, 'Young Herb', unable or unwilling to see his point of view.

Colston had been a close friend of H W, Sr, whose idea it was that Young Herb should put himself in Colston's hands. The younger Hoover differed with Colston—over the 'A' share business, over the trust which Colston established with his own money for Hoover employees and former employees, and over the independence of the British company.

Life at Hoover's became increasingly tense and in 1954 Colston, aged sixty-three, decided to quit.

He received a golden handshake of £83,000 ($225,000), a record, from the US parent. Colston remarked at the time that he left 'on terms of the warmest friendship with every member of the English Board'.

It may be doubted whether this all-embracing sentiment applied to 'Young Herb' who now became boss of the entire group. As president of American Hoover in succession to his father, he took over as chairman of British Hoover in 1956.

Following a court case concerning Colston's rights to set up in business in the appliance line, Colston's portrait was removed from the board room—as were copies from the firm's factories. His achievements went unrecorded in the company's review. He became an 'unperson'. (This treatment was handsomely reversed in 1967, after Young Herb had left the top job.)

In 1966 Felix Mansager, another American, took over the British company.

Mansager took over a company of nine thousand employees, doing fifty-seven per cent of the electric cleaner business in the UK, selling about thirty-eight per cent of the washing machines and involved also in selling floor polishers, spin dryers, refrigerators, electric fan heaters, gas fires, electric irons, food mixers, electric blankets, kettles, toasters, hair dryers and small electric motors.

Very big business. But suppose Charles Colston had been left to manage this concern—how much bigger it might have been! Colston himself reckons that if he had stayed in command

Hoover today could be the biggest consumer durable group in Britain—bigger than Thorn, AEI or GEC.

If Hoover UK had been hived off from its US parent it would not have been subjected to interference which almost certainly hindered its progress. If Hoover UK had produced the vacuum cleaners under licence—as it produced the Czech washing machines—far faster economic growth might have been achieved.

Colston, with thirty-five years as a servant of an American-owned concern, firmly believes that the head of a subsidiary must be a national of the country in which it is operating. A company operating in Britain should have a Briton as its boss.

Indeed, Colston goes further. He thinks that wherever possible the entire board ought to be made up of the host country's nationals. Certainly this would dispose of the feeling—prevalent in a number of US-owned concerns in England—that the American executives are set to watch over their British fellow executives. This 'commercial apartheid' is not good for personal relationships.

Moreover, where the Americans exercise control mistakes may be made through insufficient familiarity with local conditions.

Colston recalls an example from the early days of Hoover when the American then in charge objected to the firm advertising in the newspapers. All advertising, he insisted, should be in magazines.

This was a perfectly feasible policy in the US where there were no national newspapers, and magazines such as the *Saturday Evening Post* had a sale of many millions. But it was nonsensical in Britain where the magazines had a relatively small circulation and the daily newspapers covered the whole country. US companies and US advertising agencies still tend to think of the British Press as being as parochial as the American. Hence their preoccupation with the television network when seeking to influence the public.

Just as irritating to British executives is the insistence of some American firms—not Hoover—in having 100 per cent US ownership of a subsidiary. British investors were invited to take a stake in Hoover Ordinary shares in 1937. The Company's progress was greatly aided by publicity given in the British newspapers to rising share values, annual general meetings of shareholders and so on. Even in Hoover, however, British shareholders with a 45 per cent financial stake have only 30 per cent of the votes.

But Hoover is still much better than Ford and Vauxhall where there are no British shareholders. Without them these companies lack a spur and the American chiefs are denied the benefit of home-brewed criticism. In the long-term that is quite a price to pay for hogging all the capital—and the dividends—of the subsidiaries

13

Snap! Crackle!! Pop!!!

KELLOGG'S, LIKE HOOVER, is a word that has entered the English language. However much competitors may dislike the fact Kellogg is synonymous with breakfast cereal.

Most people looking at the packet, and the packet is always worth looking at, would conclude from the 'stories about Regiments of the British Army' and the address of the factory (in Manchester) that Kellogg's was as British as roast beef. In truth it is as British as Cooper's Oxford Marmalade and the Encyclopaedia Britannica. That is to say, it is hundred per cent American! With a history that is as uniquely American as the Wild West—where it all started.

Battle Creek, Michigan, was a rough frontier village of a thousand souls when the Kellogg family settled there in the middle of the last century. They were poor folk and rather sad too, for Mrs Kellogg had lost a number of babies, due—so the Kelloggs believed—to bad doctoring.

The Seventh Day Adventists were strongly established in Michigan. And the Kelloggs were attracted to the sect, not only because of natural piety but because the Adventists possessed a water cure for many diseases and practised strict rules about food. Piety and physical fitness seemed a righteous combination. Mr Kellogg helped to make Battle Creek the headquarters of the Adventists. One day it was to win fame in another way and become known the world over as Health City.

In the course of time two sons were born to the Kelloggs. John and Will Keith. Both survived and grew strong.

John trained as a doctor and came to the sanatorium, which his father had helped to found, as a physician. Will Keith at fourteen became a salesman in his father's tiny broom-making factory. In 1879 when Will Keith was nineteen and John twenty-seven the two brothers began an association which was to carry one of them to great riches. Significantly it was the salesman, not the doctor, who was destined for wealth-through-cereals.

For years the two worked at the sanatorium—John as physician, Will Keith as general dogsbody and book-keeper (at six dollars a week).

The normal breakfast of an American frontiersman at this time consisted of meat and fried eggs, fried potatoes, bread topped with molasses and a dish of fried corn meal washed down with rivers of boiled coffee. A load like that, according to one commentator, took twelve or more hours of sledgehammer toil to utilise. But as the frontier advanced westwards, and finally vanished, fewer and fewer people were engaged in sledgehammer labour. Sedentary habits required sedentary style diets.

Fortunately for the Brothers Kellogg, Battle Creek Sanatorium, according to the rules of the Seventh Day Adventists, operated a self-denying diet which excluded coffee, tea, alcohol, tobacco, spices and meat. By mortifying the flesh the Kelloggs were to discover the way to fortifying the revenue.

John began experimenting. He aimed to produce food which would be natural and health-giving. Nuts and grains were his raw materials. And in 1894 the Kelloggs came up with the world's first pre-cooked flaked cereal. The flakes were tough and tasteless, but they proved popular with the patients at the sanatorium, one of whom was an unsuccessful hardware dealer called Post who was later to win commercial immortality as the inventor of Post Toasties and Instant Postum.

Kellogg's flakes were winning converts to the cult of healthy-living. Former patients kept ordering supplies after they had left the sanatorium.

To cope with the demand Will Keith started a small factory. It prospered. John, gifted and temperamental, however, did not prosper with it. He broke with his brother in 1901.

And now the wheat-flake boom really got going. By 1904 no

109

fewer than thirty companies were busily engaged in turning out flakes for diet-conscious Americans. 'Families invested their life savings in cereal manufacturing machines and set up plants in sheds or even in tents,' says Kellogg's biographer. 'New companies mushroomed overnight.'

The real winner however, the breakfast food destined to become the most popular ready-to-serve cereal in the world, was Will Keith Kellogg's toasted corn flakes to which he added malt flavour and sugar (an additive of which brother John would not have approved as he had banned sugar in the old sanatorium days).

In 1906 Kellogg incorporated the Battle Creek Toasted Corn Flake Co solely for the production of corn flakes (the name was changed to Kellogg Co in 1925, the year the firm came to England).

To guard against imitations Will Keith Kellogg's signature appeared on every carton. The 1906 slogan, 'none genuine without the signature', became known all over the globe.

Will Keith was not a particularly happy man. He had constant legal tussles with his brother. He suffered domestic tragedies. At the age of eighty he went blind. But his business thrived exceedingly. He did for the food industry what Henry Ford did for the motor car.

The salesman in him was never dormant. Each improvement in food processing was marketed with consummate skill. The wax-tight package to keep his products fresh was launched with a mighty trumpet blast of publicity. Dynamic selling ideas poured from his lively, questing mind. He was a leader in premiums ('give aways'), competitions and all sorts of promotional schemes.

Not for nothing was the joke told—in many languages, too— of the American salesman who asked the Pope how much he wanted to alter the Lord's Prayer from 'Give us this day our daily bread' to 'Give us this day our Kellogg's Corn Flakes'.

When Will Keith Kellogg died in 1951 at the age of ninety-one he had accumulated a fortune of well over $300 million (transferred to the Kellogg Foundation for charitable purposes).

Part of this great food-making empire had spilled into England in the 'twenties. The era of the Bright Young Things demanded easy-to-cook breakfasts, or better still, breakfasts that required no cooking at all. Slimming was also gaining in popularity (women had to be slim to suit the fashions of the 'twenties) so the climate was just right for W K Kellogg.

The opportunity was taken with a vengeance. Kellogg's are naturally shy about profit margins, though they are said to have at least half of the British cereal market, worth some £40 million a year. But the scale of profit-making may be gauged by one interesting little incident. In 1951 a British businessman, supplying Kellogg's with baking equipment, was paid, not in cash but in stock. Two £1 shares to be precise. But each of these shares was worth £9,103 10s, for the equipment bought—coolers and dryers—was priced at £18,207.

The reason for the fantastic price of the £1 share was that the US parent of English Kellogg's had never bothered to bring the capital of its subsidiary, registered in July 1924, into line with its steadily increasing business and expanding assets. Thus by 1951 profits had reached nearly £1,500,000 a year but the capital of Kellogg's, England, had remained at 1,000 £1 shares.

The astonishing price paid to the fortunate supplier of coolers and dryers was handsomely beaten in 1954 when a single share was issued at the fantastic price of £23,104 'in satisfaction of the purchase price of two top sealers, one bottom maker, two sackers, two fillers and one cooker purchased from the allottee'. The file at Companies House, London, records that the price was made up of £1 capital plus £23,103 premium! That must constitute something of a record. And it was a bargain for the unnamed supplier of 'bottom makers, sackers, etc,' for in 1954 Kellogg's net profits were returned as £2,496,000 of which £1,102,000 was paid out in dividend. Ten years later profits had soared past the £4 million mark and the dividend had increased to £1,895,000. A slight recession brought the dividend down to £1,604,000 in 1965.

On a percentage basis, this works out at 160,000 per cent! Each £1 share was subdivided in 1956 into twenty one-shilling shares, so that the capital (£1,003) consists of 20,060 one-shilling shares, of which 19,957 are held by the American parent, the Kellogg Co of Battle Creek, Michigan.

In comparison with the tiny capital of £1,003 the company's total assets total £10,855,000 (approx. $30 million)—and are probably much understated at that figure. Reserves alone amount to £3,858,000 (nearly $11 million).

On the basis of a five per cent yield each one-shilling share would cost about £1,600 to buy. Fortunately for the directors of Kellogg, they are not, unlike the directors of most companies, required to hold shares in their own concern.

The scale of Kellogg's success in Britain is a tribute to the American's brilliant business sense and an indictment of the British domestic industry for failing to see the lush pickings at the breakfast table—or the tea- and dinner-tables for that matter.

Kellogg's and its US rivals Nabisco and Quaker Oats have won virtually complete dominance of the English breakfast food market. Heinz, with its tinned foods, is in a commanding position at the dinner-table—'Beanz Meanz Heinz' is not so much a slogan, more a statement of fact. And the giants of the English larder are being joined by still more giants from across the Atlantic.

Campbell's soups have come over in a big way. And so have General Foods Corporation. This is our old favourite, the Post Toasties firm, but Mr Post's companies have come a long way from that sanatorium in Battle Creek.

General Foods bought the old-established business of Alfred Bird & Sons in 1947, for a price said to be about £500,000. Bird's major product was the famous custard, invented by a chemist whose wife could not eat egg custard.

Bird's under the tutelage of General Foods has branched out in many directions—cake mixes, artificial whipped cream, etc. But the company's biggest seller in the UK is its Maxwell House

Coffee, which holds about thirty per cent of the instant-coffee market.

The company changed its name from Bird's to General Foods Ltd to identify itself more clearly with its American parent—the usual process after a transatlantic take-over.

Another General to appear on the British scene in the 'sixties was General Mills of Minneapolis. Already well known for its Betty Crocker cake mix, it announced in May 1967 that it had bought an eighteen per cent stake in Smith's Crisps which had been hard-hit by intense competition from Imperial Tobacco's Golden Wonder Crisps. General Mills' vice-president was appointed joint managing director.

When questioned about the possibility of a complete take-over of Smith, General Mills' finance vice-president replied: 'When a boy meets a girl on their first date, he doesn't usually ask her how far she is prepared to go.' But General Mills seems ready to go pretty far. As the second largest cereal firm in the world it would hardly hold back from pushing into the British market after it has seen how well its US competitors have fared.[1]

While American food firms pre-empt television adverts, an excellent British breakfast food, 'Force', can at least claim one distinction. It has found a place in the Oxford Dictionary of Quotations. The words from one of Force's early adverts: 'Since then they called him Sunny Jim'.

Britain is nestling in the book of quotations. America is rampant in the kitchen. There's the contrast. And there's the rub!

1. The take-over of Smith's has now been completed

14

Big $—Little £

'I WILL SUPPORT him as the rope supports a
man who is being hanged'—Lenin.

It is in much the same way that the US $ supports the £,
though, to be fair, the Americans are motivated not by malice
but by the accident of history.

From the time of the Imperial Conference at Ottawa in 1932
which established preferential trading arrangements among Empire lands at the expense of third countries, America has been
resolutely opposed to exclusive trading blocs, and in particular
to the one based on sterling.

The fact that the US economy itself was built by excluding
the manufactures of other countries does not deter the Americans
from denouncing discrimination as a sin against the light. This
puritan strain of selective hypocrisy is one the English should
understand, considering that they bequeathed it to America. But
it is still difficult to swallow.

Nonetheless it is a constant factor in US policy and America's
attitude to sterling has had a profound effect on the British economy and hence on Britain's vulnerability to transatlantic take-
overs.

The history of the nineteenth century could reasonably be called
the history of sterling. Once Newton had established the gold
rating of the £ (which remained unaltered until 1931) Britain's
currency enjoyed a primacy unequalled by that of any other
nation.

Judd Polk, a perceptive US economist and sympathetic observer
of the £, remarked in his book *Sterling*[1] that 'the nineteenth cen-

1. *Sterling,* Judd Polk, Harper and Row, 1956

tury was the only protracted period in which the credit facilities provided by a single country (Britain) met the needs of a lively and expanding world commerce. This had not happened before and it has not happened since.'

Of course the situation was exceptional. Britain was a natural banker eager to extend credit so that she could sell her manufactures to the rest of the world; ready to absorb the food and raw materials that the rest of the world could offer. A happy combination of circumstances and also, as Lord Robbins the British economist has said, 'an inherently fragile one. For the nature of Britain's trade involved a specialisation of resources in response to a fortuitous lead which could not be indefinitely retained.'

The American economist Warren Thomson went further. In *Population Problems*[1] he charted Britain's inevitable decline : 'Conditions which make it possible for any city or country to attain great pre-eminence in industry and commerce and to support a large part of its population by trading with other areas are necessarily uncertain and temporary because as a rule, they arise out of the exercise of some monopoly of skill in production or experience in trade or in the possession of certain material resources which make for low production costs. These advantages can seldom, if ever, be long maintained in the face of competition from other peoples and other areas. . . . They flourish for a time and then decline in power. Sometimes they disappear altogether.'

It is hard to avoid the conclusion that, like Warren Thomson, the Americans were not averse to hastening the 'inevitable decline'.

Their opportunities to displace the £ with the dollar came first with World War One and then, in far greater measure, with World War Two.

At their Atlantic meeting in August 1941, four months before Japan's attack brought America into the war, President Roosevelt tried to persuade Premier Churchill to abandon Imperial

1. *Population Problems,* Warren Thomson, McGraw-Hill, 1965 (5th ed)

Preference. The President suggested that a clause in their joint declaration should uphold 'the right of all nations to have access to raw materials without discrimination and on equal terms'. In effect to outlaw preferential blocs. Churchill relates the episode in his war memoirs[1]:

'With regard to this, I pointed out at once that the words "without discrimination" might be held to call in question the Ottawa agreement, and I was in no position to accept them.

'Mr Sumner Welles [US Secretary of State] indicated that this was the core of the matter, and . . . embodied the ideal for which the State Department had striven for the past nine years [ie since Imperial Preference was established].

'I could not help mentioning the British experience in adhering to Free Trade for eighty years in the face of ever mounting American tariffs. We had allowed the fullest importation to all our colonies. Even our coastwise traffic around Great Britain was open to the competition of the world. All we had got in reciprocation was successive doses of American protection.

'Mr Welles seemed to be a little taken aback. I then said that if the words "with due respect for their existing obligations" could be inserted and if the words "without discrimination" could disappear I would be able to refer the text to HM Government with some hope that they would be able to accept it. The President was obviously impressed. He never pressed the point again.'

Roosevelt did not press the issue then in view of the over-riding need for Allied unity. But his obsession with this matter indicates how much the dismantlement of the imperial trading area meant to Washington.

When the war ended the US Government tried to force exhausted England to accept the free convertibility of sterling as another means of undermining the Empire system.

These two steps were in line with American thinking since the early 'thirties. As Judd Polk, who was a senior adviser in the US

1. *Second World War,* Winston S Churchill, Cassell, 1950

Treasury, says: 'The official policy of the US has been to oppose import restrictions and support the convertibility of currencies at fixed exchange rates. Where, as a result of the policy, finance for the development of foreign countries has fallen short of needs ... the finance has been met by US aid' ... and, though Polk does not say so, the effects of that has been to turn the recipients into dependents.

Now, no nation—short of military occupation—can be made to do what it does not want to do. Churchill successfully resisted Roosevelt's economic gambit at the Atlantic meeting; the UK reneged on the free convertibility clause of the loan agreement because of a severe financial crisis. Yet, basically Britain has tamely followed American policy even at times when it has manifestly not been in her interest to do so.

Thus Britain succumbed to American arguments at the various conferences which preceded the General Agreement on Tariffs and Trade (GATT). The nub of this agreement, concluded in 1948, was the 'no new preference rule'. This laid down that no additional preferences—charging a smaller rate of tariff on one nation's goods than on another's—should be permitted. Effectively this sealed the fate of the Empire trade system, for many of the preferences were specific (ie 1s on the ton, etc) and as inflation continued apace their value withered. By GATT rules they could neither be extended nor replaced. At long last the US had achieved her major objective of prising away the foundation stone of the Imperial Preference system.

Although Britain showed her resentment when, at the first Commonwealth Conference called after Churchill's return to power in 1951, the communiqué referred to the need for Commonwealth countries to press for the removal of the 'no new preferences' rule, nothing was done.

And the Commonwealth as a trading force began its steady decline. Strangely enough the Americans, who had hunted down Imperial Preferences with relentless fury, actually welcomed the establishment of the European Common Market which built a whole new tariff wall against non-members! This strange contradiction apparently did not strike British policy makers as unusual. At any rate, by the time the Common Market was set up in 1957, Britain was hell-bent on pursuing an international economic policy which chimed exactly with US plans.

The man who steered the UK into the open waters of free trade was Harold Macmillan. As Chancellor of the Exchequer in the previous year, he had been frightened to death by America's threat to end support of sterling at the time of Britain's Suez venture. Macmillan's policy in theory was geared to re-establishing the special relationship with the US and in fact led to the acceptance of US measures without qualification and usually without argument.

To launch into convertibility of sterling and eschew all import controls might have been a defensible programme, but not at the moment when the Commonwealth was being dismantled as a political economic force. And that was precisely what Mr Macmillan was engaged in doing.

Writing in 1956 Judd Polk stated: 'The future of sterling lies primarily in the future of the Commonwealth . . . international monetary arrangements are the result rather than the cause of international associations. An association without a satisfactory world money might find commerce with the rest of the world uncomfortable. But an international money without a strong association to support it would be an anomaly.'

Yet Mr Macmillan, whether he knew it or not, was weakening the Commonwealth association by granting independence—and financial freedom of action—to state after state in Africa. He was alienating one of the Commonwealth's strongest economic props, white-ruled South Africa. And all the while he was trying to make sterling an international currency with all the perils that that involved. It was like completing a massive skyscraper while hacking away the foundations. The result was predictable: financial crisis after crisis.

It is no coincidence that the years 1956–64, which saw sterling immersed in its deepest troubles, constantly requiring US aid, also saw the period of the biggest take-over of British firms by Americans.

The pattern was simple and deadly. Conforming to the twin dogmas of free convertibility and unrestricted imports, Britain was doubly vulnerable. As soon as domestic demand rose, imports flooded in to fill the gap between home production and demand. A little discrimination between what was essential and what could be postponed, in other words some form of import limitation, might have avoided recurrent balance of payment crises. None was applied. 'No discrimination, no import curbs' was the rule of free trade and the official policy of Washington.

As a result Britain's gold reserves had to bear the whole strain of the trade deficit. Now these reserves—which rarely amounted to more than £1,500 million in the post-war years—were clearly inadequate to the task.

As soon as £40 or £50 million were abstracted from them to meet, in a single month, overseas payments, confidence in the £ began to sag. Funds were switched out of London; red lights flashed in the Treasury; Bank rate was jerked up to re-attract foreign investors and home demand was ruthlessly clubbed by a credit squeeze chiefly directed at consumer spending.

The principal victims of these sudden and catastrophic fiscal measures were firms which had optimistically expanded production to meet a demand which was no longer there. Overcommitted and undercapitalised they had nowhere to go but into the hands of the liquidators—or take-over bidders. A good many of the take-over bidders were American. While Washington advanced dollars to succour the sickly £—and get the UK Government still deeper in pawn—US businessmen moved in on British industry. It was a classic envelopment, engineered not by the Americans, but by the plastic politicians of England who chose to sell the nation's assets in order to purchase popularity and office.

In doing this, the politicians were able to call to their aid a vast amount of doctrine which had the appearance of holy writ. Summarised, their arguments were as follows :

Britain must not impose restrictions on imports because other countries may retaliate and inflict grievous harm to our international trade.

Britain must not object to large-scale American take-overs because the UK is also a major investor overseas and it would set other countries a bad example if we were to complain.

Britain must support all American economic policies because America supports sterling. And (this unspoken) because it is a lot more comfortable to lean on America than to do anything which might upset our Gallup Poll ratings.

The French have a word for such a policy. It is *immobilisme,* incapacity for independent action owing to commitments to others.

In a world where everyone played the free-trade game according to the rules there might be something to be said for elegant passivity. But in the real world no one was playing to the rules.

A number of nations, France and Italy among them, had limited imports when faced with external deficits without provoking retaliatory measures. England, proportionately the biggest importer of all and a valuable market for many lands, was actually in a stronger bargaining position than any to restrict purchases temporarily. And her need to do so was greater, too.

In the past century Britain's natural resources had declined drastically. Thus in the 1850s Britain produced 100 per cent of her lead requirements; 88 per cent of tin; 71 per cent of copper; 58 per cent of wool. By the 1950s home production of these commodities had practically vanished. As dependence on raw materials from overseas grew, so the need to economise on imported manufactures in periods of strain became imperative. The substitution of home manufactures—and food—for foreign produce ought to have been a prime objective. Nothing was done.

Instead of pursuing a sane nationalism England pursued an insane internationalism. Instead of exercising authority where it mattered, she pawed the air and elevated futility into a principle.

The idea that other nations would kick out British investors if England limited American take-overs in the UK is an example of Westminster delirium tremens.

Certain countries have indeed liquidated British holdings—notably Communist China, Persia, Egypt, Tanzania—but it is not on record that they did so because the UK had set them an example. They could not care less what the UK does. So it therefore behoves the UK not to care what others think.

The belief that if Britain does not look after her own interests foreigners will be induced not to look after theirs is one of the great fictions of the twentieth century. And it is this which has helped vastly to weaken England.

The same tradition of negative thinking has affected Britain's approach to gold.

Seventy years ago the American politician William Jennings Bryan (who wanted to raise the price and prestige of silver) cried out that humanity must not be crucified on a cross of gold.

For the past two decades it has been sterling which has been stretched on the cross of the gold-plated dollar.

One simple theme has run through US financial policy for many years. The dollar is as good as gold. Fixed in 1934 by President Roosevelt at thirty-five dollars to the fine ounce, gold has remained pegged at that price ever since.

America's overwhelming financial supremacy ensured that there would be no challenge to this concept in the years following the war. But from 1957 onwards the US began to experience balance of payments deficits; gold started to seep away and other countries, notably France, started to convert dollar holdings into gold at the official US price.

Early in the 'sixties the question began to be asked: 'Why doesn't the US review the price of gold?' 'Why should the medium of exchange for the world's goods be pegged at 1934 prices when the price of all other goods has risen threefold in the interval?' 'Why'—this mainly from France—'should America continue to dictate international monetary practices when she is no longer the biggest holder of gold?' (The US having been overtaken by the European Common Market.)

To these questions successive US Administrations returned dusty answers. Asking America to revalue gold was like asking Russia to repudiate Marx. Sometime it might have to be done— but not in our time, O Lord!

In this controversy England has merely echoed America's arguments: 'Do not rock the boat; do not disturb the delicate balance of international monetary arrangements; trust the £, trust the dollar, trust God.' Such has been the scarcely inspiring refrain of successive Chancellors.

Now if the gold price were ideally suited to Britain's interest this placid acceptance of the US line would be right and proper. But there is abundant evidence that the reverse is the case.

The £ is an international currency standing on a very narrow base; an inverted pyramid. The base, the sterling area's gold and convertible currency reserves, is lodged in London. If gold were to be revalued the size of the reserves would be doubled or trebled and the base would be that much more secure. Losses on the balance of payments of £40 or £50 million would assume much less significance.

Why should Britain go to the stake for the principle that the dollar is as good as gold?

Because, it is said, the £ and the dollar are the props of world trade. Knock one and you knock the other. This is only partially true. The dollar is overwhelmingly the reserve currency; sterling is largely a trading currency. But what is undeniable is that the £ bears a disproportionate number of knocks. In twenty years the UK has gone through eight major financial crises requiring the most savage check to domestic expansion. The US has suffered no comparable setback.

Part of this is because the United States' interest in foreign trade is peripheral. America exports four per cent of her national output against Britain's twenty per cent. But mainly it is because the weaker partner in any association is inevitably the one who suffers the hardest blows when the going gets tough. Those who seek to cut the dollar down to size direct their fire first at sterling. The £ is the dollar's front line of defence.

And when US Presidents squeeze the arm of UK Premiers and murmur 'We're both in this together' it resembles nothing more than the World War One General telling the front-line Tommy that he is right there behind him—well behind him.

As Judd Polk has remarked: 'It has long been argued in the sterling area that the price of gold should be raised in the US as a means of providing a greater amount of credit. Lack of credit for financing international trade probably accounts more than any other factor for the arbitrary measures which most of the major trading nations have taken in handling their balance of payments.'

English politicians, by clinging to the status symbol of partnership with the dollar (in reality dependence on it), have inflicted needless sacrifices on their country's economy and have passed up the opportunity to create a hard national currency—on the Swiss and German models—which would be internationally acceptable.

It is a worthless exercise to blame others for national failings. If the Americans have exploited Britain's folly by encouraging her to shoulder burdens beyond her resources and inimical to her interests, the responsibility is squarely with Westminster, not with Washington.

British politicians, bankers, industrialists have failed to gauge the real changes in this world. They have seduced themselves with catch phrases, 'world opinion', 'interdependence', 'freedom of trade'. Ready enough to cast away the imperial ardour of the nineteenth century they have held fast to nineteenth-century economic conceptions which existed to serve an empire that has vanished.

Adamant for drift, resolute for irresolution, the British have happily acquiesced in America's bold and purposeful economic leadership even when that leadership has been most to their disadvantage.

In 1952 Hugh Gaitskell, who later became Labour Party leader, assured a US audience: 'You think of the sterling bloc as something which moves as a unit, directed from the centre by instructions from someone. Whether from the Governor of the Bank of England or some mysterious body, or even from the Chancellor of the Exchequer, which all members of the sterling area obey. It does not work like that at all. No formal authority or body controls the sterling area.'

His words were meant as a defence of the sterling area; yet they came close to being its epitaph. For deprived of central direction the parts tend to gravitate towards the nearest strong grouping. London has continued to be used as the banking centre of the sterling area states because of its unrivalled services and because membership of the sterling bloc confers certain benefits. But in trying to run the loosely reined sterling area in harness with the much more powerful dollar, tightly controlled as it is by a single government, Britain has yoked herself to a hopelessly unequal partnership which generates a feeling of subservience on the one hand and of embarrassed contempt on the other.

At any rate the Big $—Little £ association is doomed. Sooner or later the whole financial system of the West must be reorganised in the light of the changed realities of power in which the strength of continental Europe looms.

Whatever sterling's role is to be in the future it will command small respect, and less influence in financial counsels if its relationship with the dollar remains one of pathetic deference and debt.

The British should realise on what sterling's supremacy was founded. W M Clarke puts it thus in *The City in the World Economy*[1]: 'In striving for convertibility and the restoration of London's role as an international financial centre, people seemed oblivious of the fact that the rise of London to the centre of an

1. *The City in the World Economy*, W M Clarke, Institute of Economic Affairs, 1965

international economy was based on Britain's mercantile supremacy as an Imperial Power.' The Empire made sterling internationally welcome. The stability and wide-ranging activities of the Empire attracted funds to London and so contributed to England's balance of payments. But times change. . . .

Indeed the changed relationship between England and the US can perhaps be judged by reference to differing conceptions of empire. The territorial Empire of Britain, and the commercial Empire of America.

15

Empire No More

'TAKE UP THE White Man's burden—Send
forth the best ye breed.'

Appropriately Kipling's words were written for the Americans
who had just, in 1898, taken the first halting steps in empire-
building by annexing Puerto Rico, the Philippines and Guam.
America had acquired a colonial empire of 120,000 square miles
and 8,500,000 people and now occupied a position of prominence
in world affairs, particularly in the Caribbean and Far East.
According to an American history 'the sympathetic British attitude to the United States did much to enhance Anglo-American
goodwill'.

The British did indeed welcome America to the Imperial Club
—as a junior probationary member. There is an undeniable
parallel between the patronising manner England adopted to
the US then and the one which America adopts towards England
today. When the Americans were 'good boys' (as they were when
they co-operated with England in frustrating German designs
in Samoa) they were patted on the head. But when they were
naughty (as when President Cleveland challenged British interests
in Venezuela) they were treated as fractious children.

To win the attention of American Presidents today British Premiers scurry across to Washington. So many have gone so often
that they have worn a path, a kind of Pilgrim's Way, on the White
House Lawn.

To win Britain's attention, seventy years ago, the Americans
adopted a more manly stance. They were as rude as could be.
President Cleveland's Secretary of State, Richard Olney, delivered
a note to the UK Government stating that disregard of the

Monroe Doctrine (no European interference in Western Hemisphere affairs) 'would be deemed an act of unfriendliness towards the United States which is master of the situation and practically invulnerable against any and all comers.' Olney later excused this remarkable outburst by explaining: 'The United States was then so completely a negligible quantity in English eyes that only words, the equivalent of blows, could be effective.'

Britain's Prime Minister, and acting Foreign Secretary, Lord Salisbury, treated the Olney note with disdain—as well he might considering that the Royal Navy protected America from foreign interference. He did not answer it for four months. 'Lord Salisbury,' it was said, 'was no more disposed to respond to this kind of prodding than he would have been if his tailor had suddenly challenged him to a duel.'

Such was the gulf that separated mighty Imperial England with its Empire of 14 million square miles and 500 million souls from the jumped-up newcomer with its negligible possessions of 120,000 square miles and 8,500,000 souls.

The envy which Americans felt for England was partly assuaged by reflections on how well the US was doing at business (just as England's present-day envy of America is partly consoled by reflections on Britain's longer history and shorter skirts). But there was an effortless superiority about the English in world affairs, a conviction that the globe was England's oyster that made Americans irritated beyond measure—and wonder how they could one day be in a position to emulate it.

The Empire was the outward and visible sign of England's inward, invisible grace. Passengers in British ships sailing round the world via Gibraltar, Malta, Port Said, Aden, Bombay, Trincomalee, Singapore, Sydney, Auckland, Fiji, and Vancouver saw only one flag—the Union Jack. And every second ship they passed displayed the same pennant.

The high noon of imperial splendour was marked by Queen Victoria's Diamond Jubilee celebrations. That was the year when the Poet Laureate, Alfred Austin (author of the imperishable lines on Lord Tennyson: 'Across the wires the baneful message came, he is no better he is much the same'[1]), confided that his dream of heaven was to sit in a garden and receive a flow of telegrams announcing alternately a British victory at sea and a British victory on land.

In that same year the world was afforded a demonstration of imperial glory the like of which no other state, not even Rome, had been able to boast. A quarter of the globe came to London to pay tribute to Queen Victoria.

The American historian, Barbara Tuchman, has painted the scene in glowing colours.

'On 22nd June 1897 the living evidence of imperial dominion marched in splendid ranks to the thanksgiving service at St Paul's. The occasion being designed to celebrate the imperial family under the British crown, none of the foreign kings who had assisted at the Golden Jubilee in 1887 were this time invited. In their place, carriages of state carried the eleven colonial premiers of Canada, New Zealand, the Cape Colony, Natal, Newfoundland and the six states of Australia. In the parade rode cavalry from every quarter of the globe: the Cape Mounted Rifles, the Canadian Hussars, the New South Wales Lancers, the Trinidad Light Horse, the magnificent turbaned and bearded Lancers of Khapurthala, Badnagar and other Indian states, the Zaptichs of Cyprus in tasselled fezzes on black-maned ponies. Dark skinned infantry regiments, "terrible and beautiful to behold" in the words of a rhapsodic Press, "swinging down the streets in a fantasy of variegated uniforms: The Borneo Dyak Police, the Jamaican Artillery, the Royal Nigerian Constabulary, the giant Sikhs from India, Houssas from the Gold Coast, Chinese from Hong Kong, Malays from Singapore, Negroes from the West Indies, British Guiana and Sierra Leone; company after company passed before a dazzled people, awestruck at the testimony of their own might". At the end of the procession in an open landau drawn by eight

1. Another version says the quotation refers to the Prince of Wales and 'electric' is substituted for 'baneful'.

cream horses came the day's central figure, a tiny person in black with cream coloured feathers nodding from her bonnet. The sun shone, bright banners rippled in the breeze, lamp-posts were decked in flowers and along six miles of streets millions of happy people cheered and waved in ecstasy of love and pride. "No one ever, I believe, has met with such an ovation as was given me", wrote the Queen in her Journal. "Every face seemed to be filled with real joy. I was much moved and gratified".[1]

'There was at this time,' said Rudyard Kipling the poet of imperial grandeur, 'a certain optimism that scared me.' And on the morning after the parade his poem 'Recessional' appeared in *The Times*:

> *God of our fathers, known of old.*
> *Lord of our far-flung battle line,*
> *Beneath whose awful hand we hold—*
> *Dominion over palm and pine—*
> *Lord God of Hosts be with us yet,*
> *Lest we forget—lest we forget.*

His warning: 'Lo all our pomp of yesterday Is one with Nineveh and Tyre' went largely unheeded by a population which had seen the Empire grow in the previous twelve years by an area twenty-four times the size of Great Britain.

Well might Lady Salisbury, wife of the Premier, remark shortly before her death at the turn of the century: 'The young generation may criticise us as they like; will they ever provide anything as good as we have known?'

The Empire was not merely a source of power, military and economic. It had a real and deep meaning for those who served it and a meaning, though more vague, for England's unlettered millions many of whose sons served its outposts.

No great nation can truly express itself without some ethos, some core of belief.

1. *The Proud Tower,* Barbara Tuchman, Hamish Hamilton, 1966

It was expressed by John Buchan, speaking through characters in *A Lodge in the Wilderness*,[1] 'Empire is not to be regarded as a mere possession, as the vulgar rich regard their bank accounts—a matter to boast of and not an added duty . . .

'It is a spirit, an attitude of mind, an unconquerable hope. You can phrase it in a thousand ways without exhausting its content. It is a sense of the destiny of England. It is the wider patriotism which conceives our people as a race and not a chance community . . .

'It is the closer organic connection under one Crown of a number of autonomous nations of the same blood, who can spare something of their vitality for the administration of vast tracts inhabited by lower races—a racial aristocracy considered in their relation to the subject peoples, a democracy in relation to each other . . .

'It is the realisation of new conditions for all our problems, an enlarged basis and fuller data . . .

'It is not England plus a number of poor relations but one organic whole whose centre is to be determined by the evidence of time . . .

'It is the task of developing the wilds, uniting the scattered settlements, bringing the whole within the influence of England's tradition and faith.

'Empire building above all things is a labour of peace. The ideal is not Dominion, not even Pax Britannica, but the spread of civilisation.'

Of course the Empire was other things, too—easy plunder for early merchant adventurers, cheap servants for jumped-up memsahibs, a safe haven for remittance men. Yet having deducted the debits a vast credit remained. And the Empire provided young Englishmen with an opportunity for service-beyond-self on a tremendous scale.

The Times in 1905 drew a portrait of Lord Milner (adminis-

1. *A Lodge in the Wilderness,* John Buchan, Blackwood, 1906

trator of newly-conquered South Africa) which might have served as a model for all aspiring district commissioners.

'We possess a public servant of a very rare and remarkable type, not merely a competent man or a strong man but a man with tempered steel-like qualities of will and intellect. Lord Milner's power is high strung and spiritual in its essence; his resolution is unfaltering because it is the fruit of profound mental toil and a high devotion to duty. . . . He has no care for his reputation, only for the accomplishment of his task. More than once he has risked everything for a principle when a lesser man would have hesitated and hedged. He has the gift of complete mental detachment when face to face with a problem. He can isolate it from all adventitious circumstances, delete the emotional and irrational, and work out the solution with unswerving logic. He is incapable of deceiving himself or becoming a prophet of smooth things.'

Behind Lord Milner and the young men who yearned to follow in his footsteps, or those who had gone before, stood an educational and class system attuned to the needs of empire.

Eton and Harrow and a few others apart, the great 'boom' in public schools came about during the middle of the nineteenth century with the aim of producing empire builders out of sons of successful businessmen.

Even by the rather forbidding standards of the Victorian era the public schools were spartan to a degree. Qualities of leadership were inculcated as the by-product of a system which placed older boys in authority over younger ones to the extent of demanding their immediate obedience and beating them if they failed to come up to the mark. Obedience was taught as a necessary apprenticeship to command.

The most popular picture in sixth-form studies was Lady Eleanor Butler's reproduction of a young officer advancing to certain death at Majuba Hill with the cry '*Floreat Etona*'.

The poems of Henry Newbolt—'Play up, play up, and play the game' echoed the same philosophy.

Nor was it confined to a small ruling caste. The nation in general approved passionately the role of building an empire on Christianity, impartial justice and growing trade. It was the working classes who demanded vengeance for the death of General Gordon at Khartoum. It was the same class which lustily sang 'We don't want to fight, but by jingo if we do, we've got the ships, we've got the men and we've got the money, too.'

Tommy Atkins on his shilling a day was the lord of creation in vast tracts of the globe. The wonder is not that he felt superior —he did—but that he acted, on the whole, with commendable restraint. The same self-discipline which his officers had imbibed at school was transmitted to the ranks. The responsibilities of empire drew forth a response from all levels of society and gave purpose to many lives.

The Empire is gone. The age of colonialism is over. Today the most powerful nation in the world is America. But what motivates her young men? Where is the spur to glory? What is the call to service?

For all their assumed cynicism the Americans have a deep respect for the stiff upper-lip nonchalance of the old Empire hands. American film companies glorified imperial ways, while taking considerable liberties with history, in epics like *Lives of a Bengal Lancer, Charge of the Light Brigade, The Sun Never Sets.*

In a well-ordered world, England might have passed on the torch to the US; the British Raj giving way gracefully to the American Raj.

Some people believe this has actually happened. It hasn't.

There is no American Empire and there is no possibility of one being erected. The nuclear bomb, the great equaliser, has seen to that. The US arrived at the summit of world strength at the very moment when might could no longer be effectively exercised.

In place of the British Empire ruled by London, subject to the will of Parliament owing allegiance to a single crown, there are, at the time of writing, twenty-six independent states of the Commonwealth and another hundred or so outside which will, quite naturally, take what they can get from the United States but feel in no way obliged to render any corresponding service, let alone demonstrate loyalty to American interests.

Britain ruled the East with 100,000 soldiers and a squadron of warships, symbol of the power that could be brought to bear.

It is America's misfortune that she has inherited responsibility without power. The trappings are there—the great fleets sailing the seas; the mighty air armadas darkening the skies, but to what purpose?

A sweeping atomic attack on the US would in a matter of hours reduce the whole lot simply to an instrument for wreaking posthumous revenge.

There is little reality behind the outward show, not because America lacks the will, capacity and courage (she has all three in abundance) but because technical changes have rendered nine-teenth-century conceptions of power politics obsolete.

As a super state the US can launch rockets to the moon, but the nuclear equation with Russia, the balance of terror, renders fruitless her efforts to impose her will on tiny Cuba, or the fractious Middle East, or the Vietnam guerrillas or backward, menacing China.

There is no real outlet for America's ardent youth to match what ought to be America's hour of destiny.

Certainly there is the Peace Corps composed of idealistic, sincere young folk offering their skills to the underdeveloped world. But they do not control the governments to which they are accredited. Unlike the young British district commissioners of imperial times, the American Peace Corps representative cannot execute his reforms, he can only recommend. And then watch in frustration as local politicians mock his best efforts by displaying their talent for graft.

Professor Kenneth Galbraith, one of America's most thoughtful economists, has said that Britain gave up her colonies at just the right time. In the same way America has inherited colonial problems at just the wrong time; when the climate of world opinion—to which the US attaches a rather exaggerated importance—is opposed to anything which suggests one nation having dominion over another.

Even in territories where Washington exerts overwhelming influence, such as Vietnam, political decisions remain in the hands of non-American authorities. They undo much of what the Americans are trying to accomplish. This leads to a growing disillusionment which eventually permeates the ranks of the armed forces, reinforcing the home-sickness to which Americans abroad so easily succumb.

The amazing thing is that the Americans have stuck to so many thankless tasks for so long. By temperament and training they are not particularly suited to administration of foreign lands.

Public service, at least until recently, did not attract the best elements in the US. Great families, with one or two notable exceptions, did not take to politics. Business attracted the keenest minds, the most daring personalities. The challenge of a vast untamed continent lay in building railroads, exploiting coal and oil, raising herds of cattle, making the prairies fruitful. And when the basic needs of society were met the successors of the pioneers turned to devising new methods of satisfying undreamed-of wants. Indeed, they created the wants. Smart gadgets came before good government.

America has no tradition of established service to the State. President Kennedy tried to create a kind of court and was roundly abused for his pains. Instead of an Establishment he was accused of setting up a Mafia.

The idea, still strongly entrenched in England despite recent attempts to overthrow it, of a continuing responsibility to the community is alien to the US except perhaps in a strictly local context.

Who, for example, can imagine this description of a statesman who was still at the helm in the twentieth century, being applied to an American : 'Having entered the legislature in the customary manner from a family-controlled borough in an uncontested election at the age of twenty-three, and, during his years there, having been returned unopposed five times for the same borough, and having sat for twenty-seven years in the House of Lords, he had little personal experience of vote-getting. He regarded himself not as responsible to the people but as responsible for them. They were in his care. What reverence he felt for anyone was directed not down but up, to the monarchy.'

That was said of Lord Salisbury. And he was followed in the premiership by his nephew, Arthur Balfour.

It was this feeling of being responsible for people rather than accountable to them which made the British such superb colonists. They didn't believe in democracy so they didn't try to make it work.

Salisbury did not believe in equality either. 'There are the multitude,' he said, 'and there are natural leaders. Always wealth, in some countries, birth, in all intellectual power and culture mark out the men to whom, in a healthy state, a community looks to undertake its government. With leisure and fortune in their hands, struggles for ambition are not tainted by sordid greed. They are the aristocracy of a country in the original and best sense of the word. The important point is that the rulers of a country should be taken from among them. As a class they should retain that political preponderance to which they have every right that superior fitness can confer.'

The Americans have been brought up to believe almost the exact opposite of this credo. Namely that there is a peculiar virtue in being lowly born and that the self-made man is worthy of the people's trust.

Log cabin to White House is a success story (even as recently as the 1960 election Richard Nixon's bull point was that his parents had been poor while Mr Kennedy's had been wealthy). But an even bigger success story is newspaper boy to company president.

Achievement in business is *the* achievement in America. And just as Americans' passion for popularity contests has made them unfit for ruling fractious little countries, so their swift response to public demands in material things has made them superb businessmen. So much more effective than those aristocratic (or pseudo-aristocratic) Englishmen with their disdain of customers and shareholders.

With Britain trade followed the flag. With the Americans the flag has followed trade.

This truism was well illustrated by an incident in one of the recurrent Middle East crises. When American marines landed on Beirut's beaches in 1958 they were greeted, not by shot and shell, but by Arab boys offering the soldiers bottles of Coca-Cola at the monstrously inflated price of one dollar a bottle!

Not colonisation, but coca-colonisation has been the major US contribution to lesser breeds without the law!

All the energy, the skills, the initiative and expertise that might have gone into making an American Empire to outstrip the British has gone into making American business the Big Boss. It will not be America's fault if the ultimate aim of two television sets in every bathroom in the free world remains unrealised when the last trump sounds.

To the accumulation of material possessions and their distribution by free market means the US has bent its magnificent talents.

Here America's gifts are unmatched. The men that US companies send abroad to staff their plants in the UK and elsewhere are first class. In this they are keeping faith with Kipling's admonition to send for the 'best ye breed'.

Why should the Americans be so much better equipped, in human terms, to direct mammoth industrial operations than the English? What is their secret?

There is no simple answer; there are a host of possible explanations. But a tremendous zest for the job is one.

16

Status and Contract

AMERICANS LIKE WORK. Dr Adenauer, the late German Chancellor, once remarked that the English were really lazy and had founded an empire which they could leisurely exploit rather than compete with their lean and trade-hungry Teutonic neighbours. Perhaps the good doctor was right. Certainly, the British, in general, do not have the same urge to toil which grips the Germans and the Americans (many of whom, of course, are of German descent).

Also the Americans take a vast delight in material things. They want passionately to own large cars, swimming pools, sailing boats. To get these they are prepared to sacrifice leisure. The British are content with fewer possessions and tend to put greater emphasis on free time. This goes as much for the factory worker who knocks an hour off his earning time in order to go to a mid-week football match as for the company chairman who skips off early on Friday to get in a round of golf. So far as work is concerned the British do not take it as seriously as the Americans.

These instinctive attitudes are unlikely to change, and therefore the American businessmen in England have a built-in advantage over the domestic product.

But there are other causes of deeper importance to explain US superiority in work performance. Chief among them is the matter of labour relations.

A great gulf separates English and American labour practices. The reason for this is rooted deep in history.

America never experienced the feudal system. She was, from the start, a free-ranging land of free-ranging people. Ancient ties, first of law then of habit, did not tie them to particular localities. Always the urge was to be on the move. And while the restless spirits in England, Scotland and Ireland had to move out altogether, to the colonies, the Americans had millions of square miles of their own in which to wander.

To the Americans, the dignity of labour was a robust fact, not, as in Europe, a political theory inextricably mixed up with Socialism.

Self-reliance was a doctrine in both England and America (Samuel Smiles, the author of the classic *Self Help,* was after all English of the most English) but in practice self-help was far more widespread in the States than in England because the opportunities were so much greater.

Lacking a feudal heritage, and believing wholeheartedly in the right, nay, the obligation of every individual to make his own way in life, the US took to capitalism with gusto. Contract, not status, was what mattered. The dustman's son or, for that matter, the dustman, might become the boss of a vast business enterprise and money would give him entry into the society of his choice. Such at any rate was the theory. It did not always work out like that in practice, but at least there was no unalterable barrier to acceptance; no fossilised caste system to bar the road.

American society was fluid and America was very big. Fail in one place and you could move to another. This mobility gave American workers an alternative to organised strife against the employers. It weakened the appeal of militant trades union leaders and encouraged rugged individualism as opposed to labour solidarity.

Entirely different were the conditions in England. There status was held in high esteem. Better to be a craftsman on slender resources, firmly set in the local community, than an unapprenticed rolling stone, no matter how much moss be gathered.

When the Industrial Revolution devalued the old crafts and set men to work in the factories, the proletariat sought, through the trade union organisation, to preserve new skills against dilution. The demarcation system was a reflection of the defensive nature of British trade unionism, in contrast with the more hopeful and trustful attitude of American employees.

A further and still more profound difference between the two countries rose with the advent of Socialism.

The radical element in England grasped the socialist ideal with enthusiasm. Instead of seeking to benefit by capitalism, an increasing number of British workers were persuaded that it lay in their interest to abolish capitalism altogether. The Labour Party codified discontent with the existing social order and by adopting a clause in its constitution advocating the public ownership of all the means of production, distribution and exchange, challenged the entire free enterprise system.

Truculence and a bloody-minded reluctance to toil for the 'boss class' were added to the natural conservatism (in working methods) of British labour. Together they produced the class-war outlook. Profit was regarded as a dirty word. New machinery as a means of displacing workers; work study as a crafty move to speed output. The word 'productivity' was not then in popular currency, but if it had been it would have been laughed to scorn. It was 'them' and 'us'.

Management in England in the latter part of the nineteenth and early part of the twentieth centuries did little to heal the wounds in labour relations. Rather the reverse. As the workers stubbornly defended their skills so employers barricaded their property. They were in mortal fear of losing it to Godless Socialism and preferred to conserve what they had rather than expand into new fields.

Labour troubles were no less bitter in the States—and they were frequently a great deal bloodier—but the American workers did not embrace Socialism. Their ideal of equality remained the right, one day, to become a boss. The free enterprise system, though reviled by certain writers, was never seriously challenged as it was in England. American unions sought to lay their hands on the goose's golden eggs while the British trade unionists aimed to lay theirs round the goose's throat.

Given these opposing philosophies is it any wonder that, from the 1890s onward, American output per head, and US living standards, steadily increased over England's?

Even today, when the class war has almost receded into memory, American businessmen in England are astonished at how easily labour's ancient passions can be aroused and how near the surface lie old suspicions of management.

Some US managements, impatient of outdated views and the mythology of industrial warfare, plunged in with dewy-eyed innocence to rebuild British industry on go-getting, fast-buck-making 'Yankee' lines.

They were rudely and swiftly disenchanted.

The making of money is not the overwhelming preoccupation of British workers as it is of American. Other factors are as important: keeping to the conventions of labour-management relations; due time off for tea; not too-high a pace of work, and proper respect accorded to all union representatives and shop stewards. Status again!

To crew-cut, horn-rimmed, sales-orientated American executives (not all of them are like that, but some of them are) this British view of work is intolerable. There is an immediate and understandable reaction of 'let's get tough'.

When this happened at Vauxhall in the autumn of 1966 it provoked near-riots. The new managing director, David Hegland, an American, was blamed for ruining decades of model peace which had been established by a series of British managing directors. Mr Hegland might reasonably have pointed out that the years of tranquillity had not yielded the hoped-for return on capital.

Two irreconcilable views: one that there is no higher activity than money-making and that profit alone is the final criterion; the other that some loss of efficiency should be accepted in order to enjoy an easier pace and a more natural life.

American concern for efficiency, for cost effectiveness, is occasionally carried to extraordinary lengths.

The Celanese Corporation of New York, which purchased

British Paints, distributed a questionnaire, consisting of nine hundred questions, to the sixty top executives of its British subsidiary. Among the questions were 'Would you object to being kissed by a member of your own sex?' 'Would you prefer to be a paint executive or a Caribbean fisherman?' It was explained that this type of probe was 'not unusual' in US corporations, and was designed to 'test the aptitude, intelligence, aggressiveness and independence of employees'.

Another US-owned firm in Lancashire advertised for men 'who can't stand red tape'. The form which applicants had to fill in included questions such as: 'Can you remember your examination results at primary or elementary school?' 'Do you own or rent your house?' 'What is the sex and age of your children?' 'Have you any other dependants?' Presumably the firm was aiming to find men who owned their own homes (responsibility and commitments), had children and other dependants (further obligations) and had scored good marks at school (intelligence and ambition). Such men would tend to fit into the organisation and not make trouble.

Indeed the firm's obsession with efficiency and co-ordination (the German word, *gleichschaltung,* is probably more appropriate) was carried to such extremes that it provoked a strike lasting many months. In the course of which the local managing director was forbidden by head office in the US to negotiate with the unions and was limited to issuing a statement which said 'I recognise the right of trade unions to withdraw labour if the circumstances are unsatisfactory. By the same token employers have the right to engage labour of their own choice. Negotiation cannot begin till hostilities cease. There must be no violence.'

What is rather pathetic is the lack of authority possessed by the man on the spot and this is a growing feature of American control. The US parent of one big British subsidiary was itself swallowed by a still larger concern in the States, making all kinds of goods ranging from machine oil to headache powders. No sooner were the new owners in command than they required their British subsidiary to file expenditure accounts in septuplicate, and no capital expenditure of any kind, even for typewriters, was permitted without authorisation from New York.

'Of course,' say the Americans, 'we must impose this close surveillance both in the interests of our shareholders and for the sake of the backward British. Is it not a fact, attributed by your own productivity committees, that British industry lags far behind America's because labour is lazy and management slovenly? It is for us Americans to put this right.'

One American businessman, William Keafer, gave tongue to his feelings, by contrasting in withering tones the performance of American workers in his plant in Carolina and English workers in an exactly similar plant in Durham. With the same machinery and comparable social facilities, English output was only one third as great as the Americans'. Commented Mr Keafer, vice-president of Warner Electric Clutch and Brake of Illinois, and director of Westool, Co Durham:

'With the same machinery the American turns out three times as much as his British counterpart. Even though we pay our workmen more than twice as much as yours, even though we're four thousand miles from Europe and you're not two hundred, we each make the same product and undersell you all over the continent. Do you wonder Britain is going bust?'

Yearly output per worker in cash sales: Westool—£2,400 (UK); Warners—£9,280 (US).

Warners own one third of Westool and both companies make components for computers. Both sell at about the same price.

Westool spends far more on welfare and improved working conditions. Warners men want more cash.

The Westool worker takes home £22 a week.

The Warners men take home £47 a week.

No strikes are permitted at Warners for any reason, by order of the Union which has concluded a three-year no-strike, compulsory arbitration agreement. Regular pay increases and profit sharing are included in the agreement.

Westool would not accept an American speed-up system by which workers' wrists were attached to the top of a machine by straps to avoid their arms being cut. British safety measures are much more stringent, but they reduce production by fifty per cent.

A US union leader at Warners sums up : 'The company's profits are open to inspection by our union and we do inspect in order to get our slice of the pie. I've been with this factory thirteen years and I can remember a bad time when we held a union meeting and decided to take a pay cut to keep things going.'

In another sphere, a report by a working party of the Economic Development Committee for the British Chemical industry confirms Mr Keafer's findings. After discounting the advantages of scale enjoyed by the Americans it concluded that 'even if the American chemical industry were reduced overnight to a British scale of operations, it would still need only sixty-four men to obtain the same output British chemical manufacturers obtain from a hundred employees.'

'The Americans,' said the committee, 'would manage with one fifth fewer production workers, a third fewer people in control of laboratories, forty per cent fewer maintenance and chemical staff and with only one worker on packing and despatch for every twenty employed by British firms.'

Demarcation between crafts added twenty per cent to the British labour force. And the diminished authority accorded to foremen in Britain contributed substantially to the poorer performance on the factory floor.

What the chemical investigators found, it is said, applies to other British industries, and explains why US productivity generally is two to three times better than Britain's.

Overstaffing certainly is a curse in the UK. It is carried to ludicrous extremes in deference to the tradition that 'full employment' is the categorical imperative of British politics. Memories of the slump (the period between 1930–35) are constantly dredged up to justify three men for one man's work. No such obsession grips American (or German) workers; though surprisingly the

Americans and Germans suffered proportionately much more than British workers from the depression, the percentage of US and German unemployment at the worst of the slump being half as much again as in the UK. The fact that unemployment was made a burning political issue in England during the 'thirties and 'forties, and was exploited mercilessly for party ends, probably accounts for the stubborn refusal of British trade unionists to face the truth about over-manning.

Still, some progress is being made. Not least by some American-owned firms which, in contrast to others, have approached labour relations cautiously and empirically.

If Keafer of Durham can find little good to say of his British workers, Burroughs Adding Machines in Scotland, for example, have established an excellent association with their employees (a former American managing director became chairman of the local football team) and could report that its products from the Vale of Leven plant were underselling the products of the US plant in America.

Perhaps the most outstanding and best publicised example of labour-management relations is the Fawley Agreement concluded by Esso and a score of trades unions.

Under the terms of the agreement, which took five years to reach, a high degree of labour mobility was achieved.

Where before there were three mates to every five craftsmen, the agreement abolished the mate system altogether. At one stroke the wasteful tradition of one man virtually watching while the other worked was eliminated. Costly overtime which prior to the settlement accounted for eighteen per cent of time worked was reduced to just over two per cent.

In exchange for these concessions the workers won wage increases which yielded them more pay for a forty-hour week than they had previously earned for working fifty hours, including overtime. Because demand for Esso products was increasing normal wastage, retirements, etc, took care of those workers who otherwise would have been displaced by the new measures. Productivity almost doubled.

Four years after the Fawley Agreement (named after the company's refinery near Southampton) went into operation the National Board for Prices and Incomes reported : 'The consolidation of overtime pay and incentive payments are major contributions towards raising the status of manual workers by diminishing the difference between white collar and "blue collar" workers. The Esso agreements show an overall gain.'

Clearly, British workers can and do work happily in US-owned plants. This is especially the case where the firm seeks to identify itself with the local needs and loyalties and where approach to labour problems is tactful, well considered and in no way doctrinaire.

Where these conditions are not fulfilled, the presence of American executives undoubtedly exacerbates the situation. In the Vauxhall disturbances, for instance, the cry 'Yanks out, Yanks out' became the dominant refrain. Similar expressions have been heard during disputes at Fords, Roberts-Arundel and other US-owned concerns.

Henry Ford recounts in his autobiography, *Today and Tomorrow*,[1] how much change he wrought when he established his first UK plant in 1917 at Cork (his ancestors' home):

'In Cork the best a man could hope for was to work three days a week in the docks, for which he would receive 6os for the hardest kind of stevedoring. If he went out as an agricultural labourer he could not expect to get more than 3os or 32s a week. None of this work was steady.

'The men and their families did not really live. They had no homes—only hovels. No clothing but what they had on.

'We started our plant with three men from Detroit to direct operations.

'Now (in 1926) we have under regular employment 1,800 men.

1. *Today and Tomorrow*, Henry Ford, Doubleday, 1926

They work eight hours a day, five days a week, steadily. The average wage is 2s 6d an hour, £5 a week. We have no labour turnover whatsoever and always have a long waiting list. The Irish are supposed to be temperamental. We have never had a complaint about the repetitive work.

'The payment of these higher wages had an immediate effect on the homes of the men. You can see it in the wife of a new man. For the first few weeks the wife will be wearing a shawl over her head. Then she will have a hat, and a few weeks later she will be in a frock or a suit.'

These circumstances will not be duplicated in the comparatively affluent Britain that has emerged in the last forty-five years. There is no place for gratitude to American technology. It will be accepted and adapted, but it will call forth neither wonderment nor indebtedness.

American firms which remain in the UK and those which come in the future will have to earn good relations with their work force. It will not be granted them by paying high wages or providing pastel-coloured wash rooms.

An intuitive grasp of what is required may be more important than the management techniques which are taught at business schools.

In this aspect, the qualifications, background and aspirations of America's younger generation of executives assumes much significance for the American stake in Britain.

17

The Dedicated Ones

THE WALL STREET JOURNAL has reported that 'the corporate caste system is being formalised and rigidified in more and more American companies'.

Certainly the old free-wheeling atmosphere, with the possibility of catching the boss's eye and zooming to the top (and later, possibly plummeting to earth), has largely disappeared from American business. Nowadays promotion is highly organised, almost on civil service or army lines. This is hardly surprising considering that American corporations in the numbers they employ and the budgets they dispose of are equivalent in size to the civil service of many countries.

In US industry two per cent of the firms employ more than all the rest put together. These groups, each with hundreds of thousands of employees, have no choice but to codify their advancement procedures.

Naturally, paper qualifications assume greater significance, just as they do in the British Civil Service where entry into the top, administrative, grade is virtually confined to university graduates with first- or good second-class degrees.

So it is, or at least is increasingly becoming, in US business.

Only two per cent of leading executives in the three hundred largest industrial, transport and public utility undertakings in the USA had working-class backgrounds and almost all the top men under fifty have college or university qualifications or have been to 'good' schools and show exceptional personality and promise.

The business schools, Harvard, Yale, Princeton, the Massachusetts Institute of Technology, the bigger state universities are the breeding grounds of the new-style aristocracy of American business.

Just as a spell in the Empire was considered fine training for young Englishmen fifty or more years ago, so aspiring US executives do well to 'get their knees brown' by service overseas. Indeed it goes further than that. Joining the foreign operations department of a big US corporation can be tantamount to joining the Foreign Legion so far as the difficulty of getting out is concerned. Once in, American executives are obliged to remain overseas for years, sometimes in the one posting, sometimes flitting from country to country. If he quits the foreign service, he quits the company. There is no discharge in the trade war.

Only the dedicated can take this life. But then a great number of young American executives are dedicated to the pursuit of business in much the same way as the Inquisition was devoted to the pursuit of truth.

The material attractions are of course somewhat more tempting. Those who are on the overseas circuit are compensated for their Flying Dutchman existence by excellent pay and company welfare services.

The most attractive districts round London, Glasgow, or Manchester always have a high percentage of American executives. The most expensive golf courses enjoy much American patronage. Travel and hotel accommodation are simply 'the best'. The treadmill is lined with mink.

At the same time, a fervent loyalty to the corporation is cultivated. The company assumes the mystique by which the regiment commands the lives of professional soldiers and this mystique is gilded with gatherings which, in disciplined panoply, resemble ceremonial parades.

When National Cash Register holds a convention it stands comparison—at least in massive organisation—with Trooping the Colour.

Thus at their 1967 sales congress in London, the Dorchester, Hilton and Europa hotels were almost taken over to accommodate the one thousand or so delegates. The Pigalle and Talk of the Town night clubs were wholly absorbed, at a cost of £6,000, to

148

minister to their wants. And the Ashcroft Theatre and Fairfield Hall in Croydon were mobilised for the grand rallies and pep talks from the top men.

'You can have no conception of what it is like,' rhapsodised one NCR rep, 'until you have taken part. It is not only the trip. You become one of the leading men and take part in the event.'

For all the easy informality, the back-slapping, the first-name exchanges, there is, to British eyes, just a touch of idolatry about all this, as though it were a sort of Business Nuremberg Rally. Banners play their part, company flags, and the Stars and Stripes, too.

America's national identification with business is demonstrated to quite a remarkable degree, by the display of the American flag (along with the national flag of the country concerned) at Rotary meetings.

It is claimed that as the US invented Rotary (and Rotary International) it is only right that Old Glory should have the place of honour whenever Rotarians meet together.

Much the same argument could be used by Britain to justify displaying the Union Jack by the world's Boy Scouts, a movement founded by the British. That however does not happen.

'America's business is business', is a spirit inculcated in all who serve US firms. It is as much part of the training system as, say, motivational research or cost effectiveness. It helps to explain the conformism which has produced the Organisation Man as a phenomenon of the US scene.

In his book, *The Hidden Persuaders*,[1] Vance Packard quotes a US engineering journal : 'One vital branch of engineering has, until recently, been woefully neglected—the science of human engineering.

'Human engineering is the science of moulding and adjusting the attitude of industrial personnel. By this process a worker's mechanical ability and know-how will be balanced by equal skill

1. *The Hidden Persuaders,* Vance Packard, Longmans, Green, 1957

in the art of demonstrating a co-operative attitude towards his job, employer and fellow employees.'

To control this aspect of human engineering demands utter devotion by the managers. If they are to instil enthusiasm in the workers they must be enthusiasts themselves. Cynicism, which is like a blight across so much of British industrial thinking, must have no part in the make-up of the American executive. Equally the man who is too much of an individual, who does not accept that his own advancement can come about only through the progress of the firm, is increasingly unacceptable. As Charles Wilson, former head of General Motors, former US Secretary for Defence so pithily put it : 'Anyone who doesn't play on the team and sticks his head up may find himself in a dangerous spot.'

Avoiding these dangers has produced the Organisation Man, the Man in the Grey Flannel Suit who says the right things to the right people at the right time.

Technically he must be of high quality and ideally his original thoughts should be how to make or sell his firm's products more efficiently.

Family life is not neglected in moulding the business-orientated man.

According to Packard, a group of US management consultancy concerns reached this conclusion in the mid-'fifties : 'Important men may not be recommended for the higher-priced jobs because the wife may be too flirtatious, or she may not drink her cocktails too well, or she may be an incorrigible gossip.'

Fortune, the American business magazine, said : 'Management has a challenge deliberately to plan and create a favourable, constructive attitude on the part of the wife that will liberate her husband's total energies for the job.

'Management knows exactly what kind of wife it wants. With remarkable uniformity of phrasing, corporation officials all over the country sketch the ideal wife who is (1) highly adaptable; (2) highly gregarious; (3) realises her husband belongs to the corporation.'

The Harvard *Business Review* added its quota of requirements : 'A study shows that the American wife of an executive must not demand too much of her husband's time or interest. Because of his single-minded concentration on his job, even his sexual ability is relegated to a secondary place.'

It would be absurd to imagine that US executives are de-humanised, de-sexed automatons. Those who represent their corporations in the UK are, on the whole, a livelier set than their British counterparts. But they do look at issues—political, economic, social—from a company point of view. 'How will this or that country's fiscal changes affect my organisation's operations?' 'How will the overthrow of this or that government affect my firm's projects?'

This emphasis on one compelling interest makes the American businessman a most formidable force. At a cocktail party or a dinner he is still 'on duty'. If he is impressed by a young guest's command of his subject or facility in selling an idea, the American is quite likely to mark the young man down as a potential recruit, and act on that assumption.

The English businessman, with his more diffuse interests and his readiness to separate social occasions from business requirements, is much less likely to seek out talent at non-commercial gatherings. Indeed the average English businessman is just less concerned with spotting talent.

Once upon a time this indifference might have been attributed to the old-school tie, to the idea that 'breeding' rather than ability should determine a man's advancement. That is no longer the case, if ever it was, because the old-school tie has lost much of its glamour.

It is apathy rather than snobbery which affects recruitment in England. The British practice is to wait for the man to come to the firm, not for the firm to go to the man.

Many young scientists, technologists and aspiring executives today lodge their names with management consultants. These organisations sift the qualifications and marry the applicant to the company which meets his requirements.

This is the modern, scientific way of job hunting—and again the Americans score, for a fair number of the consultancy firms are American-controlled and, being familiar with American methods, have a natural tendency to give first consideration to US firms which make considerable use of management agencies.

There is no question of favouritism. It is just that management consultancy being a US development, American firms are more attuned than British to stating their requirements and making sure they are met.

The result however is that zestful, questing, young men are more likely to be snapped up by American organisations than British.

The American approach to promising material on a personal level is direct, encouraging and tempting. As can be seen from the following story :

A young man who failed to get sufficient qualifications to enter a university took himself to France for a year and returned to the UK well versed in French and with sufficient Spanish, too, to be proficient commercially in that language.

He wanted to go into business, but had no very clear idea what he wanted to do once he was in. So he contacted a number of firms. He visited ten in all. Each one was interested only in his paper qualifications, which were so sparse as to be almost non-existent. Not one was impressed by his initiative in equipping himself in French, although the chairman of one of the companies he consulted had made a speech on the need for his young sales-men to be able to speak a foreign language.

Finally, greatly disillusioned, he wrote off to an American firm based in England. He was interviewed thoroughly, made to be-lieve that he was needed, carefully selected for a job suited to his talents and personality and as a result he advanced rapidly.

The training scheme and the job evaluation methods for that firm had been worked out by an Englishman but it was an Ameri-can firm which put them into practice. It was an American firm which gauged that academic qualifications alone were not enough to judge a young man's potentialities, an American firm with its sensitive antennae for selling ability which put a premium on character.

Said a US executive : 'A degree is like a girl's pretty face : one hell of an advantage at first, but it doesn't necessarily go very far.'

In most British concerns the personnel officer is a minor figure : his rating comes well below that of the lawyers and accountants, who are, too often, the dried mandarins of British business. Technical sales and personnel chaps are not highly regarded in England.

Consequently the personnel officer goes by the book. He considers an applicant's paper certificates. If they meet the job qualifications he gets the job; if not, he doesn't. Not being highly regarded himself, the personnel officer rarely exercises his initiative to consider what other posts an applicant may fit in the organisation.

Lack of enthusiasm is the biggest curse in British industry. It is contagious. It affects every department in an organisation. It can lead to promising inventions being abandoned; able individuals being neglected and workers losing pride in the job.

A most startling contrast to the lackadaisical English outlook in industry—not universal, but widespread enough to cause anxiety—is provided by the American Avon Corporation.

Enthusiasm bordering on fanaticism distinguishes this enterprise. Its business is beauty. No nation had made such a fetish of womanly features as America. The bust there is practically a national symbol. So naturally America now owns most of the famous beauty preparations firms—Elizabeth Arden, Max Factor lipstick, Camay soap, Coty perfume, Limmits slimming biscuits, Frosted Velvet moisturising body fragrance; Silk 'n Satin hair Shampoo and countless more.

Right in the forefront of this care and maintenance industry is Avon. It has, says one newspaper, 'found it comparatively easy to convince bored or broke British housewives that calling on neighbours to introduce glamorous American products though, of course, British made is a fine way to make friends and earn money'.

The company which started in England in the late fifties has been phenomenally successful. With that instinctive capacity for turning human frailties or aspirations to the business of selling goods, the Americans utilised loneliness and the desire for more income in the cause of salesmanship.

Lots of women, housewives especially, are lonely. So why not invite them to call on their neighbours with a box of lovely Avon cosmetics? They meet new people; they talk about something that interests all women and they make a bit of pocket money.

This winning combination explains why Avon sales in the UK now exceed £11 million a year. More than 40,000 happy house-wives form their sales force (guided by two hundred area managers) and the average earnings of the part-timers work out at £4 10s for a twelve-hour week—7s/6d an hour—not a great deal more than a very good charwoman would get.

Avon's ingenuity does not end with utilising women's natural curiosity to minister to their vanity. It extends to the humdrum job of building warehouses. The company urgently needed more storage space for raw materials and finished products. Because of the housebuilding boom at the time it could not get the contract completed in anything like reasonable time.

So it organised a competition for local bricklayers, with valuable cash prizes for the ones who could lay most bricks in an eight-hour stint. Bricks, mortar and ancillary equipment were provided on the site. Hundreds entered the competition (which was, of course, in the bricklayers' leisure hours) and the result was a ware-house built in record time.

But that was not the end of the story. Avon was also short of factory workers. So an opportunity was given to all employees to bring along their wives and teenage daughters, together with their closer friends, to tour the factory. A splendid meal was laid on, a firm was shown and by the end of the day Avon had signed up so many women and girls for full- or part-time work that it had filled most of its vacancies—and this in an area, Northamptonshire, of over-full employment.

Sometimes Avon's all-embracing grip on its employees' loyalties is too much.

The dedication of its sales executives came into sharp focus in December 1964 when Mrs Terese Patten threatened to sue Avon for enticing her thirty-three-year-old husband Peter away from her and their two children. Mr Patten was the Midlands Divisional Sales Manager for Avon. According to Mrs Patten he had left home a year earlier, influenced by 'a sales policy which demands all his time and attention'. Bitterly she sighed that 'he is married to his job.' (In fact, she did not sue.)

Clearly Mrs Patten would not meet with the approval of the high priests of American management techniques, being neither adaptable, gregarious, nor willing to subordinate herself and her family to 'The Corporation'.

Nonetheless the ability of American-owned firms to command the zest and devotion of their British employees must be accepted as a basic reason for their success.

Unless and until British companies in general match the American achievements in management they will continue to trail behind the US companies in performance.

18

'Give Me Your Tired, Your Poor'?

'THEIR GERMANS ARE better than our Germans'
—Bob Hope on Russia's first satellite launching.

Planned American recruitment of European technicians began in the months immediately following the end of World War Two. German rocket scientists had astounded the world, and almost wrecked Allied plans, by landing V-1 and V-2 missiles on London in the autumn of 1944. It was obvious to governments and their military chiefs that the rocket was now a weapon of immense, perhaps decisive, significance.

By swiftly overrunning Eastern Germany in the early months of 1945 the Russians captured a large number of German rocket experts and straight away put them to work on Soviet projects. The Americans followed suit and coralled as many rocket engineers as they could. Britain, which had neither the ferocious will to seize nor the money to buy missile technologists, missed out completely.

What started as a military feud between the Soviet Union and the United States has now developed, so far as America is concerned, into the deliberate recruitment of the best scientific talent in the world—the 'brain drain'.

The extent of this recruitment has not yet been fully measured. Professor Titmuss of the London School of Economics has however estimated that 'since 1949 the USA has absorbed the import of 100,000 doctors, scientists and engineers from developed and developing countries. In eighteen years the US will have saved some 4,000 million dollars by not having to educate and train or train wholly their vast quantity of human capital.

'In medicine alone, foreign doctors now account for twenty per cent of the annual additions to the American medical profession. The world now provides as much, or more, medical aid to the United States in terms of dollars as the total cost of all American medical aid, private and public, to foreign countries.'

US educational experts reckon that the value of foreign skills lured to the US since the war equals, in terms of the money it cost the contributing countries to train their people, about as much as the US has provided in civilian relief subsidies.

Not unnaturally the Americans have no inclination to do anything to halt this windfall.

A special study group under the chairmanship of Dr Charles Frankel, Assistant Secretary of State for Education and Cultural Affairs, reported that, in the year ending June 1966, 24,953 scientists, engineers and technical specialists were signed on by American industry. The comment on this immense brain gain was : 'While recognising that this migration may be of concern to developed nations, the council doubts that steps to regulate the migration would be effective or would be in the best tradition of an open society.'

Ah, the open society! A fine noble conception, a resounding phrase, signifying precious little.

Since 1921 the US has operated a quota immigration system based on nationality. The chance of an unlimited number of illiterate Sierra Leonians or Nigerians or Indians getting into the US is considerably less than a camel getting through the eye of a needle.

Rejecting any suggestion of diminishing the flow of skilled whites to America Dr Frankel's committee declared : 'Limitation would deny that freedom of movement which has always been a cornerstone of United States policy.'

The committee went on to say that it did not find evidence to support complaints that the migration of special talent to the USA was 'overwhelmingly large'.

It all depends on what you mean by 'overwhelmingly'. Mr

Quintin Hogg, a leading spokesman for the Conservative Party, puts the loss of British talent—mainly to the USA—at 350 doctors and up to 4,000 scientists, engineers and technicians a year.

Britain is the target for the most concentrated recruiting campaign. Mr William A Douglass, at the head of an Invasion Task Force called Careers Incorporated, was splendidly blunt about his aim : 'We're going to hit you British hard. We are draining you blind of some of your most promising talent.' He claimed to have recruited more than a thousand technologists and exulted that the British Government did not have a clue, did not even keep figures, on the talent the country was losing.

In financial terms the drain is prodigious. It costs £20,000 of the taxpayers' money to train a PhD. In 1966 one third of those taking their PhD degrees in physics at British universities went off to the United States.

It takes £10,000 to produce an honours degree graduate and a large number of these also take off for America.

If any society can be called 'open' it is the British. Talent pours out of the door marked 'exit' and vast numbers of unskilled immigrants pour through the door marked 'entrance'. In twenty years, if present trends continue, England will lose 100,000 highly skilled, expensively educated citizens and gain 2,500,000 unskilled citizens.

There is no shadow of doubt that the Americans approve of this 'open' society which gives so generously of its skills and accepts such a copious flood from the underdeveloped world.

Whether Britain benefits is entirely another matter. Yet the fault is largely England's own. As one American smilingly put it : 'You train 'em—we drain 'em. If you're stupid enough to do that why the hell should we stop you?'

Britain is the principal victim of the brain drain. But she is far from being the only one. To fill hospital and scientific vacancies left by departing British doctors, Asian specialists come to the UK, although their own countries, India, Pakistan, Ceylon, desperately need them.

Thus a lunatic roundabout operates by which the wealthiest society in the world gains skills it does not really need while the poorest societies lose skills they cannot do without.

America pours out billions in aid to the developing countries, and vitiates much of the aid by drawing away the talent which alone can put the aid to proper use.

So prodigal is America of brains that her Government estimates the US will be 'short' of scores of thousands of technologists by the early 'seventies. In which case the brain drain will intensify. And the advertisements which already appear in prominent positions in the Sunday newspapers for skilled British engineers to work in Seattle, Cincinatti or Chicago will vastly increase.

What does Britain mean to do about this? What can she do?

If the 'open' society theory holds then of course she ought not to do anything. The public would presumably continue to subsidise students who on gaining their degrees would be free to accept posts in the United States or elsewhere. Britain would be free to compete for other nations' talents and lacking the resources to rival the US she would turn to Africa and Asia, with possibly just a soupçon from France and Germany.

All this presupposes that everyone else is operating an 'open society', which is manifestly not the case. Some countries require their students to repay the grants they have received either by working for a certain 'service' period at a lower salary than they would otherwise command or simply by paying back the money and remaining on their native heath until they do so. No country will allow scientists or engineers engaged on defence contracts to circulate freely. And of course one third of the world—the Communist bloc—is outside the scope of the enquiry, being a closed society.

Like that other beautiful theory, free trade, the open society is so riddled with qualifications as to be meaningless.

The fact of a common language makes the recruitment of Englishmen a priority for US firms. There is no need to acclimatise the newcomer to the American idiom. He is already attuned and fit to start working from the moment he arrives. Long years of technical collaboration, dating from the wartime partnership, has also familiarised British engineers with American industrial terms. Both nations use basically the same system of weights and measurements.

Even more important is the willingness of Britons to venture overseas. For nearly two centuries British people have been emigrating in large numbers to new countries like Canada, Australia, New Zealand and, of course, America herself. In contrast with France, for example, there is a tradition in the UK of seeking one's fortune across the seas. The danger is that as Britain's national identity is weakened by constant propaganda, largely self-inspired, against nationalism, the USA will come to look on Britain simply as a repository of talent; to be milked in much the same way as England has milked Scotland.

Britain has an infinite capacity for inflicting pain on herself. Certain fashionable ideas are repeated *ad nauseam* by pundits and, lo! become fundamental verities.

Freedom without obligation is now a very popular verity. This means that anyone is entitled to take what he can get from society without incurring any debt to society. Thus, a young man may be educated at the expense of the taxpayer, to gain a PhD. He then immediately joins the brain drain to the United States and helps to design an aircraft which drives its British competitors out of business. He and his wife may return to the Old Country from time to time, perhaps when a baby is due, so that it can be delivered 'free' under the National Health Service!

The extraordinary thing is that British Government policy, under both parties, has encouraged this process. The placid toleration which passes for a policy in England today has produced the worst of all worlds.

Talent is not rewarded as it should be. Up to £5,000 per annum the tax levied on an individual in the UK is not all that different from the taxation in the States. Beyond £5,000 there is a much steeper rise in England so that by the time an Englishman is earning £15,000 a year he is paying more than double the tax borne by his opposite number in America.

The Ministry of Health ladles out medicines to everyone regardless of their income, but keeps doctors on short commons so that, proportionately, they form by far the biggest element in the brain drain.

Yet while stern limits are imposed on professional earnings and tax-paid incomes, no restrictions whatsoever are placed on newly graduated technologists taking their newly acquired knowledge to another country.

If England were a dictatorship no outward flow of talent would be permitted. If she were devoted to free enterprise her native talent would not want to leave. As it is, Gresham's Law of politics operates : Equality drives out quality.

Alone among the major industrial nations Britain maintains a policy calculated to produce anti-national results.

Russia keeps brains by compulsion. America tempts brains with money. France binds brains by patriotism. Germany woos brains with prosperity. England worships mediocrity—and calls it social justice.

Is it any wonder that Britain is bottom of the economic growth league? Can there be surprise that US recruiting teams do so much better in the UK than in any other European country?

Mr Douglass of Careers Inc says that one big reason why so many young Englishmen choose to emigrate is that they lack scope and opportunities in the UK. 'They just haven't enough to do.'

American firms established in the UK are also very well aware of this alleged frustration. When they go 'head hunting' they make a point of offering responsibility early to the right men. And anyone who is really outstanding is likely to be offered a still bigger appointment in the States.

Thus a concealed brain drain is added to the open one. And this hidden transfer of talent is far more serious for England than for other nations because there are far more US subsidiaries in the UK than on the Continent.

In attracting talent to the States, whether from US-owned companies or from British-owned concerns, money is certainly the strongest temptation. Mouth-watering sums are bandied about. Awestruck young men of twenty-five are told they will treble their salaries from £1,400 to £4,200. At the fixed rate of exchange that may be so. But the pound's parity with the dollar is artificial. It was fixed, by God and by guess, in 1949, and again in 1967 when England was trying to stimulate exports through devaluation. The £1 = $2.40 formula does not represent relative purchasing power. It does not mean that 2.40 dollars in New York would purchase the same amount of goods as £1 in London.

Comparing the living costs in one country with another is an extraordinarily difficult exercise. In some parts of the States it appears that $2.40 actually buys more consumer goods than £1. Generally speaking however, when medical costs (privately borne), insurance, pension contributions, housing are added in, the $2.40 = £1 figure is seen to be unrealistic.

A survey in the *Sun* newspaper contrasted the household budget of a young couple with two children in Hythe, Hants, with an American couple of the same age and family size in Buffalo, New York.

The conclusion was that, in purchasing power, the pound was equal to seven dollars—given the fact that the British couple wanted to remain in the same social bracket. This meant they would have a telephone (which they didn't have in England) and a newer car. Telephones and fairly new cars are so common in the United States that they rank, socially speaking, with television and radio sets in Britain.

Putting the pound at seven dollars would be fiercely contested by most Americans. The fairest thing, and probably the most accurate, would be to split the difference between the official rate of 2.40 and the *Sun's* estimate of seven and put the purchasing power of the pound at somewhere around $4.70.

At that rate an offer of $12,000 (£2,550), though good, is hardly the glittering prize it is held out to be.

Nonetheless a great many young scientists and engineers take it. They are lured too by the prospect of boundless wealth to come —sometimes justified, more often not—and by the belief that they are going to the centre of power.

Superbly self-confident American executives exude this aroma of authority. They give the impression, it is not a spoken commitment, that no man can test his capacity to the full unless he tests it in the heart of Capitalism. American business is so much bigger, it commands such infinitely greater machine and human resources that it is almost on a different planet compared with British business.

Twenty years ago an entertainer who had toured in America, however humbly, was introduced to a British audience as though he had come from paradise. Since the Beatles, British show business is not quite so Uriah-Heepish.

But in commerce, American superiority is readily, somewhat fawnishly, acknowledged. Some business journals, eagerly scanned by aspiring young technologists, almost take the line:

> *God bless the Yank and his relations*
> *And keep us in our proper stations.*

This spirit of wonder is naturally transmitted to potential recruits. They are half-won over before the interview starts.

Once they have experienced a demonstration of US salesmanship combining as it does the casual take-over of the most expensive hotel suites with hospitality which is generous without being vulgar the potential emigrant is usually won over. Nothing succeeds like success. And the Americans are obviously, almost painfully, successful.

Like a magnet the US draws the eager, energetic, try-anything-once people to her shores. Nothing excites Americans like a challenge to technical skills. 'Shoot the moon, Ike,' cried the crowds when the Soviets sent their first satellite hurtling into space in 1957.

America has been devoting billions upon billions of dollars to hitting that target ever since. And recruiting the world's brains to help her do it.

Lord Bowden, Principal of Manchester's Institute of Science and Technology, burst out angrily in 1966: 'Because of the preposterous and insatiable desire to put a man on the moon, the US wants more scientists and engineers than she can possibly produce herself. America is stripping other countries of their technologists.'

As an illustration of how hard the US is trying to strip the UK, many members of the 5,000-strong Royal Aeronautical Society, a most distinguished body, have been circularised by American firms offering them jobs in the States.

It is entirely within America's competence whether or not she continues with her massively expensive manned exploration of space. The results may be toweringly successful for mankind or they may merely increase the options for delivering nuclear bombs.

The point is: should scientific talent trained in England, financed by the British taxpayer, be available at no cost to the US?

The stock reply that England is free to attract Americans is irrelevant. Everyone is free to buy a Rolls-Royce; but only people with lots of money actually buy Rolls-Royces. The Americans have lots of money because their country is thirty times bigger and many times richer in resources than England. There is no equality of factors.

There is, however, a deadly logic in the brain drain across the Atlantic.

The more that able individuals are tempted to quit Britain, the less competitive does British industry become—and the more vulnerable it is to US take-overs.

'Hit Britain hard,' says William A Douglass the Brain-drainer in Chief. From the American point of view it is shrewd advice.

When, if ever, will the British decide to hit back?

19

Enter the International Company

IN 1934 MR Clement Attlee, leader of the Labour Party, announced that he regarded himself as a citizen of the world! That was very noble of Mr Attlee, but he might have saved his breath. For no one else regarded him as a citizen of the world. His status was fictional. The reality, which Mr Attlee from 1940–45 proved with customary courage, was that he was a British citizen.

There is, or was, an unfortunate individual who haunted the United Nations proclaiming himself to be the first member of a World State. So far as is known he remained the sole supporter of this exclusive club. 'Where there is no vision the people perish' is doubtless a profound saying. An even sounder one is 'Where there are no people the vision perishes'.

And the vision of a World State is further away than ever. In 1914 there were 50 sovereign nations. Today there are nearly 150 and at the rate existing states are breaking up there is likely to be a good many more before the century is much older.

Yet while political fragmentation continues apace, lo! there appears on the horizon a new internationalism—the international company! Busily, persuasively, advocates promote the merits of this phenomenon.

It appears that very large companies do not really belong to any one nation. They are above all that, existing in some kind of wide blue yonder where men of many races contribute their skills to a benevolent corporation which distributes largesse to the four corners of the globe (three if you exclude the Communist corner).

This beatific picture has as much relation to actuality as Mr

Attlee's 'world citizen' ploy. There is no such thing as an 'international company'.

True it is that there are concerns which operate in many lands and employ many thousands of people of different race, creed and colour. But somewhere there is a boss. Somewhere there are shareholders who control a majority of the equity. And where the treasure is there is the heart and mind and soul of the corporation.

Most of the 'International Companies' are, of course, American. Mr G Keith Funston, president of the New York Stock Exchange, informed a Scottish audience that 'the growth of the multi-national company in recent years has been one of the greatest things in international business.

'Most of America's large companies are now involved, or are about to become involved, in either partly or wholly owned subsidiaries in other lands. Of the 200 largest companies in the US an estimated 84 per cent now has one or more foreign subsidiaries.'

Mr Funston felt it would be 'most advantageous to people everywhere to encourage truly international ownership of these companies'.

The Americans have a penchant for multi-national solutions. There was once a proposal for a multi-national nuclear fleet in which all the nations of NATO would co-operate. French engineers would take commands from Dutch officers; German gunners would salute Belgian commanders; British stewards would distribute spaghetti prepared by Italian cooks. There was just one proviso. The Americans alone would decide when the weapons were to be used.

So it is with the 'truly international corporation'. Ultimate authority rests with the country whose citizens provide most of the capital. And, in nine cases out of ten, that is America.

Of the 200 biggest companies in the world 170 are US-owned. Perhaps the greater significance is the fact that some of these companies are 'general stores' ready to buy up concerns anywhere regardless of what they make.

These firms are basically management enterprises. Their stock-in-trade is financial flair, spry administrative capacity, vast money-raising capabilities and a highly-tuned sense of what the public wants, or can be encouraged to want.

Such a firm is Litton Industries, whose products range from nuclear submarines to typewriters. It was Litton which finally put an end to the last remnants of the British typewriter industry, thereby turning it into the only trade—so far—that is 100 per cent controlled by foreigners. Litton (which already owned Royal) bought out Imperial in the autumn of 1966.

Mr George Evans, Imperial's chief executive, enthused over Litton's gifts : 'It has been able to bring the latest advances in technology to bear on all the companies in its orbit and so produce the finest goods at the lowest cost. . . . We have already felt this vital urge.'

Certainly poor old Imperial needed urging. It had the old-fashioned aim of making things to last.

Once the firm received a letter from the Mother Superior of a Convent in Eire. She complained that she had bought an Imperial thirty years ago 'and the ribbon is now completely worn out' !

Planned obsolescence nowadays takes care of these little local difficulties.

Another US firm which spans a wide range of products is American Home Products, owners of such diverse products (in the UK) as Three-in-One oil, Anadin and Prestige Kitchenware. Prestige, itself an American firm, was acquired by American Home Products in 1965.

Concerns such as AHP and Litton are ready and willing to pounce anywhere. Diversification is their business and be it ever so ailing there is no company that cannot be revived by brisk management.

The trouble is that colossal businesses with tentacles reaching out into perhaps a hundred different trades can exercise dangerous power. Litton could step into trade after trade in the UK without ever rousing the ire of the Monopolies Commission or the Restrictive Practices Court because its share of the market constituted no more than, say, ten per cent. But from that base it could push outwards and use its mammoth resources to squeeze out native producers. Maybe it wouldn't do that. But it could, and what is to prevent amalgamations of US firms in America leading to ownership of subsidiaries here being concentrated in very few hands—and foreign hands at that?

Of course anti-trust legislation in the US may forestall certain mergers, but a decision affecting British business would be made by American courts, concerned only with American interests.

Thus does the 'International Company' work on the commercial level.

What about the political implications? Professor John Dunning, in his scholarly and detailed work *American Investment in British Manufacturing Industry*,[1] states: 'One must remember that it is the larger US corporations who are mainly the interested parties (in the UK) and these can often exert considerable political influence in the American House of Representatives and Senate. To further this point a recent supplement (in the early 'fifties) listed the 500 largest US companies. Of these, 85 had subsidiary manufacturing interests in the UK and between them accounted for no less than 35.4 per cent of the total sales of the 500; 35.2 per cent of the total assets and 43.3 per cent of the net profits. Of the largest 200 US companies alone, 55 operated branch units in the UK.'

The political influence of these giants is significant. But in turn they must heed the wishes of American politicians, as is shown in the case history of the Viscount airplanes. Lord Francis-Williams told the story in his book on the American Invasion:

'Consider the Viscount case. In December 1961 it was announced that as part of a purely commercial transaction orders had been placed in Britain for six Viscount airliners for delivery to China. The planes concerned were civilian planes, free from strategic embargo. The sale of the six Viscounts had the full

1. *American Investment in the British Manufacturing Industry*, Professor John Dunning, Allen & Unwin, 1958

approval of the British Government. It did not, however find favour in American eyes, and on December 8 Mr Dean Rusk, the US Secretary of State, made it known publicly that the American Government disapproved of the transaction. . . . The British Government very sensibly ignored this protest. It repudiated the suggestion that it should intervene against a perfectly proper commercial transaction fully in line with official British policy. . . .

'What followed has a more sinister connotation, especially when seen in the context of the immense expansion of American interests in a number of big British industries. The British company which is the main supplier of equipment for the instrument landing system and VOR navigational beacon receivers fitted in the Viscount is the Standard Telephones and Cables Company. This equipment is recommended for world-wide navigational aids as a major contribution to air safety by the International Civil Aviation Organisation. But Standard Telephones and Cables, one of the biggest producers of telecommunication equipment in Britain, is wholly owned and controlled by the International Telephone and Telegraph Co of New York and, governmental pressure having failed, this economic power was now invoked. In January 1962 it became known that the International Telephone and Telegraph Co had been alerted and 'cautioned' by the US State Dept regarding the Viscount transaction, although it had no direct concern with the equipment involved, none of which was even manufactured under American licence or patent; it had been designed in the British factory. Thereupon the International Telephone and Telegraph Co sent instructions to its British associate, Standard Telephones and Cables, warning it that it must not provide equipment for any Viscounts intended for China.'

Comments Francis-Williams : 'By these means, to put it plainly, a deliberate attempt was made to use American control of a British company to subvert British Government policy.'[1]

British computer firms have penetrated deeply and successfully

1. *The American Invasion,* Francis Williams, Anthony Blond, 1962

behind the Iron Curtain. American-owned computer firms in the UK have made no effort to sell to Russia and Eastern Europe. The reason for this coyness is the American Government's embargo on the export of advanced technical equipment to the Soviet Union and its satellites.

American Government pressure has also been exerted against the sale of British supersonic aircraft (containing certain US-made elements) to South America on the grounds that this would start an arms race. Curiously, the same argument was waived in the case of Saudi Arabia, to which country Britain sold Lightning fighters, perhaps because that contract was part of the package deal whereby Britain bought a huge number of planes from America in return for the right to sell in Saudi Arabia, long regarded as an American client state.

Does anyone imagine that one thousand buses would have been sold to Castro's Cuba if the company making the buses had been Fords or Vauxhall and not the entirely British-owned Leyland?

The truth is that, in the end, US companies in Britain and Europe must conform to political decisions made in Washington. As the French discovered when their reliance on US computers slowed down their nuclear weapons programme.

Lord Shawcross, an ex-Socialist who has become a blunt, vigorous and highly engaging champion of free enterprise and is also a director of Shell Oil, the Anglo-Dutch concern, operating on a world-wide scale, has said: 'The fear of American investment in Britain is due to a misconceived, if not frightened, spirit of nationalism. What is more important nowadays than the ownership of an industry is its actual operation . . . Subject to the laws, the loyalties and the economic and social policies of this country (*ie* the UK).'

There is nothing wrong, and much that is admirable, in British, Dutch, American, Japanese, German firms which operate globally. What is wrong is to pretend they are 'truly international'. They are not. They are national companies with branches in other countries.

If there is a conflict between the economic policies of Britain and America an American subsidiary in the UK is bound to follow orders from the parent board. And the parent board will follow the instructions or advice of the American Government. And short of seizing the plant there is nothing Britain can do about it.

Lord Shawcross's reference to 'loyalties' must be heavily qualified. Loyalty to the laws of the country in which the firm is operating—yes! But ultimate loyalty in commercial practice goes to the one who pays the piper, the parent company.

One of the most extraordinary examples of the complete control exercised by headquarters over a foreign subsidiary concerned the French branch of Remington Rand, the US typewriter firm.

An order was sent by teletype from the US to fire 800 of the 1,200 employees of Remington Rand's factory near Lyons in order to facilitate the concentration of production at Remington's more modern plant in Holland. This casual disposition of foreign labour roused the French to fury and goes a long way to explain President de Gaulle's animosity to American capital.

Indeed, so fervent was the Gallic reaction to this and other episodes involving American firms that a US businessman (a Chrysler executive) was appointed to investigate the complaints. He reported that :

'In a significant number of companies on policy matters touching upon activities vital to the French economy there was little delegation of authority to subsidiary management. The centralisation of the decision making process in the US appears to be particularly objectionable in view of the offhand manner in which decisions of great consequence abroad are taken.'

Nowadays many American concerns go out of their way to be tactful; to identify themselves with the 'host' country. Mention has already been made of the UK branch of Bechtel, the chemical engineers, flying the Union Jack on their advertisement. Honeywell, the US computer concern operating in Scotland, stresses its Britishness at every opportunity. This laudable attempt to smooth the susceptibilities of foreigners shows that Americans are very much alive to the dangers of Gaullism and are anxious to achieve happy relations with their host countries.

Unfortunately kindness is not enough. However much American businessmen try to win the approval of foreign governments they must ultimately obey the orders of their bosses back in the States.

They may carry out these instructions with greater aplomb than their more tough-minded predecessors. But they cannot avoid the final crunch; which is to say to the workers and the host government: 'Sorry, but these changes, though they may not suit you, or us, as an operating concern in your country, are nevertheless in the interest of headquarters. Orders are orders.'

Somehow or other the basic concept of the 'American International Company' must be altered to meet the legitimate grievances of other countries. And that may mean a wholesale reorganisation to end a dependence which has become insupportable.

20

The Ballad-Makers

'IF A MAN were permitted to make all the ballads, he need not care who should make the laws of a nation.'—Fletcher of Saltoun.

'Ballad-making' in England today is almost a US monopoly. The only general interest picture magazine circulating in Britain is the American journal *Life* (circulation in the UK 95,000 in 1967). The only news magazines circulating in Britain (with the exception of *Time and Tide*) are the US journals *Time* (circulation about 85,000) and *Newsweek* (21,000). The only pocket magazine is the American *Reader's Digest*. One of the two twice-weekly serials on British television is the story of an American small town, 'Peyton Place'. In 1967 nineteen of the twenty-five first-feature films being made in British studios were partly or wholly American-financed. Thirty per cent of the paperbacked books sold in Britain are American-owned. Half the encyclopaedias, notably the *Encyclopaedia Britannica,* which enter British homes are American.

The American take-over in the media of communication is staggering. The effect on British tastes, attitudes and opinions is not easily gauged but it must be formidable, for American-owned companies are not interested in promoting purely British products. They want to sell world-wide—and always their principal objective is the American market. It is four times larger in population; seven times greater in wealth than England. Every magazine article, every paperback, every film must be slanted to give it American appeal. In this Britain and other European nations are not discounted. They are merely given a rating according to their position in the international market schedule.

The sad demise of the British magazine industry is due entirely to excessively bad management and the onset of television. One after another the magazines—*Picture Post, Illustrated, Everybody's, Lilliput, Strand, Sphere* went out the window as the television set came in the door. There was no real attempt to fight back; no long-term effort to endure until the novelty of television had worn off. When that did happen in the early 'sixties there was nothing left. So the Americans stepped in and stepped up their 'Atlantic editions' of *Time, Life, Reader's Digest,* dispensing a certain amount of local interest with the bulk of American-style material.

Like the 'International companies', the 'International magazines' are the projection of America across the water. The British comedian Spike Milligan was very upset when he was criticised for complaining about things in Britain to *Life* magazine. It was pointed out to him that he shouldn't 'knock' his own country in a foreign journal. He indignantly replied that the magazine was not foreign, it was the 'British' edition which had contained his strictures!

It is argued by some people, who are not necessarily disinterested financially, that to object to the influence of the 'International magazines' is to adopt a narrow nationalism, unworthy of this contracting world. This is a very odd argument, for *Time* and *Life* are ardently, stridently, pro-American—as they have every right to be. If the subjection of one's own nationalism to that of another nationalism just because it is larger is to be the test of internationalism then the Chinese, who have infinitely more nationals than anyone else, are going to be the ultimate winners.

There is something rather pathetic about the eagerness with which the British seize on any mention of themselves in US journals. They warm themselves in the glow of a patronising smile and when *Time* actually wrote of London being the swinging city joy was unconfined. The fact that Babylon might also have earned the swinging epithet—or epitaph—went unnoticed. If London had not swung before she now bent every effort to earning *Time*'s good opinion. And with the self-consciousness of a middle-aged woman stripping in public, gave herself up to being the 'fun-loving' capital of the Western world.

One story, perhaps unfounded, was that the Americans gave London the 'swinging' title in order to demote Paris which, as the capital of de Gaulle's France, had earned black marks.

True or not, the story is perfectly conceivable. For where America's interests are concerned US magazines, especially of the strongly right-wing stamp of *Time, Life,* will do all they can to help. British journals in the days of imperial sway would have done no less for England.

An even more significant episode concerned the Anglo-American literary periodical *Encounter*. This intellectual magazine devoted an entire issue to the decline and fall of Britain under the heading 'Suicide of a nation?'

Whether the analysis was profound or superficial is beside the point. On intellectuals, or people with pretensions to being intellectual, it was bound to leave the impression that Britain was in a bad way. If its aim was not to spread pessimism like the plague that was certainly its effect .

Encounter has always had a particular attraction for left-wing writers, who viewed British imperialism as an unhappy memory and American imperialism as a crude and rude reality.

Imagine then their dismay when they discovered that for years *Encounter* had been receiving funds channelled from the American secret service the Central Intelligence Agency, the dreaded CIA.

It may well be that the aid was given for altruistic purposes and that no hint of editorial advice accompanied it. All the same, it would be interesting to know what other 'objective' magazines also receive a helping hand from Washington.

It is not the American attitude that is difficult to understand in all this, but the British. To seek an historical parallel for such subservience to another's will one would need to go back to Charles II's relations with Louis XIV. Then, too, England was in debt most of the time. And London was indubitably swinging !

This anxiety to please America was born in the days of the war when US goodwill was essential to England's survival. It has endured for a less praiseworthy reason : because of the pull of the dollar. Even British authors writing for British publishers are apt to think first of the marketability of the book, play, film script in the States. Britain, as a market, is barely big enough to sustain her own talent. And as Americans have the same language and other similarities exist between the peoples, it is to the US that British literary and dramatic talent looks.

So the assault on England's mind is twofold. From American-owned publishing and film companies determined to exploit the British market as a valuable subsidiary, and from British writers eager to sell their works to the largest English-speaking market, America, and to adapt their thoughts and style to that end.

As long as Britain is content to remain a branch of a dominant outside culture this situation will continue. And for American magazines the only question worth asking concerning England will be 'Is London hippier than San Francisco?'

For pretty well everyone in the nineteen-twenties and -thirties Hollywood meant films and films meant Hollywood. Any movie that hadn't come out of Hollywood was regarded as an oddity; a subject of intense curiosity which prompted cinemagoers to reach the same conclusion as Dr Johnson on women preachers : 'like a dog walking on his hinder legs, it is not done well; but you are surprised to find it done at all.'

British pictures, certainly in the 'twenties, fell into the category of women preachers. No one expected them to be good; the miracle was that any were being produced at all !

Once again 1914 is the watershed. England plunged into war at the very moment when film-making was emerging from the penny show to the status of a great industry. While British producers concentrated their slender resources on war propaganda films, the Americans were able to use peacetime conditions, the sunshine of California and the genius of Charlie Chaplin (born in London), to make the silent films which were to sweep the world.

By the end of the war there was not really a British film industry worthy of the name. Sir Michael Balcon, who was to become one of the outstanding personalities of the British industry, recalls that when he started in 1922 most cinemas had booked American films generally for years ahead. British film production was frozen out and earned a poor living on the fringes where the rather sticky reticence of English actors and actresses did little to raise its reputation for quality.

Help was slow in coming. First, the chaotic system of renting which had allowed the Americans to get a stranglehold on the exhibition side of the industry was reformed. Then, in 1927, Parliament moved to safeguard domestic movie-making by imposing a quota which required every British cinema to show at least 5 per cent—later 20 per cent—British films. Under the Quota Act, to qualify as 'British' 75 per cent of the wages and salaries had to be paid to UK personnel and all studio scenes had to be shot in England.

British production began to revive. Lively, creative minds were attracted to the craft; distribution and exhibition were rationalised and such was the vigour now displayed that British films began to make inroads into the US itself. The US moguls took a somewhat jaundiced view of this and a 'Clean Film' campaign was launched in the States which slated many foreign films as 'indecent, immoral and unfit for public exhibition' while giving a clean bill of health to American movies that hardly differed in kind from the 'wicked' foreign products.

Here was glittering testimony to the new robustness of British film making. At last it was making ground; not only at home, but in the Empire and the US.

Alas, the progress was not sustained. Once more war intervened and although some excellent movies were made in England during the hostilities, the country was in a tired and weakened state when the fighting ended.

To conserve dollars the then Labour Chancellor, Hugh

177

Dalton, imposed a tax on US films. But under pressure from the American film makers, who did not see why they should be singled out for punishment when America was pumping aid into England, the tax was abandoned in 1948 and a backlog of American movies flooded into British cinemas.

Desperately the British producers turned to the government. 'How,' they asked, 'can we stand up to Hollywood when they can sell films here which have already recovered their production costs in the States?'

'Why,' they demanded, 'cannot we have the State support afforded Italian producers by their government?'

Initially the British Government returned a stony answer to the film men's plea, but in 1950 it promoted a voluntary levy known as the Eady levy after the Treasury official who worked it out, whereby cinemas paid the producers a fraction on each ticket sold at the box office above a certain minimum.

With the levy tucked under their belts and the quota system (now raised to thirty per cent) to protect their markets, the British film makers happily launched into a new phase of expansion. This was the period of the famed Ealing comedies which rivalled the best that studios anywhere were turning out.

Then things turned really sour for movie makers everywhere. Television dealt the industry a staggering blow. The number of cinemas in America and Britain slumped by sixty per cent. The glitter, and most of the stars, deserted Hollywood. And a great melancholy descended.

Two courses of action, it was decided, were needed to revive the industry. One, costs must be cut; two, spectacular films must be made to lure the customers away from their television sets.

Both courses led to the same end: A large-scale American movie invasion of England: where there was no language barrier and top-class films could be made much more cheaply, owing to lower wages.

So began the take-over of the British film industry. One after another the famous studios fell before the invader. Within a few years, Shepperton, Pinewood and Elstree were occupied, four fifths of the time, by American companies. Borehamwood was already the property of Metro-Goldwyn-Mayer.

Of course, this was not the first time American film interests had penetrated England. As soon as the barriers of protection had gone up with the passing of the Quota Act in 1927 US business had moved in to secure its UK market. Warners had long owned a large slice of Associated British Picture Corporation. Indeed the Treasury had given encouragement to the American concern even when it bid for the shares owned by the estate of the Scottish film magnate John Maxwell against competition from British interests represented by Courtaulds and associates. Fox had also come close to controlling Gaumont-British. In addition US producing companies had established subsidiaries in England though, up to the mid-fifties, on a comparatively small scale.

Now they were bustling in in a big way. And being subsidised by the British taxpayer to boot !

To comply with the provisions of the General Agreement on Tariffs and Trade (surely the most beneficial document from America's point of view since the Declaration of Independence) the Eady levy—made statutory in 1957—did not discriminate between British-owned and foreign-owned film companies. So long as the foreigners did most of their work in the UK they qualified for the levy and for the quota.

Considerable chagrin was caused to British film makers by this provision, but there was nothing they could do about it.

Thus the Yanks came, saw and conquered. Just as they had some years before 'discovered' Rome, so now they 'discovered' London.

Why, they crooned, the British were just bursting with artistic talent! Deprived of their empire, they were proving excellent minstrels; making just the dandiest cameramen, the sexiest actors, the lushest actresses. All over the world the bells were set ringing for London Town. But the cash register was tinkling for the US corporations who owned all that colourful property.

179

James Bond may have been invented by Scotsman Ian Fleming, acted by fellow countryman Sean Connery, directed by Englishman Lewis Gilbert, produced by Canadians Harry Saltzman and Albert Broccoli, but the profits went to America's United Artists.

So long as non-discrimination remains the rule Britain will remain an appendage of the American film market. For England simply does not have the resources to compete effectively with the US in an international movie free-for-all. The National Film Finance Corporation, a State-sponsored body established in 1949 to aid British film production, had £1 million of disposable capital in 1966. By American standards this is 'peanuts'. *Cleopatra* alone cost £15 million to make.

Lord Willis, the Labour peer and script writer, has quoted an example of the salary differentials which explains why Britain lags behind. A British film star received £15,000 for a film made in England. He then went to work for an American concern. The next time his services were required by a British company he demanded £75,000—because that was the kind of money he had been getting from the States.

Who can blame him for raising his sights? Who can blame the Americans for paying him what they regard as the going rate?

The fault lies not in the stars, but in the system which permits wealthy American corporations to raise money in the City of London and benefit from the proceeds of a levy designed to succour the British film industry.

Not merely benefiting from that levy, but practically monopolising it. In 1966 the UK subsidiaries of US corporations received eighty per cent of the Eady fund. For every £100 profit made on their films shown in England the US companies pocketed an extra £56 from the levy. Thus are rich foreigners made richer —by Act of Parliament.

The American answer to this charge is that the Americans bring work and high wages to a British industry that would otherwise be moribund.

But would it be moribund if there were clear financial discrimination in favour of purely British-made films, combined with a powerful national authority to promote commercial development?

The experience of British commercial television suggests there may be a solution on these lines for the British film industry.

When independent television was launched in the UK in 1955 the temptation, and the maximisation of profits, lay in buying American programmes which, having already earned their keep in the States, could be purchased very cheaply.

Peak viewing time could then simply be filled with US fare.

The Independent Television Authority however intervened. With its absolute powers over the allocation of licences its word had to be heeded; the amount of US material was swiftly scaled down and domestic production rose accordingly.

It is surely not beyond the bounds of possibility for the television companies, which are wholly British-owned, to make films for the cinema, to benefit exclusively from the Eady levy and to be kept on the path of rectitude by an authority, like the ITA, which is neither over-paternal nor over-indulgent.

At least something must be done before the home-based British film industry disappears altogether.

Nor should it be imagined that the Americans will remain enamoured of Britain for ever. The location may shift again as it has done in the past.

Or as Sidney Gilliat, director of British Lion, put it: 'American finance has snowballed here in the last six years, but of course a snowball can melt as soon as the weather changes.'

21

Bonanza

'WE MUST MAKE these women so unhappy that
their husbands can find no happiness and peace'—
B Earl Puckett, Allied Stores Corporation of the US.

One Sunday evening the American feature film on British television was interrupted for the advertisements. Of the six 'spots'
five were advertising American goods and each one of these products was advertised by an American-owned advertising agency.
The Sunday in question was April 23—St George's Day!

No British industry has been so thoroughly Americanised as
advertising. It is not just that eight out of the fourteen largest
agencies in the UK are US-owned; nor merely that many of the
remainder have associate links with US concerns, but rather that
the development of twentieth-century advertising has coloured
British lives and twentieth-century advertising is overwhelmingly
American in origin and appeal.

The point is made well by Sargeunt & West in their book
Grand Strategy[1]: 'America's rise to industrial supremacy has
been at least partly due to the fact that her advertising methods
—the most effective in the world—encourage the desire always to
possess the latest improvement or novelty necessitating the constant use of scientific research in industry in order to keep pace
with popular demand.'

The mass market generates mass production and competition
ensures that the consumer is kept constantly aware that alternatives are available to him.

With the world's biggest market in terms of buying power;
with the world's most highly organised machine for mass pro-

1. *Grand Strategy*, H A Sergeaunt and G West, Jonathan Cape, 1942

duction and the most intensely competitive system it is no wonder that America has by far the mightiest advertising industry in the world.

Every hour of every day nearly £1 million is spent by American advertisers persuading people to buy goods: a grand total of £6,000 million a year, or about one half of the budget of the British Government.

Famous names in American advertising are now firmly established in the UK. At the top is J Walter Thompson with an annual billing in excess of £20 million (a number of British MPs are employed by this company); Pritchard Wood International (part of US Interpublic Group); Young and Rubicam; McCann-Erickson (part of US Interpublic); Hobson Bates (merged with Ted Bates & Co); Erwin Wasey; Foote Cone and Belding; Crane, Norman Craig and Kummel; Benton and Bowles. Plus many smaller ones like Leo Burnett and Kenyon and Eckhardt.

It would be quite wrong to imagine that the native English industry has been knocked out of the ring. It is fighting back vigorously, but it is, perforce, fighting with weapons chosen and perfected in America.

There a whole way of life has grown up around advertising, extending beyond mere commerce into politics, mass management, the professions, the services, religion. 'Advertising in the Service of God' is not an invented slogan. It is a genuine one in the US which may explain why an American theologian, Rheinhold Niebuhr, felt obliged to warn his fellow countrymen: 'We are in danger of developing a culture that is enslaved to its productive process, thus reversing the normal relationship of production and consumption.'

Advertising in the US has long had practitioners in the esoteric realms of motivational research and deep analysis. They are now at work in the UK. In advertising, more than in any other business, it is true to say 'What America does today, England will do tomorrow.'

This is so because so many of the American-owned products

in England are consumer goods which are advertised direct to the public by American-owned agencies. Sometimes the US agency will not even change the 'copy' from that used in the States and the same 'strong, compelling, dynamic' American accent on television tells girls in England to buy that special hair spray. Research, however, has disclosed that the transatlantic tone has lost appeal and US advertising generally adapts itself to local conditions.

But behind the local gloss beats the mighty engine of an American industry which determines taste and applies findings of what makes people buy to the whole Western world.

Would packaged meat sold in supermarkets have spread so rapidly in England if American researches had not discovered that women were secretly scared of entering into discussions about cuts of meat at the butcher's shop?

Would advertising of cake mixes take the form it does without this gem of motivational analysis from Edward H Weiss probed by Vance Packard in *The Hidden Persuaders*?

'A single advertisement for ready-made cake mix might appeal to one woman, then in her creative mood, to try something new, then at the same time appeal to another woman whose opposite emotional needs at the moment will best be satisfied by a cake mix promising no work, no fuss, no bother.' This conclusion is based on a psychiatric study of women's menstrual cycle and emotional state.

Would 'Swinging London' be quite so swinging without the discovery by American ad men (again calling psychologists to their aid) that 'the wish to appear naked or scantily clad in a crowd is present in most of us and represents a beautiful example of wish fulfilment'? This particular piece of research—conducted as long ago as 1954—gave rise to an advertisement dubbed: 'I dreamed I stopped the traffic in my Maidenform bra.'

As far as undressing is concerned England has now advanced beyond America. It is doubtful if a girl in a Maidenform bra, or even without one, would stop the traffic. Still the initial impulse to try came from across the Atlantic.

Packard, in his books *The Image Makers* and *The Hidden Persuaders*, gives example after example of the devoted care lavished on finding out what makes people choose one product instead of another. Take the case of tea, one of the few remaining British influences in the US. A Dr Dichter made a close study of the decline in the tea drinking in the USA. It appeared that by 1960 Americans per head were drinking only one third the tea they had consumed in 1900. So the doctor went to work and he came up with this astonishing answer: It was all the fault of the Boston Tea Party!

Americans, it seemed, had been subconsciously resistant to tea since the night, nigh on two centuries ago, when colonial patriots tossed a cargo of British tea into Boston Harbour. The continued gloating over this episode had inspired Americans with an anti-tea attitude.

Dr Dichter suggested that Americans should be taught that the Boston Tea Party was not a protest against tea but rather a dramatic expression of the importance of tea in the life of the American revolutionaries!

The obverse of this is that a well-known Scotch whisky firm has discovered that British consumers reacted against an advert claiming that the whisky was selling particularly well in the US. British whisky drinkers were loth to believe that the Americans were capable of judging whisky!

But tea and whisky, which have special nationalistic connections, apart, the Americans are pretty sure that what goes down in the States will prove a sure-fire winner overseas.

Sex and the motor car are the symbols of the 'sixties, and are likely to be in the 'seventies, come to that.

The Americans have in their advertising exploited both to a quite remarkably successful degree. Sex, in its relation to cake mixes and underwear, has been dealt with. What of the car?

That, too, has, according to the psychiatrists, sexual overtones. American research discloses that we tend to think of a fixed-top saloon as a wife and an open roadster as a mistress.

The car however has other attributes. It is, to quote a US advertiser : 'A portable study of our personality and our position, the clearest way we have of telling people of our exact position. In buying a car you are saying, in effect, "I am looking for the car to express who I am".'

A glorious note of triumph was struck by the general manager of Chevrolet who trumpeted : 'We've got the finest door slam this year we've ever had. A big door slam !'

It would be nice to think that the psychologists and motivational researchers and deep analysts were fooling themselves. But the evidence does seem to show they are right most of the time. And that their findings are as valid to England as to the US.

With the tie-up between American agencies and American manufacturers in Britain there is every likelihood the volume of advertising for American goods, and therefore their sale, will rise swiftly and steadily.

In many cases indeed the saturation advertising of certain products has swept all local competition out of the market. In breakfast cereals, for example, the US companies now have a virtual monopoly. In car-hire the big fight in England is between two American-owned concerns. The word 'Hoovering' is more commonly used in England than vacuum cleaning.

In advertising, the colossi are American. And they have a 'Mankind or nothing' approach to promotion. Tom Sutton, president of the giant J Walter Thompson American advertising agency, has said : 'Companies are going international and this is becoming the rule rather than the exception. Virtually every top US agency has made moves overseas, often via acquisition of a local agency.' He estimates that by 1980 Americans will be exposed to two thousand commercial messages a day by television, press, posters, mail and magazines. Britain can expect much the same.

This really is saturation. And it will be combined with a still more messianic approach.

Eugene H Kummel, president of McCann-Erickson International, says : 'Creativity is the one world-wide, universal fact of life.' He cites the Esso Tiger as 'A powerful example of how an essentially non-verbal image can communicate to any individual regardless of the language he speaks.'

Then there is Coca-Cola. 'The tool here,' says Mr Kummel, 'is something as universal as creativity—youth. The sight of young people enjoying Coca-Cola while enjoying the particular pleasures of their own environment is one of the classics of selling-symbolism. No one can be said to own youth . . . but the Coca-Cola Company has come pretty close.' Both Esso and Coca-Cola are of course American companies. It is estimated that of the top 200 companies selling consumer goods round the world, 180 are American. If each is to capture one certain quality—youth, creativity, etc, there won't be much left for anyone else.

In terms of advertising appropriations, the Americans have an unassailable lead. Gillette alone in 1965 spent $95 million selling its razor blades round the world—and Gillette is by no means the largest US advertiser. Big companies mean big advertising which in turn means still bigger companies.

If the present rules are kept, there seems nothing to prevent the bulk of Western commerce being dominated by a handful of organisations most, if not all, American.

22

Right Honourable Ad Men

THE INFLUENCE OF US advertising methods
on British life is all-pervasive. And nowhere is
that seen more clearly than in politics.

Consider this description of a political leader: 'He appears to be a politician with an advertising man's approach to his work. Policies are products to be sold to the public—this, one day, that one, tomorrow, depending on the discount and the state of the market. He moves from intervention to anti-intervention with the same ease and lack of anguish with which a copy writer might transfer his loyalties from Camels to Chesterfields.'

This is not a description of Harold Wilson, but a pen portrait of Richard Nixon, drawn in the mid 1950s when he was Vice-President of the USA. Yet it bears an uncanny resemblance to the accepted image of British politicians in the mid-'sixties. What American advertising did to American politics in the 'fifties has been repeated in England ten years later.

A US beauty columnist gave this advice on a television presentation to President Eisenhower when he was campaigning for re-election in 1956: 'Those pale-rimmed spectacles must go. They enhance the natural pallor that comes to everyone after forty winters have besieged the brow. Also pale rims tend to wash out when worn by anyone with fair colouring.'

Here again there is a remarkable similarity to the advice offered by newspaper columnists (concerned with politics rather than beauty) to Sir Alec Douglas-Home, the Conservative leader in 1965. He must be the only party leader in history to have resigned over a pair of spectacles. So intense were the complaints that his television image was wrong—especially the half-moon spectacles he kept putting on and taking off—that the poor man finally flung up the job.

His alleged inadequacies in economic science (which is about as much a 'science' as astrology) was the purported reason for hounding him. The actual one was his disengaged, faintly quizzical manner. This was held to be a disadvantage compared with the 'dynamic' 'abrasive' qualities of his opponent, Mr Wilson.

Consciously or not, Home's critics were adopting the advertising man's techniques; judging the product by its packaging; delivering their verdict on the size of the shadow thrown by the television screen rather than the substance of the man.

As far back as 1952 Adlai Stevenson, Eisenhower's Democratic opponent in the Presidential contest that year, said: 'I feel as if I am competing in a beauty contest, not a solemn debate. The idea that you can merchandise candidates for high office like breakfast cereal . . . is the ultimate indignity to the democratic process.'

Unfortunately for Mr Stevenson (defeated both in 1952 and 1956) the merchandising process was highly successful. The US Chamber of Commerce in 1956 confidently predicted that, in future, 'both parties will merchandise their candidates and issues by the same methods that business has developed to sell goods. These include scientific selection of appeals; planned repetition. No flag-waving faithfuls will parade the streets . . . Instead ads will repeat phrases with a planned intensity; billboards will push slogans of proven power . . . candidates need, in addition to a rich voice and good diction, to be able to look "sincerely" at the television cameras.'

Leonard Hall, businessman, and national chairman of the Republican Party, gleefully endorsed the Chamber of Commerce forecast by proclaiming: 'The Republican Party has a great product to sell . . . You sell your candidates and your programmes the way a business sells its products.'

Harold Macmillan, never one to hesitate about adopting American methods, hired an advertising agency to handle the

Conservative Party's 1959 election campaign—with, for him, the most gratifying result.

From the Labour Party there rose a growl of synthetic rage at this 'debasing of the political coinage'. And for some months after the Conservatives' election victory, their third successive triumph, the argument rumbled on about the ethics of using professional advertisers to promote a political policy.

The argument missed the point. Advertising is a wonderful servant, and the more professional the service the better it is. The danger arises when it becomes the master and candidates are selected, policies propounded, promises made *not* for inherent worth, but because they have 'appeal'.

Having delivered themselves of a stern lecture on the wickedness of advertising, the Labour Party promptly imitated the Conservatives by getting their own advertising agency. And were so successful in marketing their brand that a television producer was prompted to comment that Harold Wilson was 'a natural actor'.

The similarity between British and American politics, even to the extent that in both countries the main contest is now a competition between two leaders, is given added emphasis by the effect on the UK of that other American innovation in the art of political persuasion : the Gallup Poll.

Dr Gallup won fame, or perhaps notoriety, with his forecast that Mr Truman would lose the 1948 US Presidential election. Truman won. Suitably abashed, the doctor tightened up his organisation, improved his sampling techniques and restored the reputation of public opinion polling. To such an extent that his poll was adopted by a British national newspaper and his methods were transplanted to England and used, with modifications, by British pollsters.

Thus an instrument suited to the American political scene was projected across the Atlantic where it distorted the British political scene.

In the US electioneering is a continuing process. It has been truthfully said that America is either in a pre-election year or an election year. Congressional contests take place every two years, Presidential ones every four. The full life of a British Parliament is five years. The period of actual campaigning at a General Election is no more than four weeks while in a US Presidential tourney it is some eight months—from the first primaries to polling day.

It is a built-in feature of US politics to refer constantly to the people, so naturally pollsters play a prominent part in the process. In England, with the much longer periods between elections, the pollsters fill in their time taking the public's pulse on all sorts of issues and conducting regular popularity contests between the Party leaders. Inevitably this has enhanced the prestige of the chiefs at the expense of their followers, the MPs. The esteem of Parliament has declined as the image of the leaders has grown.

It would be ridiculous to imagine that the Gallup Poll has decisively altered the balance of power in British politics. A host of other influences has been at work.

Nonetheless one element undoubtedly has been the attraction of the polls. When the public is asked every five minutes : 'What do you think of the Prime Minister [or the Leader of the Opposition] ?' there is a natural tendency among the top man's followers to be guided by the public's answers.

If the Party leaders have had the limelight drawn to themselves as a result of the polls, they are also far more vulnerable in consequence. A stream of adverse poll findings can erode a leader's authority as effectively as a series of wrong decisions. The pressure to be popular at any cost is intense.

Curiously enough the Americans, who invented the whole thing, are less affected. An American President is elected for four years and no matter what happens there he stays until his term is completed. Death alone intervenes. Not even incapacity may terminate a Presidency. Woodrow Wilson remained President for a year after illness had robbed him of the capacity to work. His wife maintained the elaborate pretence that he was still in control.

So, however the polls may chart his ups and downs in public

opinion he remains at the helm and really only needs to worry about 'repairing fences' in the few months leading up to his re-nomination.

In contrast, British party leaders are wholly dependent on the support of their followers in Parliament. If the MPs think their chief is losing too much popularity in the country (and thereby endangering their chances of re-election) they will move to have the leader replaced. The Conservative Party achieved some kind of record by ousting two leaders, Mr Macmillan and Sir Alec Douglas-Home, within a period of twenty months largely because both men had been doing badly at the opinion polls and were giving the Party 'a poor image'.

Thus an unthinking acceptance of American market research methods and popularity ratings had led to a subtle shift in British politics.

Politicians are even less inclined than heretofore to take unpopular courses; to risk upsetting anyone. They are more concerned than ever to veer with every changing wind and to be fashionable at all costs. If anyone believes England has benefited from this super-responsiveness to the market of demos they should compare Britain's performance in the 'sixties with that of France under Charles de Gaulle, a statesman not noted for his responsiveness to the momentary whims of public favour.

The fact is that over-emphasis on political salesmanship—a direct consequence of relying on public opinion polls—has proved a baneful influence on British political life. It is one more example of the unfortunate effect on English society of blindly absorbing features of the American way of life.

23

Which Way?

'THE CHARACTER OF a nation is more important
than its opulence'—Joseph Chamberlain.

The title of Canada's national anthem is 'O, Canada' and a
whole world of meaning can be derived from that single letter
'O'. It could be an exclamation of awed admiration that this land
of 20 million people, most of whose towns are strung along the
United States border, most of whose people live in close proximity
to their giant neighbour, should have maintained their political
independence for a century.

Or the 'O' could stand for disappointment that Canada should
have allowed herself to become so economically dependent on
America that the whole area of Canada and the US is frequently
referred to simply as North America. As far back as 1924 the US
Commerce Department briskly dismissed Canada with the words:
'Economically and socially it may be considered a northern extension of the United States.'

Certainly the degree of Americanisation is overwhelming. More
than 50 per cent of Canada's entire productive economy is American-owned. Twenty-five of Canada's 36 fuel companies (oil and
coal) are American; 60 per cent of Canada's gas industry, 62 per
cent of her mining and smelting, 25 per cent of her railways, 13
per cent of her utilities are in American hands. It is hard to quarrel
with the verdict of Canadians themselves that they have passed
from being a British colony to being an American satellite.

Of Canadian companies owned by overseas investors in 1911
the UK controlled 72 per cent, the US 23 per cent. Now the positions are reversed. UK holdings are down to 15 per cent; US
holdings up to 80 per cent.

In the ten years from the end of World War Two America's direct investment in Canada doubled. Canadian commentators claimed that primary products were being sent to the US for processing instead of being processed by Canadian secondary industries. The long-term development of the country, it was argued, was being sacrificed for short-term gain. Canadians were being denied the opportunity of commercial leadership within their own land. It was estimated that, of the 4,253 branches of foreign organisations operating in Canada, only seven per cent had Canadians on the board of directors.

Tim Buck, secretary of Canada's Communist Party, admittedly highly partisan, observed: 'American monopolies are developing the Canadian economy solely to serve their own interests and not the interests of Canada and her people. They have reduced Canadian industry as a whole to the role of a branch plant economy . . . Little if any research or development work is done in their Canadian subsidiaries. In the main the decisions as to what shall be produced in Canada are made in the US.'

He went on: 'Two thirds of US expansion in Canada is being financed out of the lush profits American companies are making. They are buying up the country with part of the profits they are making by exploiting its rich material resources and its productive working class.'

Mr Buck's tirade was not just Communist Party propaganda. It was echoed by others. Lionel Chevrier, a Liberal, and Canadian High Commissioner in London, told a British audience that no other country in the world would tolerate the degree of American financial penetration which Canada had experienced. 'We Canadians,' he declared, 'wish to see the trend of foreign control of Canada's industry arrested and reversed.'

John Diefenbaker, when Canada's Conservative leader, declared: 'Canada's economy is altogether too vulnerable to sudden changes in the trading policy of Washington. Canadians do not wish to have their economic, any more than their political, affairs determined outside Canada. Moreover we have become dependent on the USA which now largely controls our iron, petroleum, copper and the like.'

Diefenbaker won the biggest landslide election in Canadian history on a platform which called for the reduction of American control of Canada. He proposed switching fifteen per cent of Canada's external trade away from the US (with which Canada had $1,200 million a year deficit) to England (with which she had a $450 million surplus). He failed. America's economic grip on Canada was too tight, her power to retaliate against discrimination by Ottawa too great. The big attempt to heave Canada free of American influence was abandoned.

In the years following Diefenbaker's abortive Declaration of Independence, US investment waxed mightily. By 1961 it had gone above the $20,000 million mark. An attempt to dam the flood of capital into Canada by imposing a thirty per cent tax on the sale of assets to foreigners was defeated following pressure from Washington. Higher and higher rose the level of dollar inflow. By 1967 the Canadian banks, last bulwark of financial sovereignty, were threatened with inundation.

Even Lester Pearson, the Liberal Prime Minister, and a devoted adherent of free trade and the unimpeded movement of capital, was compelled to do something. The Bank Act was amended to require seventy-five per cent Canadian ownership of shares in the chartered banks. Mr Pearson went on to promise a 'deep study' of the whole structure of Canadian business with special reference to foreign ownership and control. The study, when it is completed, will no doubt show in minute detail what everyone knows already—that, economically, Canada is virtually part of the USA. Nothing illustrates this dominance more clearly than the case of the Canadian tractors :

A group of Canadian automobile companies, with the strong encouragement of the Canadian Government, negotiated a contract for the sale of a substantial number of tractors to China. At once Detroit stepped in; declaring the transaction to be contrary to American (although not Canadian) policy, US automobile manufacturers ordered all their Canadian affiliates to repudiate the contract without further notice. So the Canadians were forcibly reminded of the fact that their motor industry was owned by, and obeyed, the orders of a foreign power.

Some Canadian businessmen would like to take their country right in and become an American state. Their argument being that secondary status is worthless and if you are going to be part of the American system you should become an integral part, with some share in the decision making. This view is still not widespread and is countered by the example of the Republic of Ireland, which is even more dependent on England than Canada is on the US, yet continues to maintain a proud separation from London. Undeniably, however, Canada is on the brink of complete commercial absorption by the US.

The road to surrender is so easy, so tempting. It is a fine broad highway offering a splendid vista of prosperity. Simply take the money, and enjoy the fruits without the risks of entrepreneurship. That is what Canada has done.

She may regret it now; she may wish that she had been more selective in her choice of US capital, less eager to exploit her vast natural resources by selling her assets. But there is precious little she can do about it. Even if she wished, Canada will find it hard to escape the American grip. It is too tight. More significant, it is too comfortable.

What has happened to Canada can happen to England. All it needs is for her to adopt the same ready acquiescence in letting someone else do the saving, the investing, the working and the thinking. Then England can become a well-heeled vassal.

Canada is the most outstanding example of a nation which has been embraced so wholeheartedly by America that, economically, it is only half a nation.

It can be argued that Canada could not have advanced so swiftly to industrial strength without massive infusions of US capital, and that Canada is setting the pattern which others must follow if they wish to be commercially powerful. In other words that the price of progress is the loss of sovereignty to the strongest.

That appealing argument is used by all who favour unlimited American investment in the UK. It is, however, completely confounded by the experience of Japan.

Japan has virtually rejected foreign ownership. In 1967 the US stake in Japan was only £90 million, one twenty-fifth of the US stake in England. Yet Japan has a higher rate of economic growth than any other industrial nation. She has been advancing at four to five times the rate achieved by North America and West European states. True, Japan had further to go; she was starting from a much lower level. Even so, her progress has been prodigious. And in sophisticated industries she has made startling advances—reaching fourth place in car output, being the fourth nation to put a satellite in space and equalling England by having a substantial (more than fifty per cent) home-based computer industry.

Japan's accomplishment is even more remarkable in the context of her post-war situation. For she was occupied by the United States and subjected to a most intensive 're-education' designed to re-orientate her ideas in a democratic direction. She submitted to this with apparent willingness and adopted all the correct symbols—free assembly, free press, parliamentary opposition. So far as economic affairs were concerned, however, she kept tight control of her own industries.

In 1955 US interests tried to persuade the Japanese Government to permit foreign companies to buy up Japanese electrical, asbestos and automobile undertakings. The Tokyo Government refused. Official Washington would like to have supported the US commercial concerns but was afraid to do so because of the delicate political/military situation in the Far East.

So Japan continued on her independent way, freely purchasing licences from all over the globe, gladly admitting foreign concerns on an associate basis, but rigidly excluding foreign control in every important industrial sphere.

There were protests of course. In July 1967 the Japanese

Government bowed before the pressure and agreed that foreigners could own up to a hundred per cent of Japanese firms in seven specified trades. Another twenty were designated in which foreign ownership would be tolerated up to fifty per cent. But the Japanese obeisance to foreign opinion was more in the manner than in reality. The seven trades opened up to outside investment included motor cycles, steel and textiles in which the Japanese-owned firms were so dominant that no foreign concern had a hope of breaking in profitably. Japanese shipbuilding presented the same monolithic front to the foreigners.

Permission may be granted to foreigners to start up yards and eventually take over existing Japanese producers, but, in fact, the invitation is without substance. For Japanese shipbuilding is overwhelmingly stronger than any possible competitor.

Where there was a real chance of foreign companies getting a grip—in the growth industries of computers, electronics, aviation, communication—the Japanese maintained their bland 'no entry' policy.

For England, the contrast between Japan and Canada in their relations with the US presents a study of more than academic interest.

Canada is rich. She could hardly be otherwise, considering the splendid, thrifty, hardworking, stock : Scots, English, French, who occupy a land of immense natural resources right next door to the wealthiest community on earth.

Yet Canada is uncertain of her identity. The politicians fight against political absorption by the US while the businessmen accept commercial absorption. The result is neither happy for Canada nor satisfactory for the US. Americans show a barely concealed contempt for their northern neighbours which all the amiable talk about the 'undefended frontier' and 'common interests' and 'solidarity' cannot disguise. Indeed the Canadians are bitterly resentful of interference by US business, and US trades unions, in the affairs of Canada. They feel a sense of shame that Canada should be treated as a branch of American business and

Canadians as American customers who live on the wrong side of the tracks.

It is even possible that Canadians may one day feel envy for Japan, where 100 million people live in an area not much bigger than the British Isles and lacking most of the agricultural and natural resources in which Canada is so abundant. For the Japanese have raised their gross national product to the level of Britain's and Germany's without sacrificing one jot of their economic sovereignty to the US. Moreover, the Japanese are doing their own research and development and are repeatedly coming up with discoveries which win applause, and profit, for Japan and reinforce Japanese self-esteem.

Canada and Japan represent the two extremes.

Britain has the choice of following one or the other, of permitting unrestricted American investment in all industries, as Canada does, or strictly supervising investment as Japan does.

Abraham Lincoln once said that no nation could survive half slave and half free. It is hard to see how a nation can survive economically dependent and politically independent.

Canada is attempting that course. Japan has rejected it.

Soon Britain must decide which way she means to go.

24

Politics of Dependence

'AMERICA WILL NEVER be another Rome'—Adolf Hitler

On a cold, grey afternoon in Washington the telephone rang in the State Department. It was the secretary of Lord Inverchapel, the British Ambassador, asking for an urgent appointment with General George Marshall, United States Secretary of State. In Marshall's absence his under-secretary, Dean Acheson, accepted an advance of two dispatches which the ambassador wished to convey to the United States Government.

The notes declared that Britain could no longer carry the economic burden of helping Greece and Turkey to resist Communist subversion. Would America undertake the commitment?

According to the account given by Desmond Donnelly, MP, in his book *Struggle for the World,* Acheson and two state department officials read the British notes 'with mounting excitement'. All three men realised that Great Britain had, within the hour, handed the job of the world leadership, with all its burdens and all its glory, to the United States.

The date was 21st February 1947.

Six days later President Truman assembled Congressional leaders in his office to discuss the question of aid to Greece and Turkey. Acheson spoke. He told, in graphic terms, of Britain's declining power and the vacuum she was leaving behind as she was forced to withdraw from various positions, including her fabulous Indian Empire. He concluded : 'Only two great powers remain in the world : the United States and the Soviet Union. There has never been a situation like this since ancient times when Rome and Carthage held sway.' The allusion may have been an unhappy one considering what happened to Carthage, but the

Congressional leaders were in no mood to consider ancient history. They were too overwhelmed with the significance of Acheson's words. Now, at last, America was at the summit of power.

On 12th March President Truman unfolded the Truman doctrine to a joint session of Congress and declared: 'I believe that it must be the policy of the United States to support free peoples who are resisting attempted subjugation by armed minorities or by outside pressure. I believe we must assist free peoples to work out their own destinies in their own way.' He asked Congress for authority to provide aid to Greece and Turkey amounting to $400 million and concluded: 'The free peoples of the world look to us for support in maintaining their freedoms . . . great responsibilities have been placed upon us by the swift movement of events.'

Thus was inaugurated the era of American supremacy. To many, including Winston Churchill, it appeared a natural, heartening and happy transfer of authority from one great Anglo-Saxon community to another. If the British could not keep world power who better to grasp the torch than the strong self-confident young giant across the Atlantic? And, as the sun finally set on the mightiest empire ever known, it seemed right that it should rise above the land of the free and the home of the brave.

However, the world has changed so suddenly, so startlingly, so fundamentally, that the very word 'empire' has lost all meaning.

No nation has ever possessed so much power in the material and military sense as America. And no nation, possessing such power, has been so circumscribed in the use of it.

At the time of Truman's declaration the US alone of all nations possessed the atomic bomb. If the Americans had been intent on imposing a Pax Americana, that was the moment to do so. Under threat of nuclear bombardment it is hard to see how Russia could have resisted demands to withdraw from Eastern Europe and abandon subversion campaigns everywhere. No nation on earth could have defied the United States in those days.

If any such dazzling dreams of global hegemony passed before the eyes of American leaders, they were swiftly suppressed. By a self-denying ordinance without parallel the Americans passed up the opportunity. In July 1949 the Russians tested their atomic bomb and the American nuclear monopoly was broken for ever.

The shame is that the US has not been given credit for this act of outstanding moderation. She has been reviled for extending political dominion when, in fact, she has done nothing of the sort. She did not try to translate her overwhelming might into practical reality when it was possible for her to do so. And since the balance of nuclear terror was established she has been unable to do so.

Charles de Gaulle realised this and used his knowledge with a chilling logic to extend influence far beyond the limit of France's actual strength and in open defiance of American wishes and interests. Even earlier, Marshal Tito of Yugoslavia had sensed the restrictions of Russian power and had freed his country from Soviet control.

Mr Acheson was right when he said that the United States and Russia were the two greatest powers. He was wrong to confuse them with Rome and Carthage. Rome and Carthage could act. Russia and America could not lest they risk mutual annihilation. The giants were paralysed by fear of the H-bomb.

Britain's politicians, however, did not grasp the significance of the new order, or perhaps they did not want to.

In the late 'forties England rightly devoted all her efforts to winning American support to secure Western Europe against Stalin's blackmail and threats of force. Once that had been accomplished, as it was with the defeat of Russia's Berlin blockade and the setting-up of the North Atlantic Treaty Organisation, it was both simpler and more immediately rewarding to continue acting as America's trusted lieutenant, than to adopt any other posture. The price of this policy, however, was to make England less of an ally and more an auxiliary.

When Churchill returned to office in 1951 he tried to persuade Washington to give command of the NATO forces in Europe to a Briton. He failed. The commander-in-chief of NATO remained an American and it was made clear to him that this would not change.

The Americans, after all, provided many of the troops, most of the money and all the nuclear weapons, so why should they not have the leadership?

British initiatives were accepted only if they coincided with American wishes. Thus when the plan for a European defence community—a project for combining French, Germans and other Europeans in a single integrated army, robustly denounced by Churchill as 'a sludgy amalgam'—foundered, Mr Anthony Eden's suggestion that Britain should permanently station four divisions and a tactical air force in Germany was seized upon with delight, because it corresponded with American desires for strong military forces on the European continent. Even Mr Dulles, the American Secretary of State, was pleased, and his affection for Britain fell a good way short of idolatory.

As long as England held the front against Communism, for example, when she suppressed the left-wing government of Dr Jagan in British Guiana, she was assured of staunch American backing. But let her wander from the straight and narrow path of anti-Communism, let her try to defend what she conceived to be her own interests, as in opposing Colonel Nasser's designs, and American support withered to be replaced by outright hostility.

Alliances of course are always subject to strain. What was different about the Anglo-American alliance was that Britain lacked the countervailing power to impress America. Occasionally her advice was accepted, as when the United States refrained from using nuclear weapons in Korea in 1951 and on the Communist guerillas of Indo China in 1954, but that was because British views chimed with those held by members of the US administration. On its own, British power counted for less and less in Washington as the post-war confrontation with Stalin gave way to long-term containment of Communism.

Changes in American policy pulled England this way and that.

The United States clung to the belief that the British Empire was a positive embarrassment to the free world. President Roosevelt and his Republican opponent Mr Willkie had given voice to these sentiments during the war. After the war England was constantly exhorted to 'liberate' colonial dependencies. American propaganda to this effect was massive and persuasive and was echoed by non-European members of the United Nations.

To comply with the requirements of 'Democracy' in its struggle with Communism Britain was urged to liquidate the empire so that newly independent countries could take their place in the ranks of the Free. In the early 'fifties it was a common occurrence for African politicians to plead their case against British colonialism and receive a sympathetic hearing from the United States.

There was also a natural, though unexpressed, desire among Americans to inherit British influence in territories long under the sway of the Union Jack.

Suez was the climacteric. President Eisenhower and Mr Dulles took the view that the British and French attempt to overthrow Nasser was damaging to America's image in the Middle East and harmful to the crusade against Communism. So the utmost financial pressure was brought to bear on England to force her to call off the venture and at the United Nations America and Russia joined in censuring Britain and France. As the former French Premier, Pierre Mendes-France, wrily commented, 'A new formula has emerged, the biggest two against the two less big.' From that moment on Anglo-American relations were never quite the same.

Harold Macmillan, who succeeded a sick and saddened Anthony Eden in January 1957, swiftly set about repairing the breach with America and just as zealously set about dismantling what was left of the empire. In seven short years the imperial red was wiped off the map of Africa. It would be absurd to suggest that America was responsible for this over-hasty exit. But US arguments certainly contributed to that conclusion. Mr Macmillan was in a particularly good position to know what was in the American Government's mind, for he visited the US on no fewer than eight occasions in six years, an average of one visit every nine months. A record in commuting broken only by Mr Harold Wilson who averaged a trip to Washington every six months.

By the early 'sixties Britain was stripped of her imperial possessions. Sans empire she counted for even less in the world. Yet the newly emergent nations of Africa, much to America's disappointment, did not step forward as champions of freedom and democracy. Rather, they retreated rapidly into tribal warfare or military dictatorship, just as British colonial service veterans had warned they would.

With the disappearance of the empire Britain had lost but America had not gained. A new course had to be charted. Having helped pull England away from empire, the US sought now to push her towards Europe.

The Common Market beckoned. What better than that Britain should join the European grouping, contributing her great wisdom, stability, traditions, etc, to the New Europe? In the world jigsaw, as seen from Washington, ex-imperial Britain, the odd piece out, might be fitted snugly into Europe, thereby completing America's Grand Design. There was an additional and very important advantage to America from ensuring British membership of the Market. With her strong transatlantic connections and global trading interests, Britain could campaign for an outward-looking low-tariff community which would aid America's highly profitable exports to Europe. Britain would also cut President de Gaulle down to size. So America reckoned. So Mr Macmillan acted.

The British Premier made one fundamental error. He declared, 'I believe that our rightful place is in the vanguard of the movement towards the greater unity of the free world and that we can lead from within, rather than from outside.' By trumpeting the glories of an Atlantic rather than a European community, Mr Macmillan ensured the failure of his attempt to join. For President de Gaulle wanted no Atlantic Community and he applied the veto.

'To govern is to choose,' a French statesman once remarked. In 1962 Britain refused to choose between America and Europe and so made certain that, for some more years, she would not govern her own destiny.

The empire was gone. The door to Europe was barred. Now where? In 1965 the United States 'discovered' a new role for England : keeper of the peace east of Suez.

It was a remarkable reversal of policy.

Nine years earlier the United States had firmly aligned herself with the emergent Afro-Asians against Britain and France. England's role as policeman at Suez had been roundly condemned. Said Vice-President Richard Nixon at an election rally in New York in 1956 : 'In the past the peoples of Asia and Africa have always felt we would, when the pressure was on, side with the policies of the British and French governments in relation to the once-Colonial areas.

'For the first time in history we have shown independence of the Anglo-French policies towards Asia and Africa which seem to reflect the colonial tradition. That declaration of independence has had an electrifying effect throughout the world.'

You could not be clearer than that.

Vietnam accounted for the change in American attitude towards colonialism. In January 1965 US forces landed in strength in that country. By the year's end she was deeply committed with more than 100,000 men in the field.

The British had demonstrated superb capability in containing and finally defeating Indonesian aggression against Malaysia. The 'hearts and minds' campaign, which, after ten long years, had eventually saved Malaya itself from Communist insurgents, was another memorial to British supremacy in this area.

What more natural than that the British should collaborate with the Americans in holding back Chinese, or Chinese-inspired, subversion in South-East Asia?

Prime Minister Wilson eagerly responded to the suggestion and declared that Britain's frontier lay on the Himalayas. The defence of India, the safety of the small states bordering on Vietnam and the security of the Pacific were to be joint Anglo-US responsibilities.

But to sustain a major role in South-East Asia Britain required long-range aircraft able to take off from jungle clearings; she needed strong naval task forces which could come to the aid of threatened friends. The Americans had planes and ships in abundance and were producing them in an ever-increasing flow. It would be uneconomic and fearsomely expensive for Britain to produce planes and carriers for her own forces in South-East Asia. How much easier, how much more sensible, to rely on America for the equipment! Thus military commitments in Asia were bound to lead England remorselessly and inevitably to further economic dependence on America.

Britain's Minister for the Navy at the time, Christopher Mayhew, was the first to grasp the significance of this development. During 1965 he fought for a clear-cut decision from his fellow Ministers : 'Either increase defence spending to furnish the aircraft carriers that will make sense of an east of Suez presence or, if you are determined to curb military expenditure, abandon the role east of Suez.' When the Government refused to take either one course or the other, Mayhew resigned.

He explained : 'It was obviously tempting for the Government to lay down a ceiling for defence expenditure. It was equally tempting to make an early announcement about our intention to stay east of Suez to reassure our American allies, whose aid we were seeking to save the pound.

'What was indefensible was the Government's readiness to commit itself to both objectives before making sure they were compatible with each other . . . by insisting on the one hand on large defence expenditure cuts and on the other on maintaining a world military role, the Government was compelled to rule out all military operations not agreed in advance with our allies who were, in practice, the Americans.'

Further, he argued : 'Our policy of so-called interdependence with the US in Asia will be all the more difficult because of the disparity in power between us. In financial resources and in ships, aircraft and troops, the Americans will be ten or twenty times stronger. Even more important, their troops will be self-sufficient. They can dispense with our help but we cannot dispense with theirs.

'If we exercise influence at all in the Far East it will not be in our own right, but as an extension of American power. We shall not be the United States' ally, but her auxiliary.'

How far Mayhew's case, advanced in his book *Britain's Role in the World Tomorrow*,[1] affected British Government policy is not known. Probably it had a deal less influence than the sharply deteriorating economic situation which forced yet another 'fundamental review' of British defence spending in the summer or 1967 and led to the announcement that the UK would quit her Asian bases by 1975.

But, more significant than arguments of strategy, or the consequences of financial stringency in bringing about changes in London, was the dawning realisation that there really was little that England or, for that matter, the United States could do about Afro-Asia.

The process of disillusion was cumulative. It started at Suez. Then it seemed that Britain and France had been eliminated from the Big Power League. But events in the decade succeeding Suez demonstrated that the league itself had been eliminated.

By the summer of 1967, after two-and-a-half years of war, the Americans had half a million soldiers in Vietnam; greater fire power per mile of the front than that used by both sides in World War Two; thousands of helicopters; hundreds of supersonic aircraft; nuclear bombers (though operating in a conventional role),

1. *Britain's Role . . .*, Christopher Mayhew, Hutchinson, 1967

and still they could not subdue the Vietcong guerillas. Not only could not subdue them, but could not prevent them from shelling the centre of Saigon, capital of South Vietnam.

In the Middle East, in that same summer of '67, the Sixth American Fleet, with a mightier 'punch' than all the fleets of history combined, patrolled the eastern Mediterranean. Off its bows were countries which, in theory, owed their livelihood to American goodwill. Egypt was the recipient of billions of dollars' worth of aid and was, in 1967, beneficiary of huge gifts of food from America. Egypt's leader, Colonel Nasser, owed his very existence to American intervention on his side during the Anglo-French invasion of Suez.

Across the Sinai Peninsula lay Israel, virtually an American creation, owing its very life, in its early days, to transfusions of American capital. Israel, too, was the recipient of vast amounts of US dollars.

Here if anywhere, American influence ought to have been paramount. What happened? The Egyptians closed the Gulf of Akaba to Israeli ships. The Americans told them to open it. The Egyptians paid no attention. The Israelis mobilised. President Johnson publicly warned them not to start a war. The Israelis paid no attention. They attacked, and within five days routed their Arab foes.

The only ship of the mighty American Sixth Fleet to be involved was a radar vessel which strayed into the fighting zone and was badly damaged by Israeli bombers.

The super-colossal nuclear over-kill of the American Navy was simply irrelevant. Of course an atom bomb on Cairo or Tel Aviv would have put an end to the Middle East imbroglio. But such a bomb could have been dropped just as easily by an old British Canberra bomber or a French Mirage, or a Russian Ilyushin or a Chinese plane.

Being able to kill people thirty times over (which is what the Americans claim) does not make one thirty times stronger. With death, once is enough. And with nuclear power enough is plenty. The Bomb is the Great Equaliser and this equality has cancelled out the supremacy of material power over vast stretches of the globe.

The chilling truth is that from Cyprus to Fiji there is no real power system. The imperial cement having been removed, the whole structure is liable to subside.

Only a brave man—or a foolish one—would forecast how long India will remain a united nation, or even a recognisable state at all. Africa is a shambles. The Middle East is a powder keg.

If America can make little or no impact on the nations of Afro-Asia, why should Britain even try? And if China gets really tough what can Britain, or anybody, do?

Such thoughts must surely have influenced British policy makers.

The politics of dependence, which are the politics British statesmen have followed for the past two decades, make sense only when they contribute to a coherent system which secures peace and gains some advantage to one's own country. NATO did that in the late 'forties. But in the Middle East, Africa and Asia, the US-led effort to build associations of coloured peoples analogous to NATO has completely broken down.

The US provided arms to Egypt and Israel on the strict understanding that they would use them only against aggressors from outside the Middle East (*ie* Russia) and never, never against each other. The arms were used—against each other!

The US supplied weapons of war to India and Pakistan to help them build up their defences against external pressure (*ie* from China). The condition of providing the arms was that India and Pakistan would not use them against each other. The only time they were used was against each other!

What is the point in pretending that security pacts exist in the Middle and Far East when manifestly they do not?

The US tried to ride two horses: anti-Communism and support of violently anti-Western dictators like Colonel Nasser. It was an inherently contradictory policy and, not surprisingly, collapsed. Britain is now in the process of getting out from under the wreckage.

If she didn't, if she continued to cling to America's coat-tails in Asia, she would pursue a mistaken policy to her own grave disadvantage.

As Mayhew has said, American equipment would be needed for the British forces in Asia; IBM computers for submarine contact, F111 bombers for land-based air cover; US carriers for air-sea cover; US space satellites for communication. All at the expense of technological progress in England The politics of dependence leading inevitably to still greater economic dependence—and to no discernible purpose. England would simply be sharing America's appalling dilemma—responsibility without authority; the 'defence' of nations which do not want to be defended. The 'protection' of states intent on pursuing bloody vendettas and devoted to mutual destruction.

If America had, in fact, inherited Britain's eastern empire there might be an honourable place for Britain in providing the US with knowledge and experience acquired over the centuries in 'governing lesser breeds without the law'. But the 'lesser breeds' are on their own now. And, apart from isolated instances like Malaysia, show no wish to accept anyone's guidance.

Australia and New Zealand are in a different category. Were they to be endangered, the British people would fly to their defence, armed with whatever weapons were required, from whatever source they could be obtained.

But so far as the Asian mainland is concerned, the white man is an unwanted intruder.

For America there is no empire to inherit. For England there is no sense in continuing to act as a loyal lieutenant to a commander who cannot, by the nature of things, command.

The politics of dependence which have swayed England's fortunes for so long are exhausted. For better, or worse, for richer, or poorer, England must find a new role. And find it on her own.

25

The Road to Brussels

'OF ALL THE broken reeds, sentimentality is the most broken reed on which righteousness can lean'—Theodore Roosevelt.

Nations rarely act on fixed principles; they react to circumstances created by others. So it has been with the European Economic Community, the Common Market.

Surveying the shattered Continent in the autumn of 1946, Harold Macmillan remarked that if he were a young European he would emigrate. The Continent might have remained in this shocked and ravaged state for many years, with its best people fleeing in ever-growing numbers, had it not been for the Soviet threat. The imminent possibility of Russia, supported by large local Communist groups, taking over Western Europe prompted Britain and America to act; Britain to formulate plans for a Western military alliance, America to provide funds through Marshall Aid for the economic rehabilitation of Western Europe. The result was the North Atlantic Treaty Organisation, the military arm, and the Organisation for European Economic Co-operation, the economic arm of the new deal for Europe.

But parallel with this development, which was Anglo-American in origin, went another purely European scheme. This was to combine the French and German Coal and steel industries in a single community. Advertised as a step towards Franco-German reconciliation, the European Coal and Steel Community was actually the first step to a Common Market.

England looked on benignly. The Labour Government of Clement Attlee was in no mood to get involved with Europe— being entirely devoted to the organisation of the British economy on Socialist principles and the foundation of the Welfare State —but saw no reason to cavil at Franco-German co-operation.

Likewise the United States. The US Government gave its blessing to efforts to build inter-European understanding. The closer the European nations got to one another the better able they would be to resist Communist subversion. So the Coal and Steel Community endured and flourished.

Tentative invitations were extended to Britain to join this grouping. The seeds of European co-operation fell on stony ground so far as the Socialists were concerned, for they had no wish to tie the nationalised coal and steel industries of England to the capitalist ones of France and Germany. But what of the Conservatives? Mr Churchill had been a powerful and eloquent advocate of European unity when in opposition. Might he not be a compelling force for unity when he achieved office?

Churchill however did not conceive of Britain as part of Europe. He and his Foreign Secretary, Anthony Eden, based British foreign policy on the three magic circles: the Anglo-American alliance, the Commonwealth, and Western Europe. British influence, it was held, could be exerted most effectively by maintaining the position at the point of intersection of these three circles. Too much emphasis on one at the expense of the others would upset the balance. And, at any rate, European unity was still, in the early 'fifties, a plant of frail and tender growth.

So the years passed. Practical experience of working together in individual industries—nuclear power as well as coal and steel —led six European countries, France, West Germany, Italy, Holland, Belgium and Luxembourg, to search out a permanent framework for combining their economies. The result was the Treaty of Rome, signed in March 1957, which established the European Economic Community.

The purpose of this organisation was to eliminate tariffs and dismantle trading obstructions between the member states; to raise a common tariff against all other states; to permit the free flow of labour and capital within the Community; to harmonise taxation and social services; to prevent the distortion of competition; to create a common capital market and to protect agriculture by

213

a system which rejected cheap imported food in favour of self-sufficiency.

Britain had been invited to take part in the negotiations leading up to the Rome Treaty but had declined. It was felt that the agreements hammered out by the Six were not compatible with British economic practice. Nor were they. In order to reconcile differences between each other the Six had sacrificed the interest of the 'third party'—the outside world.

In 1957 Britain's trade with Western Europe amounted to less than one third of her trade with the Commonwealth, less than one sixth of her total trade.

To accept the rules laid down in the Treaty of Rome Britain would be obliged to discriminate against Commonwealth food producers and in favour of high cost European peasant farmers. She would have to throw over a century-old tradition of free trade and cheap food for a system which deliberately priced food higher than world costs. The road to Brussels (now the Headquarters of the European Community) was one which few Britons had any wish to travel. 'Let's stay as we are' was the general consensus in England.

What was not appreciated however was that one of the magic circles had slipped out of alignment. Western Europe, or the biggest part of it, was off on its own. Surrounded by its tariff wall; possessing its own directorate, the Council of Ministers, its own Executive, the Commission, and its own Judiciary, Europe was no longer linked by bonds of mutual interest to the Commonwealth and the Anglo-American partnership. One of the three fundamentals on which British policy was founded had fallen away.

In the very same month in which the Treaty of Rome was signed, the British colony of the Gold Coast was given independence. The territory took the name of Ghana. The dissolution of the British Empire in Africa had begun.

Within four years it had become plain that the second magic circle was coming undone. The multi-racial Commonwealth was revealed as an illusion. The independent coloured states, now in a majority, were intent on squeezing the last drop of advantage from the association. They wanted the lot—freedom to take their own line in diplomacy, economic largesse from England, and the right to interfere in the internal affairs of white Commonwealth States with whom they disagreed. In short, the 'New' Commonwealth put a premium on irresponsibility.

South Africa, a founder member of the old Commonwealth and one of its richest members, quit in disgust. That was in April 1961. Four months later Britain applied to join the Common Market.

Prime Minister Macmillan allowed his jaundiced view of the Commonwealth to show through in a television address:

'At the end of the last war the Commonwealth consisted of Britain and four independent countries, all British colonies originally, mainly of British stock, all of them subjects of the Queen.

'Although we differed about some things, we were a small united group. We had broadly the same foreign policy. We were virtually a military alliance—tested to the full in two great wars . . . but now it is all changed.

'Now there are fifteen countries. In Asia, in Africa, in the West Indies as well as the old countries of which I have spoken. Some are large, some are small. There is a great variation of opinion, of policy, of tradition. It has altogether changed the pattern of the Commonwealth.

'If you contrast it with the Common Market—that's quite a different thing. They form a great economic group and, naturally, as their economic growth comes together, so will their political.

'And so, you see, Western Europe is quite different from the Commonwealth.'

Yet the true situation was still not appreciated in London. It was not sufficiently understood that with two of the magic circles all but gone, Britain had lost her position as the linkman and was now tied to America. And the third circle, the Anglo-US alliance, was not so much a circle as a chain.

The application to join the Common Market exhibited the painful confusion of Whitehall. It was far from being a straightforward request. Instead the Parliamentary Motion—the instrument of application—instructed the British representative, Mr Edward Heath, to discover if Britain could join the Community subject to satisfactory guarantees being obtained for the 'Special interests of Commonwealth free trade.'

This was rather like going along to a club and saying you were prepared to join if they would change the rules and alter the name from 'White's' to 'Black's'. As M Couve de Murville, the acidulous French Foreign Minister, remarked at the time: 'If Britain enters the Common Market with the Commonwealth, the Common Market will be finished, if she enters without the Commonwealth, the Commonwealth will be finished.'

Month after month the negotiations dragged on. The negotiators despairingly tried to square the circle, to reconcile the irreconcilable. Where progress was made it was due to the British giving way on Commonwealth trade. Naturally so. As the applicants they were obliged to concede. But the concessions provoked strong reaction at home.

The British public still believed passionately in the Commonwealth (though when they said 'Commonwealth' they meant the old Dominions, Canada, Australia and New Zealand). What feelings they had for Europe were largely ones of dislike for the Germans and distrust of the French.

Initially the people had looked with tepid favour on the Common Market as a means of getting cheaper cars and cameras. A fervent press campaign in support of the Market, countered only by the Beaverbrook newspapers, had initially won public backing. But as the full consequences of membership became known, popular support evaporated. The Labour Party, deeply committed emotionally to the New multi-racial Commonwealth, smartly backtracked on its original, grudging approval for the application and demanded impossible conditions. At a by-election in the autumn of 1962 the Conservatives lost a safe country seat in Dorset due to the intervention of an anti-Common Market candidate.

But what finally put paid to Mr Macmillan's European bid was the demonstration that Britain was still tied to the United States.

In December 1962, America abandoned the Skybolt missile on which the Royal Air Force depended for the delivery of its H-bombs. Mr Macmillan sped across the Atlantic to warn President Kennedy of the awful effect this apparent betrayal would have on British, especially Conservative, opinion with regard to the Anglo-American alliance. He secured Polaris submarine missiles in exchange for the defunct Skybolt, but what he gained in America he lost in Europe. President de Gaulle made it crystal clear that Britain was not fit for membership of the European Community.

Remarked an American observer, Professor Hartley Clark, in a book *The Politics of the Common Market*[1]: 'The political nature of the Common Market was advertised to the world when President de Gaulle decided to terminate negotiations for Britain's membership after the British accepted Polaris missiles from the United States and refused to join with France in nuclear arms development.

'The French Government had asked to share in British nuclear technology as a gesture in the spirit of the Community. But the British had to refuse because of the treaty restrictions on technology that had originally been provided by the United States . . . To de Gaulle the whole nuclear weapons affair demonstrated British dependence on America, a dependence which was misplaced because the US could not be relied upon to come to the aid of Europe in case of Soviet attack.'

The link with Europe could not be formed because the link with America was, as yet, too strong. In trying to be all things to all men, England could not be true to herself.

1. *The Politics of the Common Market,* Prof Clark, Prentice-Hall, 1967

An interesting sidelight on the nuclear weapons affair is that Britain originally embarked on nuclear weapon development before America and handed all her discoveries to the US when the two countries became allies in December 1941. Thereafter British scientists worked in the US on the atomic bomb project under American leadership. A secret agreement, signed by Churchill and Roosevelt in 1943, pledged the US to furnish England with all information and never to use the atomic bomb without first consulting the UK.

This agreement was repudiated in 1946 when the McMahon Act was passed by Congress prohibiting the US from sharing nuclear secrets with anyone. It was later claimed that President Truman knew nothing of the agreement signed by his predecessor. Whether that is so or not the upshot was to rob Britain of information to which she was entitled.

When, later, nuclear data was passed to London from Washington it was so hedged by conditions as to prevent Britain from using it in an independent capacity.

Having given freely of her own, England was repaid with a sour mixture of condescension and suspicion. Rarely again will any British Government cast its bread upon the waters with such touching faith!

The process of adjustment following the collapse of the first attempt to join Europe proved very painful. Mr Macmillan, the man who had wished to commit political bigamy by marrying both America and Europe, was bereft of a policy. Within ten months of de Gaulle's 'Non' he was replaced as Leader of the Conservative Party and Prime Minister by Sir Alec Douglas-Home who proclaimed the Common Market to be, temporarily at least, 'a dead duck'.

When the Labour Party came into office there seemed every prospect that the dead duck would be buried with something less than full military honours. Mr Wilson, in opposition, had been one of the sternest critics of the application to join the Common Market. He was a Commonwealth man; an advocate of close financial liaison with America, an exponent of the east of Suez military posture and an outspoken foe of any nuclear weapons-sharing with the Continent.

Yet, step by step, he shed each one of these policies until, in May 1967, he, too, submitted an application for membership of the Common Market.

Now why did he do this? Why did he repudiate his publicly expressed beliefs to the detriment of his own reputation and the disgruntlement of a large section of his party?

He was not converted by some blinding light of revealed truth. He gave every indication of coming to the decision grudgingly and hesitantly. It was pragmatism which guided this most pragmatic of Premiers. Having tried the alternatives to joining Europe he came to the conclusion that there was no alternative (his anti-Market colleagues drily remarked that the alternative to cutting one's throat is not to cut it).

Each of the policies to which he was committed before winning the 1964 election led, when he put them into practice, to greater and greater dependence on America.

The maintenance of the Big $—Little £ arrangement obliged him to rely heavily on US support for sterling. This, in turn, caused him to bow to US pressure—and the dictates of sterling's frail health—and cancel the all-purpose British TSR2 aircraft. Which, in consequence, made a British aerial presence east of Suez rest on American aircraft.

No wonder Mr Wilson paid five visits to Washington in thirty months. He had to find out what he could do next!

Gradually it was borne upon him that the policy of unequal partnership with the USA was unworkable. Reluctantly he looked again at Europe as a possible power base. The prospect was daunting, for in the years following the collapse of Mr Macmillan's bid, the organisation of the Market had hardened, its members had more to lose by admitting a big outsider and its politics were taking shape under the prompting of President de Gaulle.

Public opinion in England was no more ready to embrace

219

Europe in 1966 than it had been at the end of negotiations in 1962, when the polls showed a clear majority opposed to entry. Far from seeking a new challenge, the English had retreated into a mini-England, a fantasy world where the trivial and meretricious were exalted and affairs of State received at best, a yawn, at worst, a sneer.

This lethargy however suited Mr Wilson's purpose. If one is going to reverse one's principles it is always much easier to do so when the public mood is one of apathy than when it is brim full of vigour and vigilance.

The second approach to Europe provoked nothing like the domestic storm of the first. It was preceded by technical agreements with the French on aircraft, computers and the Channel Tunnel. Not all of these agreements were successful. But they created a climate of co-operation, a sort of *entente commerciale*. Further, they provided the groundwork for the next step.

If performance did not match up to promise it could be argued that only full membership of the Common Market could bring about effective technological collaboration. If the agreements worked they could be held up as examples of what could be done once Britain was in the Market.

Just as the Anglo-American partnership had imposed its own logic on British policy, so the Anglo-European agreements gained a momentum of their own, and began to shape British policy, to draw it away from the Atlantic towards the Continent.

Mr Macmillan's bid to join Europe had assumed a continuing close association with the United States. Mr Wilson's assumed a repudiation of close association with the United States.

This does not mean that one statesman was pro-American and the other anti-American. But simply that events had imposed a pattern to which the leaders were obliged to adjust.

The basis of the Macmillan approach was the widening of the market for British goods; an expansion of free trade which would lead—and, indeed, was planned to lead—to a European-American trading pact. Britain's first application was economic in its aim and the political noises about a 'United Europe' were for effect only.

Mr Wilson's bid was dictated by wholly different reasons. The growth of American dominance in technology, the buying up of British and European scientific firms, in short the reduction of the Old World to the status of technical helotry to the New (Mr Wilson's phrase), required a radical realignment: The creation of a European counterforce by the process of excluding American economic power from Europe. Only by going the whole hog could Anglo-European technology survive.

To take an example from aviation: the United States with its long production runs and the benefit of big military spending on research could normally expect to outsell and undercut any European aircraft manufacturer. This had indeed happened again and again, the British being the principal victims. The American aircraft firms had succeeded in persuading European airlines to standardise their fleets on American equipment. In other words the Americans had used their economic power to the maximum advantage, as they were perfectly entitled to do.

But suppose the European manufacturers got together and designed a plane for European needs. The market would be large enough to justify the development costs and provide a decent return on capital invested. Then suppose too that the European airlines were instructed by their governments to buy that plane, America's competitive strength would be cancelled out.

It could be, of course, that a rival American plane was marginally better, or cheaper, but if it were simply not for sale in Europe, no European airline would be placed at a disadvantage by not possessing it, for none of its competitors would possess it either.

By applying the crude formula of 'bloc economics' the economies of scale would become possible for Europe as they have been practised for many years in the US.

Britain and France, the principal European aircraft manufacturers, would be major beneficiaries of bloc economics in aviation. To compensate other European countries, and to tempt them to buy European planes, it would be necessary to offer them concessions in other industries. And each time the concessions would be given at the expense of the outsider—America.

Thus Europe would build herself up by progressively reducing purchases from the US or from American-owned plants in Europe.

Seen in these terms, Europe offered something that Britain, in the Government's eyes, desperately needed : a mass home market, committed to purchase the fruits of Anglo-European technology; a 'captive' market which alone could justify the manufacture of sophisticated products by providing a long production run, so reducing the unit cost of manufacture and the cost of tooling.

But this kind of Europe cannot be created without halting and reversing American economic penetration. So long as US firms, geared to continental manufacture, are free to buy themselves into the European market, so long will the development of European industries be hindered.

Indeed the Common Market becomes then merely an 'outward-looking trading association', which is what the British originally sought to make it. In which case it will actually facilitate US economic dominance. For the Market will remove business barriers between European states without erecting barriers against non-European ones. The much smaller European firms will stand no chance against the much larger American ones. Just as the much smaller European countries (even the largest, Britain and Germany, have barely one third the population of the US) would stand no chance against the single, monolithic United States.

If ever the phrase 'let us hang together or we will assuredly hang separately' had meaning it is in the case of Europe.

For the British people, as Mr Wilson very well knows, the adjustments to a continental strategy will be painful and unpopular.

Painful, because food prices will rise steeply as England abandons free trade and farming subsidies for continental protection and non-subsidised agriculture. Painful as sterling is revalued to bring it into line with the franc and the Deutschmark. Painful as a number of British industries contract as the price of continental wide rationalisation of production, even though other British industries will expand for the same reason.

Unpopular because the British prefer the American people to Europeans. As Churchill once told the French, 'If you ask us to choose between the Continent and the Atlantic we will always choose the Atlantic.' When he said that, during the war, it was absolutely true. But Churchill, never one to cling to dull consistency at the cost of reality, also said, 'My views are in constant harmony with changing circumstances.' The circumstances having changed, he would be the first to admit that views must change, too.

To avoid being absorbed by American affluence, and stifled by American surpluses, the British Government seeks an arrangement with countries it does not particularly like or trust in exchange for dependence on a nation with which it has long enjoyed a special relationship.

It is a poignant irony that the British must embrace erstwhile foes to save themselves from their long-time friends!

Such appears to be the belief of Britain's two major party leaders. It can be argued that Britain is at least the equal of the two principal powers on the Continent, France and Germany. Within a European community she would attract the support of the smaller states—the Scandinavians and the Low Countries and probably Italy as well. A fragmented Africa, relying, to the extent of ninety per cent, on Europe for its trade, might also benefit from stabilising British influence, operating through the mechanism of the Common Market.

The alternative is not—more's the pity—the Commonwealth, or even an association of the English-speaking peoples. The alternative is deepening dependence on America. And because the dependence would be fairly comfortable, British society would become even sillier, more frivolous and purposeless than at present.

Up against the reality of a struggle for primacy on the Continent, Britain may rediscover her lost nationalism. She will never do so as long as she sits crooning idiot ballads to herself in the shadow of the American Eagle.

The threat of Russian aggression brought military unity to Western Europe. American commercial pressure is forcing some degree of economic unity. Just as the Europeans reacted against Soviet strength by arming themselves with military weapons, so they may well react to US economic strength by arming themselves with economic weapons.

The Common Market is either an all-out economic rival to the US—or it is nothing.

By a strange quirk it may be England, the reluctant, rejected, suitor, who will give leadership and purpose to the Market.

Mr Dean Acheson once said: 'England has lost an empire and has not found a new role.'

If England does find a new role in Europe, Mr Acheson and other Americans cannot really complain if it is not to their liking.

26

The Special Relationship

THERE IS A special relationship between the British and American peoples. It springs not from formal arrangements, which must adjust to changing circumstances, but from a million personal contacts; from experiences and dangers shared over half a century; from common traditions (at least, with an important section of America) and a certain way of looking at things. The mistake made by the professional champions of Anglo-Americanism is to claim that criticism betokens destruction. This is not so.

A certain amount of demolition there must be. Certain hallowed myths must be abandoned if the British are to see themselves as the Americans see them. And, no less important, if the Americans are to see themselves as the British see them.

One myth to go is that Britain 'counts' for something in Washington. If the Americans consider Britain at all it is to reflect how sad is her decline from the hour of glory in 1940 to the decay of the 1960s. Britain's anaemic economic performance is contrasted with the vigour demonstrated by continental Europe and the inevitable deduction is drawn that England has had her day.

America, full of strength and purpose, does not need England any more; not even for her political guile, not even for her diplomatic wiliness. America has come of age and can look after the world on her own.

But does Britain need America? Simply to ask that question invites rebuke. Britain, it is alleged, could not last five minutes without America's nuclear shield, without a steady flow of American capital, without the dollar to prop up the ailing pound.

This argument has been so widely accepted in England that it has become an article of faith : 'Subservience to America is obedience to God.' Yet it is absolutely phoney.

Britain, probably alone, certainly in co-operation with Europe, can have her own, utterly effective nuclear shield.

The pound has been the whipping boy for the dollar, receiving punishment for the misbehaviour of America finance (US payments deficits have been three or four times as big as England's for many years). It is hard to see what sterling has to lose by forfeiting the 'support' of the dollar.

As to the flow of US capital to England, that is the biggest single reason for Britain's dependence and her growing inferiority complex. If someone else is going to undertake the hard toil on the frontiers of knowledge and present you with the fruits, at a price, why undertake the toils yourself? Why not just sit back and accept a secondary role, doing a little garage work for the main contractor and providing the technological masters with Scotch whisky, and their wives with nice knitwear? If Britain were to reject this role and deliberately seek to build a European bloc to compete with America, she might regain her self-respect. And if that were to happen all kinds of things might happen in consequence—including the economic miracle that has eluded her for so long.

Events, in Asia no less than in Europe, are of course moving things this way. As the United States becomes more deeply involved in the East she becomes politically and militarily less committed to Europe. The original impulse for her commercial expansion is thus weakened. Any change in international financial arrangements which diminished the dominance of the dollar would weaken it still further, by making it more difficult for the Americans to finance take-overs.

So there is just a chance that the flow of American capital will temporarily recede slightly of its own accord. But Britain cannot rely on chance. Her policymakers must soon decide how much of British industry they are prepared to see sold to the United States. They must decide whether to engage in a political power struggle or to cling to nineteenth-century conceptions of free trade and console themselves, as a number of singularly ill-informed politicians do, with the thought that a large slice of American industry is owned by Britain.

Such consolation is poor fare indeed. Proportionately to national income, the British stake in America is one seventh of America's stake in Britain. Britain's share in America is dwindling; America's share in Britain is growing. Furthermore, UK investment is largely portfolio, that is, it does not constitute control of American firms. The Americans aim for ownership of British concerns.

To talk of a 'fair fight' on free-trade principles in these conditions is a sham. As well talk of a fair fight between a rabbit and a boa-constrictor.

Free trade was good for Britain in the nineteenth century. It is not good for her today. So why cling to an outworn theory as though it were one of the eternal verities? The Americans do not hesitate to overthrow free trade when it suits their purpose. The 'Buy America' Acts have effectively frustrated foreign competition in many fields. It is interesting to note, for example, that England's balance of payments deficits are entirely accounted for by the deficit in trade with North America.

Sebastian de Ferranti of the British electronics firm put it succinctly : 'Competing with America is like playing against a football team which has boarded up its goal.'

There is nothing more stupid than playing to rules to which your opponent does not adhere. British policy for the last ten years has been based on the proposition that 'it is right to accept rules which are bound to harm us, in the hope of being able to persuade countries still weaker to accept them though the rules would harm them even more' (Sir Hubert Henderson).

Once Britain abandons the rules of free trade and embraces bloc economics with Europe, the United States will be obliged to adjust to a new situation. It might be best for the Americans to anticipate changes in the political and economic climate, by altering relations now between parent companies and their British subsidiaries.

Continued ownership of British concerns might be exchanged

for partnership. There is no reason why the Americans should not be content with forty-nine per cent or less of a firm (as in Japan). Prompt action today may well prevent a less tolerant attitude to American capital from developing in the future.

The free flow of ideas and cash and people need not be impeded simply because due regard is paid to national sensibilities. Indeed a happier and more stable basis will be established between Britain and American business if the present imbalance is corrected.

The Americans would be dangerously in error if they imagine that Europe will remain indifferent to the rapidly increasing number of mergers in the States which are bringing together disparate concerns under a single management. And, willy-nilly, are bringing their European subsidiaries under the same all-embracing control.

Huge groupings are being formed in the US as corporations seek to diversify and to exploit management talent—a scarce commodity—to the full.

Film companies are taken over by food combines. Publishing houses are amalgamated with electronic firms. Soap is married to biscuits.

International Telephone and Telegraph is extending its grip over other industries. Ling-Temco-Vought covers a vast range from aircraft and missile manufacture to meat packaging and sporting equipment. Equally widespread are the interests of Litton Industries and American Home Products.

And this is just the beginning. Soon even greater combines will enter the field, snapping up, first smaller companies in allied production and then snatching at manufacturers which have not the remotest connection with the giant's own line of business. Management in the US has become an end in itself.

> For forms of government let fools contest,
> What e'er is best administered is best.

It is for the Americans to decide whether this is for them a desirable development or not. What concerns Britain and Europe is the fact that US-owned concerns can change their ownership without the slightest consultation with their subsidiaries, or with the governments of the countries in which the subsidiaries are situated. This ought to produce a twentieth-century equivalent to the battle cry: 'No taxation without representation'. It is another compelling argument for the Americans to share control of their subsidiaries with the nationals of the states in which they operate.

Appeals for 'fair play' by themselves are not likely to alter American attitudes. But if they are faced by aggressive business techniques, such as bidding for some of the bright young American executives in England and the threat of legislative action by the governments of the European Economic Community as well as the UK, a more accommodating view may be taken. The Americans, like other folk, much prefer half the loaf to none at all.

For Britain at least, the way ahead is clear. The status of a cringing satellite does not become England. Yet that is what England will become if she remains hobbled to the US.

It is like a three-legged race in which the bigger partner leans on the smaller, not because he wants to, but because his height obliges him to do so.

America's height and weight impose an intolerable burden on Britain and the unequal partnership doesn't do America much good either.

A century and a half ago George Canning declared that he had called the New World into existence to redress the balance of the Old.

Britain's task now is to call in the Old World to redress the balance with the New.

Appendix 1

The Arrogance of Power

EXTRACTS FROM AN address by Senator J W Fulbright, chairman of the US Senate Committee on Foreign Relations, delivered at the School of Advanced International Studies at Johns Hopkins University in Washington, DC, 5th May 1966:

"America is the most fortunate of nations—fortunate in its rich territory, fortunate in having had a century of relative peace in which to develop that territory, fortunate in its diverse and talented population, fortunate in the institutions devised by the Founding Fathers and in the wisdom of those who have adapted those institutions to a changing world.

For the most part America has made good use of its blessings, especially in its internal life, but also in its foreign relations. Having done so much and succeeded so well, America is now at the historical point at which a great nation is in danger of losing its perspective on what exactly is within the realm of its power and what is beyond it. Other great nations, reaching this critical juncture, have aspired to too much and, by over-extension of effort, have declined and then fallen.

I do not think for a moment that America, with its deeply rooted democratic traditions, is likely to embark upon a campaign to dominate the world in the manner of a Hitler or Napoleon. What I do fear is that it may be drifting into commitments which, though generous and benevolent in intent, are so universal as to exceed even America's great capacities. . . .

The attitude, above all others, which I feel sure is no longer valid is the arrogance of power, the tendency of great nations to equate power with virtue and major responsibilities with a universal mission. The dilemmas involved are pre-eminently American dilemmas, not because America has weaknesses that others do not have, but because America is powerful as no nation has ever been before and the discrepancy between its power and the power of others appears to be increasing. . . .

We have not harmed people because we wished to; on the contrary, more often than not we have wanted to help people and, in some very important respects, we have helped them. Americans have brought medicine and education, manufactures and modern techniques to many places in the world; but they also brought themselves and the condescending attitudes of a people whose very success breeds disdain for other cultures.

Bringing power without understanding, Americans as well as Europeans have had a devastating effect in less advanced areas of the world; without wishing to, without knowing they were doing it, they have shattered traditional societies, disrupted fragile economies, and undermined people's confidence in themselves by the invidious example of their own efficiency. They have done this in many instances simply by being big and strong, by giving good advice, by intruding on people who have not wanted them but could not resist them.

Have you ever noticed how Americans act when they go to foreign countries?

Foreigners frequently comment on the contrast between the behaviour of Americans at home and abroad; in our own country, they say, we are hospitable and considerate, but, as soon as we get outside our own borders, something seems to get into us and, wherever we are, we become noisy and demanding and strut around as if we owned the place. The British used to say during the war that the trouble with the Yanks was that they were "overpaid, oversexed and over here!"

I recently took a vacation in Mexico and noticed in a small-town airport two groups of students on holiday, both about undergraduate age; one group was Japanese, the other American. The Japanese were neatly dressed and were talking and laughing in a manner that neither annoyed anybody nor particularly called attention to themselves. The Americans, on the other hand, were disporting themselves in a conspicuous and offensive manner, stamping around the waiting room in sloppy clothes, drinking beer and shouting to each other as if no one else were there.

'This kind of scene, unfortunately, has become familiar in many parts of the world. I do not wish to exaggerate its significance, but I have the feeling that, just as there was once something special about being a Roman or a Spaniard or an Englishman, there is now something about the consciousness of belonging to the biggest, richest country in the world, that encourages people who are perfectly well behaved at home to become boorish when they are in somebody else's country and to treat the local citizens as if they weren't really there.

One reason why Americans abroad may act as though they 'own the place' is that in many places they very nearly do : American companies may dominate large segments of a country's economy; American products are advertised on billboards and displayed in the shop windows; American hotels and snack bars are available to protect American tourists from foreign influence; American soldiers may be stationed in the country and, even if they are not, the population are probably well aware that their very survival depends on the wisdom with which America uses her immense military power.

I think that any American, when he goes abroad, carries an unconscious knowledge of all this power with him, and it affects his behaviour just as it once affected the behaviour of Greeks and Romans, of Spaniards, Germans and Englishmen, in the brief high noons of their respective ascendancies.

It was the arrogance of their power that led nineteenth-century Englishmen to suppose that if you shouted at a foreigner loud enough in English he was bound to understand you, or that now leads Americans to believe like Mark Twain's 'innocents abroad', who reported as follows on their travels in Europe :

The peoples of those foreign countries are very ignorant. They looked curiously at the costumes that we had brought from the wilds of America. They observed that we talked loudly at table sometimes . . . In Paris, they just simply opened their eyes and stared when we spoke to them in French! We never did succeed in making these idiots understand their own language.

We all . . . enjoy telling people how they should behave, and the bigger and stronger and richer we are, the more we feel suited to the task, the more, indeed, we consider it our duty. Dr Chisholm relates the story of an eminent cleric who had been proselytising the Eskimos and said:

'You know, for years we couldn't do anything with those Eskimos at all; they didn't have any sin. We had to teach them sin for years before we could do anything with them.'

I am reminded of the three Boy Scouts who reported to their scoutmaster that as their good deed for the day they had helped an old lady cross the street. 'That's fine,' said the scoutmaster, 'but why did it take three of you?' 'Well,' they explained, 'she didn't want to go.'

The good deed above all others that Americans feel qualified to perform is the teaching of democracy and the dignity of man. Let us consider the results of some American good deeds in various parts of the world.

Over the years since President Monroe proclaimed his doctrine, Latin Americans have had the advantages of United States tutelage in fiscal responsibility, in collective security and in the techniques of democracy. If they have fallen short in any of these fields, the thought presents itself that the fault may lie as much with the teacher as with the pupils.

When President Theodore Roosevelt announced his 'corollary' to the Monroe Doctrine in 1905, he solemnly declared that he regarded the future interventions thus sanctified as a 'burden' and a 'responsibility' and an obligation to 'international equity'.

Not once, so far as I know, has the United States regarded itself as intervening in a Latin-American country for selfish or unworthy motives—a view not necessarily shared by the beneficiaries. Whatever reassurance the purity of our motives may give us must be shaken a little by the thought that probably no country in all human history has ever intervened in another except for what it regarded as excellent motives.

'The wicked are wicked, no doubt,' wrote Thackeray, 'and they go astray and they fall, and they come by their deserts; but who can tell the mischief which the very virtuous do?'

For all our noble intentions, the countries which have had most of the tutelage in democracy by United States Marines are not particularly democratic. These include Haiti, which is under a brutal and superstitious dictatorship, the Dominican Republic, which is in turmoil, and Cuba, which, as no one needs to be reminded, has replaced its traditional right-wing dictatorships with a Communist dictatorship.

Maybe, in the light of this extraordinary record of accomplishment, it is time for us to reconsider our teaching methods. Maybe we are not really cut out for the job of spreading the gospel of democracy . . .

I do not question the power of our weapons and the efficiency of our logistics; I cannot say these things delight me as they seem to delight some of our officials, but they are certainly impressive. What I do question is the ability of the United States . . . to go into a small, alien, undeveloped Asian nation and create stability where there is chaos, the will to fight where there is defeatism, democracy where there is no tradition of it and honest government where corruption is almost a way of life.

Our handicap is well expressed in the pungent Chinese proverb : 'In shallow waters, dragons become the sport of shrimps' . . .

The 'Blessings-of-Civilisation Trust', as Mark Twain called it, may have been a 'daisy' in its day, uplifting for the soul and good for business besides, but its day is past.

It is past because the great majority of the human race are demanding dignity and independence, not the honour of a supine role in an American empire.

It is past because whatever claim America may make for the universal domain of its ideas and values is countered by the Communist counterclaim, armed like our own with nuclear weapons.

And, most of all, it is past because it never should have begun, because we are not the 'engine of mankind', but only one of its more successful and fortunate branches, endowed by our Creator with about the same capacity for good and evil, no more or less, than the rest of humanity.

An excessive preoccupation with foreign relations over a long period of time is a problem of great importance, because it diverts a nation from the sources of its strength, which are in its domestic life.

A nation immersed in foreign affairs is expending its capital, human as well as material; sooner or later that capital must be renewed by some diversion of creative energies from foreign to domestic pursuits.

I would doubt that any nation has achieved a durable greatness by conducting a 'strong' foreign policy, but many have been ruined by expending their energies on foreign adventures while allowing their domestic bases to deteriorate . . .

There are many respects in which America, if it can bring itself to act with the magnanimity and the empathy appropriate to its size and power, can be an intelligent example to the world.

We have the opportunity to set an example of generous understanding in our relations with China, of practical co-operation for peace in our relations with Russia, of reliable and respectful partnership in our relations with Western Europe, of material helpfulness without moral presumption in our relations with the developing nations, of abstention from the temptations of hegemony in our relations with Latin America, and of the all-round advantages of minding one's own business in our relations with everybody.

Most of all, we have the opportunity to serve as an example of democracy to the world by the way in which we run our own society. America, in the words of John Quincy Adams, should be 'the well-wisher to the freedom and independence of all' but 'the champion and vindicator only of her own'.

If we can bring ourselves so to act, we will have overcome the dangers of arrogance of power. It will involve, no doubt, the loss of certain glories, but that seems a price worth paying for the probable rewards, which are the happiness of America and the peace of the world."

Appendix II

Uncle Sam's Roll Call

HERE IS A representative selection, totalling about one quarter of the 1,600 US-owned subsidiaries, associated companies and branches operating in the United Kingdom at midsummer 1967. The list is, of course, subject to change with the passage of time.

The classification of companies is :

1. Consumer—Generally those concerns whose branded products are well known to the public.

2. Financial and Commercial—banks, marketing, advertising, paper and publishing, public relations, films, etc.

3. Manufacturing—generally those concerns whose products, used in industry, are not well known to the public.

CONSUMER

Abbott Laboratories Ltd
Ace Radio Ltd
Simon Ackerman Ltd
Addressall Indexograph Ltd
Addressograph-Multigraph Ltd
AMF Ten Pin Bowling Co Ltd
Amoco (UK) Ltd
Anglo-American Bowling
    Builders Supply Co Ltd
Answering Ltd
Elizabeth Arden Ltd
Armour & Co Ltd
Armour Chemical Industries Ltd
Atlantic Petroleum Ltd
Audio Fidelity (England) Ltd
Avery Adhesive Products Ltd
Avon Cosmetics Ltd

Baby Deer Shoes Ltd
Joseph Bancroft & Sons
    (England) Ltd
Barcley Corsets Ltd
Beauty Counsellors of London
    Ltd
Bell & Howell Ltd
Bendix Electronics Ltd
Berkshire International (UK)
    Ltd
Black & Decker Ltd
Brillo Manufacturing Co of
    Great Britain Ltd
Bristol Laboratories Ltd
Bristol-Myers Co Ltd
British Arcady Co Ltd
Brown & Polson Ltd

237

Burroughs Machines Ltd
Cadum Ltd
Campbell's Soups Ltd
Carnegies of Welwyn Ltd
Celotex Ltd
Cessna Industrial Products Ltd
Champion Sparking Plug Co
Ltd
Chesebrough-Ponds Ltd
Clairol Ltd
Coca-Cola Co
Colgate-Palmolive Ltd
Collins Radio Co of England
Ltd
Comptometer Ltd
Continental Oil (UK) Ltd
Frank Cooper Ltd
Cosmic Crayon Co Ltd
AC Cossor Ltd
Coty (England) Ltd
Crimpy Crisps Potato Crisps Co
Ltd
Crown Oils Ltd
Cyanamid of Great Britain Ltd
Daimler Hire Ltd
Denholm Silk Weavers Co Ltd
Dextrines Ltd
Dictaphone Co Ltd
Dodge Brothers (Britain) Ltd
Dubarry Perfumery Co Ltd
Du Pont Co (United Kingdom)
Ltd
Eagle Pencil Co Ltd
Elders & Fyffes Co Ltd
Elgin Watches (England) Ltd
Elliott Addressing Machines Ltd
Escoffier Ltd
Esso Petroleum Co Ltd

Esterbrook Pen Co Ltd
Everest Co Ltd
Ever-Ready Razor Products Ltd
Eversharp Pen Co Ltd
Ex-Lax Ltd
Exquisite Form Brassieres (GB)
Ltd
Fairchild Camera & Instrument
(UK) Ltd
Firestone Tyre & Rubber Co
Fleming & British Optical
Industries Ltd
Ford Motor Co Ltd
Formfit Foundations Ltd
Frears Ltd
John Gardner (Supermarkets)
Ltd
General Acoustics Ltd
General Foods (Great Britain)
Ltd
General Milk Products Ltd
General Mills Ltd
Gift-Pax (UK) Ltd
Gillette Industries Ltd
The Goodyear Tyre & Rubber
Co (Great Britain) Ltd
Gulf Oil (Great Britain) Ltd
Hamilton Watch Co Ltd
H J Heinz Co Ltd
Helene Curtis Ltd
Hertz Rent-a-Car System
Hoover Ltd
Lederle Ltd
Kolynos (Sales) Ltd
Kelvinator Ltd
Ideal Standard Ltd
Venus Pencil Co Ltd
Dr Mackenzies Laboratories Ltd

Papersticks Ltd
Pond's Extract Co Ltd
Jet Petroleum Ltd
Knorr Anglo-Swiss Ltd
Jewelcraft Ltd
Marsh and Andrews Ltd
A G Spalding & Bros Ltd
Kodak Ltd
London Pharmacists' D & P
  Service Ltd
Photo Finishers (Glasgow) Ltd
Photostat Ltd
Prestige Group Ltd
Max Factor & Co Ltd
Petfoods Ltd
Philco International Ltd
Monogram Electric Ltd
Westclox Ltd
Lanolin Plus (UK) Ltd
Ingersoll-Rand Co Ltd
James Miller (Meat Salesman)
  Ltd
Worcester Foods Ltd
Pearl Radio (Bolton) Ltd
Radio Gramophone
  Development Co Ltd
Jantzen Ltd
Johnson & Johnson (Great
  Britain) Ltd
Kellogg Co of Great Britain Ltd
King Korn Stamp Co Ltd
Libby, McNeill & Libby Ltd
Eli Lilly & Co Ltd
Lana-Knit (Jersey
  Manufacturing) Ltd
Mars Ltd
Louis Marx & Co Ltd
H B Maynard & Co Ltd

Merck Sharp and Dohme Ltd
Miles Laboratories Ltd
Minnesota Mining &
  Manufacturing Co Ltd
Monsanto Chemicals Ltd
Monsanto Textiles Ltd
John Morrell & Co Ltd
Philip Morris & Co Ltd
Nabisco Ltd
Ritz Biscuit Co Ltd
The Shredded Wheat Co Ltd
National Cash Register Co Ltd
Kraft Foods Ltd
National Adhesives Ltd
E R Squibb & Sons Ltd
Parke Davis & Co Ltd
Parker Pen Co Ltd
Pepsi-Cola Ltd
Pfizer Ltd
Phillips Petroleum UK Ltd
Polaroid (UK) Ltd
Polythane Fibres Ltd
Procter & Gamble Ltd
Potter Drug & Chemical Ltd
Quaker Oats Ltd
Rootes Ltd
Textile Laminations Ltd
Revell (Great Britain) Ltd
Revlon International
  Corporation
Rexall Drug & Chemical Co
  (UK) Ltd
Tupperware Co
Vick International Ltd
Milton Pharmaceuticals Ltd
Ronson Products Ltd
Helena Rubinstein Ltd
Safeway Food Stores Ltd

Prideaux's (London) Ltd
Seager, Evans & Co Ltd
Schick Electrical Shaver Services Ltd
Scholl Manufacturing Co Ltd
A Schrader's Son Inc
Scripto Pens Ltd
Scroll Pens Ltd
Sears, Roebuck & Co Ltd
Seven-Up (Great Britain) Ltd
W A Sheaffer Pen Co (England) Ltd
Simmons Bedding Ltd
Simoniz (England) Ltd
Simplicity Patterns Ltd
Singer Sewing Machine Co Ltd
Smith Kline & French Laboratories Ltd
Mobil Oil Co Ltd
Socony Overseas Oil Co Ltd
Sperry Remington Rand Ltd
Remington Electric Shavers Ltd
Sperry Gyroscope Co Ltd
Sarong Ltd
Sterling-Winthrop Group Ltd

Phillips, Scott & Turner Ltd
Ulster Textile Mill Ltd
Sun-Maid Raisin Growers Ltd
Norfolk Animal Products Ltd
Swift & Co Ltd
Tampax Ltd
Technicolor Ltd
Regent Oil Co Ltd
Texas Oil Co Ltd
Texaco (UK) Ltd
Titan International Ltd
Underwood Business Machines Ltd
Upjohn of England Ltd
UK Time
Waterman Pen Co Ltd
Warner Brothers (Corsets) Ltd
Richard Hudnut Ltd
Playtex Ltd
Whitmoyer-Reed Ltd
Willcox & Gibbs Sewing Machine Co Ltd
The Wrigley Co Ltd
Yale & Towne

FINANCIAL AND COMMERCIAL

American Express
Bank of New York
Chase Manhattan
Continental Illinois National
  Bank & Trust Company
Morgan Guaranty Trust
First National City
First National of Chicago
Bank of America National Trust
  and Savings Association
Chemical Bank of New York
  Trust
First National Bank of Boston
Manufacturers Hanover Trust
Crocker-Citizens National Bank
Marine Midland Trust
  Company of New York
J. Walter Thompson Co Ltd
Pritchard Wood & Partners
  Ltd
Young & Rubicam Ltd
McCann-Erickson Ltd
Hobson Bates & Partners Ltd
Erwin Wasey Ltd
Foote, Cone & Belding Ltd
Benton & Bowles Ltd
Crane, Norman Craig &
  Kummel Ltd
Papert, Koenig, Lois Ltd
Leo Burnett Co Ltd
Battern, Barton Durstine, and
  Osborn Ltd

Anglo Allied Pictures Ltd
Bradbury, Wilkinson & Co
  Ltd
Associated Press Ltd
Bantam Books Ltd
Barber Steamship Lines Ltd
General Public Relations Ltd
Butterick Publishing Co Ltd
CBS, Ltd
Columbia Pictures Corp Ltd
Garland-Compton Ltd
The Condé Nast Publications
  Ltd
Vogue Studio Ltd
Corgi Books Ltd
Diners' Club Ltd
Dun & Bradstreet Ltd
Moody's Services Ltd
Encyclopaedia Britannica Ltd
Intercontinental Marketing
  Services Ltd
W H Allen
Hafner Publishing Co Ltd
Hallmark Cards (Great Britain)
  Ltd
The Good Housekeeping
  Institute Ltd
Carlton Tower Ltd
International Correspondence
  Schools Ltd
Women's Institutes of Domestic
  Art & Sciences Ltd

Knott Hotels Co of London Ltd
Lavship (International) Ltd
Collier-Macmillan Ltd
The McCall Publishing Co Ltd
Gregg Schools Ltd
Metro-Goldwyn-Mayer Pictures Ltd
National Screen Service Ltd
A C Nielsen & Co Ltd
Mothercare Ltd
Paramount British Pictures Ltd
British Telemeter Ltd
Penton Publishing Co Ltd
Quigley Publications Ltd
The Reader's Digest Association Ltd
Rust Craft UK Ltd
J H Sankey & Son Ltd
Screen Gems Ltd
The Selznick Studio Releasing Division Ltd
Seven Arts Production (UK) Ltd
British Market Research Bureau Ltd
Ace Books Ltd
Four Square Books Ltd
Time-Life International Ltd
Twentieth Century-Fox Film Co Ltd
United Artists Corporation Ltd
British United Press Ltd
John Wiley & Sons Ltd

MANUFACTURING

Aircraft-Marine Products (Great Britain) Ltd
British Cutting Gases Ltd
Alco Products Export Co Inc
Allied Chemical (Great Britain) Ltd
Phillips Control (GB) Ltd
Allis-Chalmers Great Britain Ltd
Alpha Metals Inc (UK) Ltd
Alcoa International (UK) Ltd
Western Electric Co Inc
British Wire Products Ltd
Borax and Chemicals Ltd
Britannia Lead Co Ltd
Ampex Electronics Ltd
Amphenol-Borg Ltd
British American Metals Co Ltd
Analytical Measurements Ltd
Arrow Electric Switches Ltd
Art Metal Inc
Associated Dry Goods (UK) Ltd
Automatic Canteen Co (Great Britain) Ltd
Diamond Blower Co Ltd
Bausch & Lomb Optical Co Ltd
Bechtel International Ltd
Beckman Instruments Ltd
Big Drum Equipment (England) Ltd
Black-Clawson International Ltd

Stafford-Miller Ltd
Borg-Warner Ltd
Hussmann British Refrigeration Ltd
Bostitch-London Ltd
Brooks Instrument Ltd
Brunswick Corporation UK Ltd
Brush Beryllium Ltd
Bulova (UK) Ltd
Cameron Iron Works Ltd
The Carborundum Co Ltd
Lancashire Grinding Wheels Ltd
United Abrasives Ltd
Caterpillar Tractor Co Ltd
The Cement-Gun Co Ltd
Steel Erectors Ltd
Consolidated Pneumatic Tool Co Ltd
Cincinnati Milling Machines
Cleveland Twist Drill (Great Britain) Ltd
Brush Crystal Co Ltd
Coleman Quick-Lite Co Ltd
Collins Submarine Pipelines Ltd
Columbia Ribbon & Carbon Manufacturing Co Ltd
Cone Automatic Machine Co Ltd
British Continental Motors Ltd
The Crown Cork Co Ltd
Cummins Engine Co Ltd
Aerograph-De Vilbliss Co Ltd

John Deere & Co Ltd
Dentsply Ltd
Electronics Control Engineering Ltd
Dow Chemical (UK) Ltd
Dresser (Great Britain) Ltd
Drilling & Exploration Ltd
Digital Measurements Ltd
ENV Engineering Co Ltd
Linotype & Machinery Ltd
Ex-Cell-O Corporation (England) Ltd
Varley Marine Ltd
Bradma Mailing Machines Ltd
The H K Ferguson Co of Great Britain Ltd
Foster Wheeler Ltd
Euclid (Great Britain) Ltd
Tidewater Oil Co (England) Ltd
Veedol (UK) Ltd
Grace Brothers Ltd
Merwyn Sound & Vision Co Ltd
Heckett (Ebbw Vale) Ltd
Harvey Hubbell Ltd
Hughes International (UK) Ltd
Industrial Acoustics Co Ltd
Industrial Raw Materials Corp Ltd
IBM United Kingdom Ltd
International Harvester Co of Great Britain Ltd
International Minerals & Chemicals Ltd
British International Paper Ltd
International Telephone & Telegraph Co Ltd
Cannon Electric (GB) Ltd

Standard Telephones & Cables Ltd
Irving Air Chute of Great Britain Ltd
Joy-Sullivan Ltd
Kaiser Aluminium Co Ltd
Lapointe Machine Tool Co Ltd
Ludlow Typograph Co Ltd
Magnavox Electronics Co Ltd
British Laundry Machinery Co Ltd
Mine Safety Appliances Co Ltd
Honeywell Controls Ltd
Cleveland Meters Ltd
Norton Grinding Wheel Co Ltd
Pan American International Oil Co (UK) Ltd
Parker-Hannifin (UK) Ltd
Quartzglass Ltd
Pitney-Bowes Ltd
The P & M Co (England) Ltd
Rubber Co of Scotland Ltd
Potter Instrument Co Ltd
John Dalgish & Sons Ltd
RCA Great Britain Ltd
Ranco Ltd
Raymond Concrete Pile Co Ltd
H H Robertson (Holdings) Ltd
Royal McBee (UK) Ltd
Smith-Corona Ltd
British Typewriters Ltd
Sangamo Weston Ltd
Santa Fe Drilling Co (UK) Ltd
Solartron Radar Simulators Ltd
Solartron Electronic Group Ltd
Seismograph Service Ltd
Sharples Centrifuges Ltd

A E Staley Manufacturing Co
(London) Ltd
Gravely Tractor (England
Division) Ltd
Warwick Chemical (Yorkshire)
Ltd
British Sun Oil Co Ltd
Sunbeam Electric Ltd
Teleprompter (UK) Ltd
Texas Instruments Ltd
Thor Power Tool Co Ltd
Timken Stockists Ltd
Todd Oil Burners Ltd
Transitron Electronic Ltd
Marchal Distributors Ltd
Union Carbide Ltd

Carr Fastener Co Ltd
British United Shoe Machinery
Co Ltd
North British Rubber Co Ltd
Universal Container (UK) Ltd
Veeco Instruments Ltd
Vanadium Ltd
Wakefield Lighting Ltd
Weatherhead Automotive
Replacement Parts Co Ltd
Westinghouse Electric
International Co
S S White Dental Manufacturing
Co (GB) Ltd
Continental Emsco Co (GB) Ltd

Index

McMahon Act, 218
McNamara, Robert, 86, 91
McNeil, Hector, 36–7, 39
  becomes Secretary of State, 37
Merck Corporation Ltd, 47–8
Milner, Lord, 130–1
Monroe Doctrine, 14, 127, 233
Mooney, Mr, 59–61
Morgan, Harry, 53–4
Morris, William (see Nuffield, Lord)

NADER, RALPH, 67–8
  Works: Unsafe at Any Speed, 67 fn
Nasser, President, 203–4, 209–10
National Board for Prices & Incomes, 145
National Cash Register Co Ltd, 37–8, 77, 148–9
National Film Finance Corporation, 180
National Health Service, 44–5, 47, 49, 52–3, 55, 160
National Institute of Economic & Social Research, 77–8
New York Society of Security Analysts, 95
New Zealand, 22, 160, 211
Newbolt, Henry, 131
Nixon, Richard, 135, 188, 206
North Atlantic Treaty Organisation, 82–3, 166, 202–3, 210, 212
North British Rubber Co, 7, 10, 39
North Canton, Ohio, 101, 103
Nuffield, Lord, 19, 57

OBSERVER, THE, 85

Olney, Richard, 126–7
Opel, Adam, 61–2, 66, 69
'Open' society theory, 158–9
Organisation for European Economic Co-operation, 212

PACKARD, VANCE, 149–50, 184–5
  Works: The Hidden Persuaders, 149–50, 184 fn, 185 fn, The Image Makers, 185 fn
Pakistan, 158, 210
Palmerston, Lord, 8–9
Patten, Mrs Terese, 155
Pearson, Lester, 195
Penicillin, 51–2
Pfizer Corporation, 44–9, 52
Polk, Judd, 114, 116–18, 123
  Works: Sterling, 114–15
Powell, Enoch, 44–5, 47, 49, 52
Private enterprise, 99
Public schools, 131

QUOTA ACT, 177, 179

READER'S DIGEST, 173–4
Remington Rand Ltd, 171
Robbins, Lord, 115
Roll, Sir Eric, 87–8
Rolls-Royce Ltd, 63, 164
Rome, Treaty of, 213–14
Ronson Products Ltd, 5
Roosevelt, President Franklin D, 23–5, 33, 115–17, 121, 204, 218
Roosevelt, President Theodore, 212, 233
Rootes, 39, 63–7
Rotary clubs, 149

251